Heavenly Bodies

Ten Plays From The 2011 San Francisco Olympians Festival

Heavenly Bodies:
Ten Plays from the 2011 San Francisco Olympians Festival

Edited by Stuart Eugene Bousel and Marissa Skudlarek
Copyright © 2014 by Stuart Eugene Bousel
All rights reserved

Boreas © 2011 by Lise Miller
Cassiopeia © 2011 by Christian Simonsen
Chronus © 2011 by Bennett Fisher
Europa © 2011 by Claire Rice
Hyperion to a Satyr © 2011 by Stuart Eugene Bousel
Joe Ryan © 2011 by Megan Cohen
Leda And The Pr0n © 2011 by Kirk Shimano
Nyx © 2011 by David J. Duman
Pleiades © 2011 by Marissa Skudlarek
Too Near the Sun © 2011 by Jeremy Cole

Published by EXIT PRESS

Book design by Richard Livingston
Cover design by Cody Rishell

CAUTION: Professionals and amateurs are hereby warned that the plays represented in this book are subject to a royalty. All rights of every kind to the plays included in this collection belong to their authors.
Please direct performance inquiries to
Stuart Eugene Bousel
www.horrorunspeakable.com

ISBN: 978-0-9856584-7-2

EXIT PRESS
156 Eddy Street
San Francisco, CA 94102-2708
mail@theexit.org

First Edition: July 2014

For Christina Augello & Richard Livingston,
our guiding lights at EXIT Theatre.

TABLE OF CONTENTS

INTRODUCTION vii
    BY BARBARA JWANOUSKOS

LEDA AND THE PR0N 1
    BY KIRK SHIMANO

JOE RYAN 9
    BY MEGAN COHEN

CASSIOPEIA 73
    BY CHRISTIAN SIMONSEN

PLEIADES 89
    BY MARISSA SKUDLAREK

BOREAS, OR HARD PACK 163
    BY LISE MILLER

CHRONUS 173
    BY BENNETT FISHER

EUROPA 229
    BY CLAIRE RICE

TOO NEAR THE SUN 239
    BY JEREMY COLE

NYX 273
    BY DAVID J. DUMAN

HYPERION TO A SATYR 281
    BY STUART EUGENE BOUSEL

ARTISTS AND WRITERS 356

ABOUT NO NUDE MEN PRODUCTIONS . . 363
    AND THE OLYMPIANS FESTIVAL

Introduction

October 2011 marked the second year of the San Francisco Olympians Festival, a twelve-night event featuring dramatic readings of new works for the stage inspired by ancient Greek mythology. Over 100 artists collaborated to present the 32 plays that encompassed San Francisco Olympians II: Heavenly Bodies at EXIT Theatre. As the festival's faithful box-office manager, I had the good fortune of seeing every one of these plays, and continuing the tradition of the box-office manager writing the introduction to the annual collection, I am pleased to present the ten plays selected for this publication.

For centuries, the stories of the Greeks have inspired artistic works throughout the world with their timeless wonder. By walking in the footsteps of a hero or experiencing the trickery of a god, we can better understand our roles in society, our values, and our insatiable drive to become more like the gods and heroes themselves. Mythological characters accomplish what we often fail to do in our daily lives, but their stories give us the confidence and assurance that we do have a spark within us that is heroic or divine in its own right.

This festival has been defined by its founder and producer, Stuart Eugene Bousel, as one that is "writer-centric." It is a unique approach to giving the writer complete control over his or her own words and letting them shine upon the stage in the best way possible. The playwrights in this book represent fascinating new voices in the theatre landscape. They have taken on the challenge of adapting, modernizing, and transforming these familiar stories, giving them new life and relevance to us today. Their inventiveness sheds new light on the nature of politics, ambition, legacy, family, love and truth.

One exciting aspect of being a vigilant audience member this last October was witnessing how the themes of these 32 plays were repeatedly touched on during the course of the festival, manifesting again and again via styles that were often radically different from one another. The experience of being in EXIT Theatre each night, watching these plays being read, was akin to watching a scientist in the lab experimenting with the same hypothesis tested against a nightly barrage of different variables. The festival itself was an expansion upon the first year's premise, moving beyond the basic Olympian pantheon of twelve gods, to include those figures inspired by the heavenly bodies and elements of the sky. Featured here are tales inspired by the myths of stars, constellations, asteroids, moons, winds, planets and the sun.

VIII HEAVENLY BODIES

In *Leda and the Pr0n*, by Kirk Shimano, Leda, a high-school student, gets into trouble when stumbling across suggestive pictures while searching for the origins of her name on the internet. Shimano's delightful comedy directs us to the absurdity of what is considered forbidden and taboo by society. Leda's teacher upholds the hypocrisy of educational institutions that maintain certain parts of history and culture need to be censored from young minds. At the same time, Shimano sheds light on the oddity of artists throughout history who preferred to depict a woman having sex with a swan rather than with a man. Leda is transformed into a heroine who rebels against her teacher's injustice by refusing to be spoon-fed her education from what has been deemed acceptable by her elders.

Joe Ryan, by Megan Cohen, modernizes the myth of Orion the Hunter by setting him in a 1970s crime-ridden San Francisco alongside Artemis (Missy), an FBI liaison, and Lieutenant Leto, Missy's mother. This world recalls the protagonists of *Bullitt*, *Chinatown* and *The French Connection*, placing Joe Ryan, a police detective, in a high-stakes world of a man trying to take down an entire crime syndicate called "Scorpio." With criminals like the Bull and the Rabbit as their main adversaries, Missy and Joe must find Scorpio's leader and bring down the evil that has plagued the city once and for all. In this world we see a true parallel to the heroism of the ancients, where the protagonists will stop at nothing in their quest for righteousness. Just like the myths of the past, however, a seamless web of interconnectedness hints at a cosmic balance keeping everything—good and bad—in line.

Christian Simonsen's reinterpretation of the story of Cassiopeia and her daughter Andromeda lends a fresh perspective to the tried-and-true archetypes of the damsel in distress and the hero who saves her. In *Cassiopeia*, the famed queen's ridiculous boast that requires her daughter become a sacrifice is further satirized by Cassiopeia's encouragement of Andromeda to make the best of it. Rather than play the victim, Andromeda calls her mother out on her backpedaling behavior, changing her from a helpless princess to a savvy young woman of the world. Perseus' entrance adds a further comedic element as he bumbles his way through defeating a sea monster, causing some unintended damage along the way. Thanks to Simonsen's re-visioning, we're left questioning what truly makes a hero, and why they are needed in the first place.

A woman's role in society is further explored in *Pleiades*, a play set in the 1970s Hamptons during an era of burgeoning feminist thought. Marissa Skudlarek's spin on the myth of the seven sisters explores the multiple perspectives of young women who are trying to define how to be free in a society whose rules keep changing. Though seemingly safe in a well-to-do society, the sisters are confronted with violence that seems so far removed from the world they inhabit. Becoming a strong woman, even in a world that one would think of as privileged, proves to be a daunting challenge. Secrets are overcome by the camaraderie of sisterhood as each of the sisters tries to etch out a role that isn't colored by how they are perceived by the rest of society. The play foreshadows a move toward a new kind of feminism through the ways the characters try to make sense of the actions that have bonded them together.

The cold north wind, personified as vengeful and lustful by the Greeks, is reincarnated in *Boreas, or Hard Pack*, by Lise Miller, as a jealous, flirtatious, snow-blowing businessman. In the play, Boreas, now "Bo," serves as the catalyst that rips a New England family apart in the dead of winter. Each family member is completely absorbed with their own interactions, with Bo leaving them to feel as though quitting the family entirely is the only option. The dynamic between the grumpy, ladder-climbing father, the ditsy, coquettish mother, and the rebellious, naïve daughter humorously plays itself out as Bo seems to have entwined himself in each of the characters' lives. Miller portrays a comic, but not altogether outlandish, world where envy flourishes and crossing someone with a violent temper proves to be disastrous. This is ultimately a comment on our own world, where incidences of envy and anger have taken their toll when acted upon.

In *Chronus* by Bennett Fisher, the question is whether we go too far when we sacrifice our ideals for the promise of power. John Chronus, an Arizona businessman, courts the Tea Party to support his run for the Senate after a loss in the 2008 general elections. Fisher gives us a timely piece that one year later still bears weight, particularly in light of the 2012 presidential elections. The changing political landscape is explored through the ruthless competiveness of the characters who will stop at nothing to get into office. Personal politics and public politics become increasingly at odds with one another as the campaign progresses. The shift toward one end of the political spectrum results in public endorsements of rules and laws that Chronus is privately at odds with, creating a rift within his family. We are left questioning where we are as a society when wooing extremist thought is seen as a means for fulfilling ambition.

Claire Rice's play, *Europa*, delves into the ways in which our personal truths can be completely disparate from another person's— even in passionate love. Zeus and Europa are at the end of their affair, vacationing on the island of Crete where they are confronted with differing opinions on the state of their relationship and what it might mean to each of them. What might be a new life for one is just a brief affair for another. Rice paints a painful picture of the longing for a feeling of closeness and intimacy that simply isn't there. The heartbreaking realization that Zeus and Europa see each other very differently is a reminder to us of the sting of a passionate love that has no future. It is the kind of break-up that leaves Europa in doubt of her future plans, when all that she had been hoping for and believed was possible is ultimately gone. The play focuses our attention on love's power over our identity and how our beliefs come crashing down at the end of a relationship that wasn't reciprocal.

Too Near the Sun by Jeremy Cole recontextualizes the myth of Icarus, who tragically flies too close to the sun on man-made wings. Dual storylines weave together the story of Daedalus, the gifted architect of King Minos who builds Icarus' wings, and Otto Lilienthal, a real-life German inventor known as the "Father of Flight." The classical myth is strangely prophetic when considering the actual events surrounding Otto Lilienthal's own pursuit of building a reliable flying apparatus. Both Daedalus and Lilienthal were visionaries who understood that just because something seems impossible, doesn't mean that it is. Their respective quests to unlock the mysteries of flight are characterized by Cole's wit and loving hand with his character's voices. Their whimsy and fascination with their shared ambition reflects our own quests to be free and to reach for the unattainable dream.

David Duman's *Nyx* displays the timelessness of the goddess of the night as she transforms from formidable deity to modern-day Everywoman. In mythology, Nyx is a goddess you don't want to cross. She has been around since the beginning of time, has given birth to Sleep, Death and the Fates, and her power over mankind is feared. Everyone starts and ends under Nyx's shadow, and with a wave of her hand she can dictate to the Fates what will happen to men. As a modern-day woman, she appears to us with the same callous indifference to the plight of others. We encounter her in our daily lives as a Wal-Mart cashier, a guidance counselor, a nurse, and a baseball-crazed girlfriend. Duman's comedic interpretation of Nyx's powerful hold on society highlights the levity that even a small action has in impacting the rest of one's life.

Finally, in *Hyperion to a Satyr*, by Stuart Eugene Bousel, we meet three generations of Greek gods associated with the sun. Transformed into a wealthy Bay Area family that owns a highly successful business,

Bousel takes us on the journey of the sun god, Helios (re-named Hal), who is at a crossroads in his life, stuck between the expectations of his family as the business's future heir, his past life with his ex-wife and child, and the possibility of a future where he could truly be the person he's wanted to become. In *Hyperion to a Satyr*, we see modern interpretations of the myth of Phaeton (Helios' son who stole his chariot), the first eclipse (when Selene, the moon and Helios' sister, drives her chariot in front of his), and the replacement of Helios as the sun god by Apollo. But the play centers itself around the relationships between fathers and their sons and the expectations that we feel we must live up to. Hal's quest to find his own personal truth reflects our own struggles in trying to find a way to define ourselves. Do we give up the past in order to achieve our vision of the future, or does it inevitably make its stamp on who we are?

The power of the Greek myths extends throughout the ages not simply because they are compelling stories about gods and heroes or because they teach us the values and ideas that we have chosen as a society, but because myths are the purest form of truth we have to illustrate the human experience. The reason they pop up time and time again and are transformed by not only the writers here, but writers throughout the world, is because of their ability to focus on the essential qualities and struggles of humanity. With these ten plays, the writers of the second San Francisco Olympians Festival have continued that endless conversation with the past, leading us closer to an understanding of what it means to live upon this planet.

Barbara Jwanouskos
San Francisco/Pittsburgh
October 2012

Leda And The Pr0n

by Kirk Shimano

Leda And The Pr0n

The first public reading of *Leda and the Pr0n* was on October 28, 2011 at EXIT Theatre, as part of San Francisco Olympians Festival II: Heavenly Bodies. It was directed by Neil Higgins and featured the following cast:

Karen Offereins	LEDA
Rachel Ferensowicz	CINDY
Maura Halloran	MRS. HUFFMAN
Brian Thomen	STAGE DIRECTIONS

Characters

LEDA, female, a high school freshman
CINDY, female, Leda's BFF
MRS. HUFFMAN, female, the school librarian

Location

A library in a public high school in a red state. The year 2012, or somewhere thereabouts.

CINDY stares into a computer screen, completely captivated. She clicks the mouse and jumps in shock… then clicks again.

LEDA enters carrying a stack of books.

LEDA The librarian said that these were the only—

LEDA notices the images onscreen and drops the books.

WHAT IS THAT?

CINDY jumps in front of the screen and attempts to block it with her body. When that doesn't work, she back-clicks furiously.

CINDY What? Nothing. I mean—oh, yeah, I think it just, like, came up by accident.

LEDA You are such a liar.

CINDY NO! Wait. Just a second.

LEDA attempts to leave. CINDY grabs her arm.

LEDA You know we're not supposed to look at stuff like that. Do you know how much trouble we could get into?

CINDY You don't even know what you saw!

LEDA I saw... (*lowers her voice*) boobies.

CINDY Geez, you sound like you're in the seventh grade.

LEDA What will Mrs. Huffman say if she catches you looking at porn?

CINDY It's not porn!

LEDA Then what is that girl doing to that bird? We're supposed to be learning about Greek mythology, not weird sex stuff.

CINDY This IS—

MRS. HUFFMAN walks by.

MRS. HUFFMAN Girls, we need to keep our voices down in the library.

LEDA Sorry Mrs. Huffman.

CINDY (*simultaneously*) I know Mrs. Huffman.

MRS. HUFFMAN Now let's get back to our research. We have to share the computer with everyone else.

LEDA We will Mrs. Huffman.

CINDY (*simultaneously*) Thank you Mrs. Huffman.

LEDA Oh Mrs. Huffman...

MRS. HUFFMAN turns around. CINDY kicks LEDA's foot.

MRS. HUFFMAN Did you say something, Leda?

CINDY No Mrs. Huffman. I was just talking to her.

MRS. HUFFMAN Well, let us get back to work then.

MRS. HUFFMAN leaves.

LEDA "We need to keep our voices down"—I hate that "we" stuff. It's so bossy. *(pouts)* I wasn't even going to tell her about you, Cindy.

CINDY That's good, because this is really about you.

LEDA If you're trying to get me to—

CINDY Do you know where your name comes from, Leda?

LEDA My parents gave it to me.

CINDY Well, duh. I mean, obviously. But the name Leda. It's Greek.

LEDA So?

CINDY So, I just Googled you and that's how I found this.

CINDY shows LEDA the computer screen.

LEDA Gross! Stop it.

CINDY Shhhh!

MRS. HUFFMAN *(offstage)* Girls!

CINDY Leda thought she saw a spider, Mrs. Huffman! It's gone now.

LEDA You're crazy! Do you know that? If she found you with this… Cindy, we're both in the abstinence club!

CINDY Leda was a queen.

LEDA Really?

CINDY She was the queen of Sparta, which was like the biggest part of Greece or something. And Zeus was the king of all the gods and he, like, came down and well, like, you know. But he knew she wouldn't let her get all close to him, so he changed into a swan first.

LEDA That looks like that really hurts.

CINDY Can you imagine how noisy that would be? It'd be like a car alarm. HONK! Honk honk!

LEDA What?

CINDY That's the noise a swan makes. HONK.

LEDA Wait, what's that link there?

>   *CINDY clicks the mouse. More images appear.*

Wow, there are a lot of these.

>   *LEDA takes over the mouse and clicks even faster.*

And it's not just paintings. There are poems and other stuff too.

CINDY I think I hear Mrs. Huffman coming back.

LEDA It's fine. She's over by the atlases.

CINDY Are you sure? She's looking at us…

LEDA So, like, five hundred years ago people would all get in trouble if they painted guys and girls doing it. So instead they painted—

CINDY Birds and girls doing it?

LEDA Yeah. It was almost like a code or something. There were things that they really wanted to say and this was their way to say it.

CINDY Whoa, that one's weird.

LEDA Actually… I think it's kind of… interesting. I mean, in a way.

>   *She cranes her neck.*

It's definitely more interesting than the abstinence club.

>   *MRS. HUFFMAN reenters.*

MRS. HUFFMAN Girls, we have to realize—WHAT IS THAT?

>   *CINDY hurls herself across the keyboard.*

CINDY What? No. It's nothing it's…

MRS. HUFFMAN We should remove that at once!

CINDY Yes Mrs. Huffman.

MRS. HUFFMAN Whose idea was this?

    LEDA continues reading silently.

Leda, I am talking to you, young lady.

LEDA I'm just reading about how the Italian painters…

MRS. HUFFMAN I said you need to stop looking at those pornographic images now.

    MRS. HUFFMAN violently pulls the plug from the computer.

LEDA *(quietly)* They're not porn.

MRS. HUFFMAN What did you say?

LEDA I just wanted to learn more.

MRS. HUFFMAN Well if we want to learn more, then school is not the place for that.

    CINDY giggles.

You know what I mean.

LEDA But you don't know what these pictures mean! All those painters just wanted to make something but no one would let them do what they wanted.

MRS. HUFFMAN That's because what they wanted was obscene.

LEDA It doesn't matter that you turned off that computer. The pictures are still out there.

MRS. HUFFMAN Leda, I am surprised at you! Where is this coming from?

LEDA I dunno. Ancient Greece, I guess? I mean can a picture that old really be that bad?

MRS. HUFFMAN Perversity is very old. That's why we must fight so hard to suppress it.

LEDA Those painters just wanted to say something and you're going to shut them up again?

MRS. HUFFMAN Leda, we are this close to suspending you.

LEDA You do realize that just thinking about sex won't make me pregnant, don't you?

MRS. HUFFMAN Pack up your books.

> *LEDA dives into her book bag. She pulls out her cell phone and begins typing furiously.*
>
> *MRS. HUFFMAN reaches for the phone but trips. LEDA ducks out of the way and continues to type.*

Principal's office. Now.

> *LEDA packs up her bags and walks toward the door.*

LEDA HONK.

MRS. HUFFMAN What?

LEDA HONK! HONK! HONK!

> *LEDA waves her phone triumphantly.*

Sometimes, the harder you try to hide something, the easier it is for everyone to find it. Look who has a new Facebook profile photo. HONK!

> *MRS. HUFFMAN fumes with rage. CINDY approaches her quietly.*

CINDY So… this means I'm off the hook, right?

> *End of play.*

Joe Ryan

by Megan Cohen

Joe Ryan

The first public reading of *Joe Ryan* was on October 7, 2011 at EXIT Theatre, as part of San Francisco Olympians Festival II: Heavenly Bodies. It was directed by Claire Rice and featured the following cast:

Matt Gunnison	JOE RYAN
Kirsten Broadbear	MISSY
John Lennon Harrison	THE BULL
Sunil Patel	THE RABBIT
Allison Payne	LETO
Benji Cooper	STAGE DIRECTIONS

Characters

JOE "Orion" Ryan — Male. 30s-40s. A police detective. Justice with a moustache and a tortured soul; nothing he does is good enough; he doesn't go to sleep, he passes out from exhaustion. Tense, tough, blunt, and brilliant; walks while he eats, talks while he drives; smells of coffee and sweat.

Ms. "Artemis" MISSY — Female. 20s-30s. An upwardly mobile FBI liason. Sharp as a tack, sexy as heck. Sees everything, tolerates no nonsense, and smells like a teenage boy's dream of what a woman might smell like.

The RABBIT— Male. Any age, so long as he's scrawny & can talk fast. Member of the Scorpio gang. A heroin addict and the best thief in the city.

The BULL — Male. Any age, so long as he's hefty & menacing. The Scorpio gang's meat-fisted enforcer.

Lieutenant LETO — Female. 40s-60s. Joe's boss, Missy's mom. Sympathetic in tone, but opaque in intent; the closest thing we have to a god.

Time & Place

San Francisco in a movie in the 1970s.

Setting

There is a police desk, where a cigarette smolders endlessly in an ashtray. A coffee pot boils on a table, where it has been boiling since the dawn of time. There is a streetlamp, which spills out a harsh yellow pool of light where characters occasionally stop to meet, or run through suddenly during chases. A steering wheel hangs in front of two empty chairs. The sun and the moon appear and disappear; sometimes, both are visible at once.

Sometimes the characters speak to us, to each other, to themselves; I've made as few specific suggestions about that as I could possibly stand to make.

JOE The buck teeth. The hollow cheeks. The big, saggy ears with the droopy lobes. The minute she rattled off the description, I recognized him. The skinny arms, the scrawny legs always poised to run. Every detail the robbery victim gave of her attacker sharpened the picture in my mind's eye until it was like I was staring at a portrait etched in steel. The Rabbit. He earned the nickname in his early days, when a call girl he ran around with started telling stories about him on the streets. There were lots of stories, and most of 'em were about the way he fucked, fast and angry, endless for days, like it was all he knew how to do. The other stories were about his heists, his thieving and his miraculous getaways, jumping over fences and disappearing into the dark. The best story, the one story to end all Rabbit stories, was the one about the time a beat cop saw the Rabbit hunched on a doorstep, shooting up heroin right into the droopy, saggy flesh of his earlobe. Who knew if it was true. It felt true. Regardless, now I knew who I was looking for. I was looking for the Rabbit.

LETO A.P.B., A.P.B. We need the Rabbit. All eyes out for the Rabbit.

JOE A patrol car sees him.

LETO North Beach, Broadway. Rabbit coming out of the Hustler Club on Broadway.

JOE I'm there in minutes.

LETO Rabbit on the corner of Columbus.

JOE And I see him. A flash of dead eyes disappearing into the throngs of drunk businessmen and Kerouac-dreaming tourists in front of City

Lights.

RABBIT Awwwww, man. Aw shit. Shit.

JOE Shit, he's made me. Red light, don't walk, Rabbit doesn't care, he's not walking, he's running, darting between the cars, chasing the dark, chasing safety.

RABBIT Get me home. Just wanna get home.

JOE I take the long way around, catch him trying to scoot down the alley, come at him from the front.

RABBIT Bye, Joe.

JOE He's up a fire escape. I'm a quarter of the way up by the time he's halfway. By the time I'm halfway, he's already on the roof.

RABBIT G'night, Joe.

JOE Not gonna lose him. Not another loss. Too many nights, too many times like this, so close, the hem of his flared pants disappearing ten steps ahead of me like a dream dissolving in the light of dawn. Not tonight. I'm on it, on the trail, leaping up the ladder two steps at a time like I'm not even walking on earth, like I'm walking on sky, floating on the night, letting it carry me up.

> *The RABBIT laughs.*

The roof, the roof, I stretch my arms up to grab the ledge, then I see the face. Buck teeth have become a sealed-closed curl of fat-lipped grin. Big pale eyes have become two chunks of blackened, gleaming pupil, and hollow cheeks turn to flaring, steaming nostrils. The face peering down over the ledge was not the face of the Rabbit. This was the face of the Bull. Not tonight, not tonight.

BULL Hey, Joe. Hey, Officer Ryan, aren't you a little far from home?

JOE Too many nights at the hands of the Bull, beaten into a pile of bloody sand under his hard, meaty fists.

BULL Aren't you a little far out of your neighborhood? I didn't think North Beach was quite your patch, Officer.

JOE Not another night like that, please, not another week of limping, another week of bruises and raw, tender insides. Backup, backup.

LETO Backup, who's in the area?

JOE Radio's too slow, retreat, retreat, run, speed down the fire escape. Fall out of the sky, run down towards the earth. This gang, always working in teams, always working in pairs, the bait and the trap and the trick, never a fair chase, never a fair fight, always me against them, always one against two, and now I'm on the run, running from the Bull and the Rabbit, side by side in the alley, ten steps behind me.

RABBIT Where you goin', Joe?

BULL Where you runnin' to? We just wanna talk.

JOE Not tonight, please.

LETO Patrol car at Columbus and Broadway, we got a black and white waiting for you.

JOE Safety. Safety ahead. I run. I lose them, the two of them, the Rabbit and the Bull, I run until I can't hear them behind me, till I can't hear the Bull snorting with effort, or the Rabbit's high-pitched snicker. I run. I jump into the squad car waiting with its door open. Slam it shut. I tell the waiting officer, "Drive, drive." He says "Where'd they go?" like we could give chase, but I know these two, and they wouldn't stick around. "Just drive." The dead eyes and floppy lobes, the flaring nostrils and meaty mouth, drive away, leave them in the crowds, let them disappear. Not tonight. Not tonight, guys.

RABBIT So long, Joe.

BULL Goodnight, Officer Ryan.

JOE Not tonight, boys. Soon. Soon I'll have you. Soon I'll have you both, have you all, find you where you live and take you away from there and never let you go back. Never let you back on the streets.

BULL Goodnight. For now.

The RABBIT laughs hysterically.

Sweet dreams, Officer Ryan.

LETO What happened out there? Thought you had him this time.

JOE Not tonight. There were two of 'em.

LETO Running in pairs, running in packs. It's a good strategy. You could learn something from them.

JOE I don't need any learning they've got to teach.

LETO I know you like a solitary life, Joe, but you can't get these guys alone.

JOE I'll do what needs doing.

LETO Any way you plan it, one guy versus a gang of guys is a shit plan.

JOE I'll figure it out.

LETO I already have. This is your new partner. FBI gang task force. Inter-agency collaboration. This is Missy. This is Officer Ryan.

MISSY Officer Ryan.

JOE People call me Joe.

LETO This is Officer Joe Ryan. Nickname's "Orion." Like the hunter. Call him what you want, it's none of my business, and none of my concern. I'll leave you two to work it out. Try not to kill each other.

JOE No promises.

MISSY Well, hello to you, too.

LETO I said, don't kill each other. That's not a request, that's an order.

JOE I get it.

LETO I'm leaving now, but if I see this girl storm out of here in a huff because of anything you said or did, I'll lock you in a holding cell overnight.

JOE Ha, on what charge?

LETO Disturbing my peace. Now get to work. I'm going to.

JOE and MISSY are left alone.

MISSY I didn't ask for this assignment.

JOE *(mocking her)* I didn't ask for this assignment.

MISSY Oh everyone look out, it thinks it's clever.

JOE Look, lady, they can give me a partner, but I'm not gonna take one.

MISSY Let me tell you a little something about where I come from. *(beat)* I come from a place where we don't put up with shit like that.

JOE Believe me, I don't care about where you're from.

MISSY Believe me, I don't care about whether you care about things or not. Now stop fucking around like a whiny child and tell me about the goddamn case.

JOE *(to us)* I'd been after the Scorpio gang for years before I even knew who I was chasing. I'd round up their low-level toads, a flunky here and a two-bit dealer there, you know how it goes. I stumbled across an under-the-table bookie out in Santa Clara a few days after I'd cuffed a crooked importer right here on our side of the bay and it wasn't until February of the next year that I saw the connections, figured out they were on the same payroll. It wasn't until February, when that one teenaged junkie squealed, poor little Robert McCoy, poor pathetic little Bobby, came from a good home but turned bad, it wasn't until he starting talking, hoping to lighten his load, hoping to shake justice off his selfish shoulders and go free, it wasn't until he talked, served up a pile of documents on a silver platter, it wasn't until that one little weakling broke that I knew I even had a gang case that needed breaking. That pile of papers, it was the best day, the worst thing that's ever happened to me. Like a Valentine card from a vengeful god. I read them all, page after page, over and over again, all through the night, and after that, I didn't sleep. I don't remember sleeping after that, because there was no difference between asleep and awake, because from that moment, everything was a dream. A bad dream. Can you… no, nobody can imagine. To find out, all at once, that running under every square inch of this city, there was an electric network of crime, and everyone, and I mean everyone, from the little schoolkid cheating on his chemistry test all the way up to City Hall, everyone who was doing wrong was one buzzing little wire on this huge buzzing switchboard, and that switchboard was named Scorpio. Scorpio. Score. Pee. Oh. I was the one.

The one to stop it. The one who found it. The one who needed to find more.

MISSY What happened to the squealer?

JOE We did the best we could. Let him out, of course, full police protection, of course…

MISSY How long did it take?

JOE Less than an hour.

MISSY Jesus.

JOE He was dead about… forty minutes after he left the interrogation room? And they did it real rough, too.

MISSY Forty minutes. Jesus.

JOE Yep.

MISSY How'd you let that happen?

JOE I don't know. I still don't know what went wrong. Poor kid. Forty minutes. And that's counting the time it took us to do the release paperwork.

MISSY I bet that took a while, too, probably took you forever to fill out all those forms, huh? Probably hurt your head, huh? After all, you're not very smart.

JOE Hell, maybe I'm not.

MISSY Spending years chasing this gang alone, like you're the only one who "gets it."

JOE I got nobody to trust.

MISSY "I got nobody?" Seriously, is English your second language?

JOE You think if you're mean to me, I'm gonna like you better?

MISSY Aren't you?

JOE You think if I like you better, I'm gonna trust you.

MISSY You got no choice.

JOE There's always a choice.

MISSY Ha.

JOE I've got choices. Keep you in the dark, tell you nothing, show you nothing… or tell you everything, tell you what's not in the files. Tell you the mess behind the reports, tell you everything. You want me to tell you, right?

MISSY It'll be easier if you do.

JOE Yeah, I don't think so. She can make me take a partner, but she can't make me tell you squat.

MISSY It'll be easier if you do. I'll only figure it out on my own anyway, then you'll just be embarrassed when I turn out to be so much quicker, so much smarter, so much stealthier than you are, than you ever thought it was even possible to be. You know why?

JOE Why?

MISSY 'Cause I'm fucking *magic*. Like a fucking omniscient magic fucking *wizard*. So, while your sorry, droopy ass is pounding the pavement with your flat feet, doing everything the hard way, I'll be sitting here in a comfortable chair, with clean shoes, looking for patterns and connections, and actually solving the case. What's hard for you, it's easy for me, easy like peeling a fucking orange, so if you don't brief me fully on this dossier, all you're doing is wasting time, and making yourself look shitty in the process. What are you protecting?

JOE Oh, I'm protecting my fucking soul. My life. My heart, my body, I don't know, you're so *magic* you figure it out.

MISSY I don't like you.

JOE Look, I'm protecting the people of this city. Trying to protect them from a menace that is so tangled up in this town, it runs like a vein next to every artery of life in San Francisco. You want to help? Fine. But this is not your case, this is not your operation, this is mine. My hunt, my prey. Play nice and you can carry my canteen.

MISSY Just shut up and give me the files.

LETO Give her the files.

JOE *(to us)* Lieutenant Leto tells me to give her the files. So I do. I might play dirty with robbers on the streets sometimes, but I never disobey a direct order from my supervisor. You choose your battles, and fighting the lieutenant who always has my back, who's made my career, who keeps me alive, keeps me holding the badge, lets me live to hunt another criminal another day, fighting her? That's no kind of battle to choose. So I give Missy the files. I don't feel good about it. I go. I walk the streets all night, or sleep all night and dream of walking, who can say. All I know is it's the next morning already, and the sky is blue like a new car, and the city is shiny and bright like it's got nothing to be ashamed of, and Missy has a lot of good ideas, and I haven't had enough coffee to deal with them.

MISSY See, Joe, the thing is that you can't just—

JOE I can, and I will.

MISSY You can't just chase these people around willy-nilly, you have to know where they're going to run, and—

JOE Thanks for the tip, let me write that down quick before I forget.

MISSY These people. These Scorpio people. Say what you will about their aims or their ethics, but their methods? Are… stunning. Beautiful. Gorgeous, even—their level of, just, you know, organization—it's like… not just clockwork, it's like gilded clockwork, like golden clockwork, it's—

JOE If you like them so much, why don't you just fucking marry them?

MISSY I am trying to tell you something, Joe.

JOE Just buy a hundred wedding rings, and marry the whole Scorpio gang, then you and them and their clockwork can all go on a honeymoon to the Bahamas, and be out of my precinct, and I can be happy for the rest of my life. I need a cup of coffee.

MISSY I'm trying to tell you that you'll never catch them.

JOE I appreciate the vote of confidence.

MISSY You'll never catch them *if* you keep on with the way you've been doing this. Well, trying to do this, anyway.

JOE Ha.

MISSY They have a system. They have planning, and strategy. They have, you know, maps. They probably have charts, even.

JOE Ooooh, charts, well let me get the President on the phone right away—

MISSY I've drawn up some diagrams—

JOE Let me call the Secretary of State—

MISSY I've drawn up diagrams of the city here, of all of San Francisco. Now, each dot represents—

JOE My ass.

MISSY Each dot represents a stakeout, we need to do a series of stakeouts—and it's something we can do in shifts, even with limited manpower—to find their leadership, what we need to do here is narrow down—

JOE I need another cup of coffee.

MISSY If we systematically eliminate each of these zones, we can zero in on their hiding place, or probably places, there might be more than one—

JOE Do you want a cup of coffee?

MISSY I have one, thanks.

JOE I'm going to get a cup of coffee.

MISSY Aren't you even going to look?

JOE At what?

MISSY At the map. It's all based on the reports you've made in the past six months, so it should be pretty current, and—and—Joe?

JOE *(to us)* She's still talking, I hear her voice following me all the way down to the break room where the coffee machine is, but it doesn't really matter. I'd stopped listening at least a couple minutes before I'd left her at the desk.

LETO Officer Ryan.

JOE Ma'am.

LETO You know what I'm going to say. Save me the trouble, Joe.

JOE You're going to say "Give her a chance, try it out, a fresh perspective, new set of eyes, blah blah blah."

LETO Great. You know the whole speech. Now I don't have to bother.

JOE I guess not.

LETO Don't make me bother. Listen, I don't want to have to take you off this case.

JOE Don't. Just… don't.

LETO Ryan, it's good that you care so much. It's good that you're a great cop, that you are committed to this chase, to this hunt, even after all these years, committed to tracking this gang.

JOE I know.

LETO But that's not enough. Hasn't been, isn't now, and isn't going to be.

JOE I'm getting closer.

LETO No. You're getting older. And they're getting away with everything. Now get back in there, and listen to that woman.

MISSY Well, you ready to work yet? *(beat)* How's the coffee?

JOE Boiled. Twice-boiled. Three times boiled, probably. Barely even a liquid. If you put it in a pair of pants, it could walk around the room.

MISSY Joe.

JOE Show me the zones. And the dots. All the fucking blue dots.

MISSY *(to us)* It's a good plan. The best plan you can have, when you don't know where they live, is to find out where they live. The best thing you can do, when you're chasing rats, is to find the nest. The grubby, grungy little hole where they hide, where they infest, where they eat and shit and breed and whine, and where they plot, where they make their plans, their gorgeous complex plans, the plans that trip you up if you don't see them coming miles ahead of when they start to happen. The plans that roadblock you at every turn as you stumble through the city's darkness and neon. I know he's not listening. I know he's gonna have to learn the hard way. It won't be the first time I've done this dance, it won't be the last. I'm used to leading. Not with force, not with power, just leading by stamina. Leading eventually. Leading, finally, because the person who thinks he's leading gives up, and just lets it happen, lets you show him how to follow. Lets you teach him how to follow. It's the oldest boy-girl dance in the book. Well, the second oldest. We all know the oldest.

JOE I don't know about this whole stakeout thing. A night here, a night there, I don't see the pattern.

MISSY It's the best way to narrow down the terrain, to find their hiding place, their leadership. Just try it. Let's just try it. And if it doesn't work, you go to the lieutenant and you tell her "I tried it, Missy's an idiot, now give me a horse and a rifle and leave me to my own numbskull devices and let me fail my own stupid too-proud lone-cowboy way."

JOE I don't like horses, and I don't shoot rifles, I shoot handguns, because I am not a cowboy, I am a real cop, which doesn't seem to be something that you know much about. Real cops don't work at desks, they work on the street, where the life is, where the crime is, and I don't know what they taught you at the CIA—

MISSY FBI, I'm from the FBI.

JOE I don't know what they taught you at the NFL or TNT or XYZ or wherever the hell they teach people to be like you, but being a cop isn't about making pretty pictures at your desk. It's about instinct.

MISSY Well, thank God you're here to teach me better.

JOE Police work is about instinct, motion. It's about criminals you deal with in the flesh, and not being afraid of them, or about being afraid but running towards them in the dark anyway, because even though your life may be on the line, your job is on the line, too, and your life is worthless without your job.

MISSY Thank you, Professor.

JOE It's not about planning, it's about the smell of piss and gunpowder in an alley where you're cornered by a thug.

MISSY Are you done?

JOE We'll try it your way. Not because I want to, but because I don't have a choice. We'll try it. But you're still an idiot.

MISSY Is that it? Is that everything you have to say? I'm an idiot, that's it? Try to bother me. Try it. You can't do it. You won't.

JOE I just want to catch these guys.

MISSY So do I.

JOE Yeah, you want to catch them with your little charts, like they're rats in a maze, but they're not predictable. They're not an experiment you can control in a lab, they're a bunch of wacked-out junkies and psych-ward thugs, crazy and insane, impulsive and wild, and they don't plot their crimes or their routes any more than a guy in a coma plots his drooling.

MISSY Joe. We're on the same team.

JOE We'll play connect-the-dots on your little dotted-up maps, and you'll see what it gets you. It's gonna get you shit on a cracker, but with no cracker to balance the shit on.

MISSY *(to us)* It shouldn't bother me. But it does. Because maybe, just maybe, he's right.

LETO So. How's the first day.

MISSY It's fine. I mean, it is how it is.

LETO There's going to be nothing easy about this, Missy. You knew that going in. Not the gang, not the case, not the cop. It's an uphill trip both ways, and it's going to stay that way until it's done.

MISSY I'll be fine.

LETO I know you will. That's why I let you take the assignment. I'm not worried about you, but I can see that you're upset.

MISSY I'm handling it fine.

LETO If you need to talk, I'm here.

MISSY I won't.

LETO But if you do…

MISSY I know. Thank you.

LETO That said, don't expect me to do you any special favors. Don't expect me to cut you any slack, Missy. This is a job, and it's about the job, and it has to stay about the job, even though I happen to be your mother.

MISSY Thank you, Lieutenant.

LETO I won't be baking you any cookies, or singing you any lullabies.

MISSY I know, Mom.

LETO Even though I'm your mother, you work for me. That's why you're here. That said… it's nice to have you around, to see you around the office. It's nice to have you home from Washington.

MISSY It's nice to be home. *(beat)* I think.

LETO And… be careful. Please.

MISSY *(to us)* It shouldn't bother me. But it does.

JOE Stakeouts are for rookies. Any wet-behind-the-ears, shoe-polish-still-on-the-boots rookie could do this job. Sitting in a car, looking out at the city, what are we, watching a movie? What is this, life is a movie to you?

MISSY You gotta think of the big picture here, Ryan. Let me see your notes.

JOE I'm not taking notes.

MISSY We're both supposed to take notes.

JOE What is this, high-school physics?

MISSY If you don't pay attention and take notes for reference, then the stakeout is worthless.

JOE Well, look at that, we finally agree on something.

MISSY This is only worthless if you make it worthless.

JOE I'm getting out of the car.

MISSY Don't you dare.

JOE I'll flush 'em out, you write it down as they run by. We can't just sit here and hope they cross the street when the light turns green. We gotta rustle the bushes and see what crawls past. These guys hide. They hide until you seek 'em out, Missy. Miss Artemis. Little Miss Missy.

MISSY Fine.

JOE Little Miss Magic Missy.

MISSY I said fine! Go, try to find 'em, chase 'em around if you want to, just make sure you remember where you found them, so we can put it on the map, so you can tell me where to put the dots on the map as you mutter from your hospital bed where you'll be lying after they beat you to a pulp.

JOE Great. I'll see you in traction.

MISSY *(to us)* The minute he slams the car door, I know I've made a mistake. An error in judgment. Nobody's perfect, after all. I'm pretty close to it, but even I'm not perfect. Not all the time. I go out after him, go looking for him. Got to make sure he's OK. Got to look out for your partner. Even when he's an asshole. Even when he's an idiot.

JOE Freedom. The familiar chill of the fog, the grunts of the exhaust pipes from the cars stuck in traffic, the feel of the city. The feel of my terrain.

MISSY Turning corner after corner, it's only been a minute, how'd he get so far ahead? How'd I lose him so quick?

JOE I swivel around corners, double-back through shortcuts, I'm covering every inch of the block, peeking in every doorway, rattling the cover of every dumpster. Come out, come out, wherever you're hiding. I'm going to find you. I'm finding you any second, I'm finding you already. I'm all ready for you.

MISSY The sky is dark. The fog is wet. The cars are loud, the people are louder. The loudest thing is my heart, pounding with each step, with each footprint I pound into the pavement. Where did he go?

JOE I see the twitch, hear the sniffle, the horrid little moan, before I see the ears, the eyes, the bony hands, the dirty shirt.

RABBIT Aw, shit.

JOE I've got him.

RABBIT I'm gone, I'm going quick, I'm gone like a firework that's already blown out in the sky, gone, not even a smoke trail left behind me.

JOE Where'd he go?

MISSY I've got him, got someone, I think it's him, the droopy ears, the hollow eyes, the buck teeth like a streetlamp taunting in the night, follow follow follow, this is not a chase to be lost. Don't get lost. I see him in front of me, but where am I?

JOE Where'd he go? Heading for a dealer, for a hideout, for a hole to crawl into? Where's your carrot, motherfucker?

MISSY Over a fence, under a staircase, through an alley then out in the open. Across the sidewalk in front of a mansion, then another mansion, then another mansion.

RABBIT Nowhere to hide, I fucking hate Pacific Heights!

MISSY There's nowhere to hide, you freaked-out little junkie, and you know it. I see you know it, I see surrender in the curve of your bony, wire-thin spine. Why not just slow down, slow to a crawl, drop to the sidewalk and put your hands out to get cuffed? You can't fight this, you can't fight my fucking magic, I know where you are, I'll follow your smell, your reek, I'll follow your footsteps echoing, no matter how fleet of foot, you can't fly from this bitch. Gaining ground, gaining speed, two more blocks and I'll have your ass.

RABBIT Oh shit, she's got me, she's almost got me.

BULL I got you this time.

MISSY Oh, shit.

RABBIT Thank God!

BULL I got this, I'll handle her. You go, little man, just go.

RABBIT I love you!

> *The BULL laughs.*

BULL Don't worry, little buddy, I always got your back.

MISSY With a high-pitched squeal and a shudder of limbs, he's gone, the scrawny junkie's gone. And it's two of us again, but not the same two as before. This new one, this new one… this is a whole other deal.

BULL Good evening, Miss. Fancy meeting you here. In the middle of nowhere. With no one else around.

MISSY Oh, shit.

JOE Where'd he go? Into the park?

MISSY Whatever you're thinking of doing—

BULL You look scared.

JOE Where the fuck did he go? She's gonna laugh her ass off when I get back to the car.

MISSY You don't have to do whatever you're about to do, we can just— we can figure something out.

BULL You sound real scared, lady. Is you scared? Of little old me? Why should you be so scared of me, what do you think I am, some kinda monster?

MISSY Should've stayed in D.C.

JOE I won't have her laughing at me, I won't let that happen, it can't, I won't let it.

MISSY Shouldn't have come here, to the west edge of this country where nothing makes any sense, to the city where the ocean and the bay bleed into each other like they got no decency, I shouldn't have come here, this is still some bullshit cowboy town, no rules no law, this is a load of shit, and I'm… I don't even know where I am.

BULL I just wanna look at you. Just a look.

MISSY Where are we?

BULL I ain't gonna hurt you, I just… look how scared you are. I like how scared you are.

JOE If I can't catch him, I'm at least gonna fake it. Run through some puddles, run through some mud, make it look like a chase, get my cheeks flushed and my brow sweaty, she'll never know, she'll never know I'm faking, she'll think it was a real chase for real. More mud, more grime, get some brambles on there, into the park, into the park and get some mud on the boots, some mud on the hems, that's the right thing, she'll never know, she'll never guess it's not for real, she'll never guess I lost him miles ago, she'll think it was a real good chase.

RABBIT Aw, shit.

JOE He's there, I see him, I see his shadow, his silhouette that I've traced in my mind a hundred times like a prayer, I've got him again now, got his trail again.

RABBIT Safety, safety, where, where, I need—help me—I need—HELP ME—

MISSY What's that sound, close by—

BULL Just look at you for one more minute, then I'm gonna… oh, boy…

RABBIT I LOVE YOU!

BULL Little buddy, where'd you come from?!

MISSY He turns toward the noise—

JOE I'm on the trail, on the track, half a step behind and then I see all of them, all three of them, and then she's—

MISSY Just enough time to go for the gun, and I—

> *Suddenly and at the same time, a gunshot and a howl of agony from the BULL.*

JOE The shot, the scream of pain, they pierce the night, fill the park like water filling a sink, it's all anyone can hear, it's all anyone's ever heard.

MISSY The smoke from the barrel swirls up like the delicate curve of a swan's neck, and I break it with a sigh. Feels like the first breath I've taken in hours, like I was drowning before and now… now I'm fine, or if I'm not fine, at least I'm breathing again. My ears are ringing. I almost feel sorry, but I don't. They're gone into the bushes, the both of them, big and small, all their skin and bones and muscle and meat and now there's dark blood, too, along with the rest of it—and suddenly Joe's right here, asking if I'm all right, and I don't know how to answer. I tell him I'm all right. I have to be. I don't have a choice.

JOE She walks all the way back to the car with her arm draped over my shoulder, not like it's on purpose, just like she doesn't know where else to put it.

MISSY I feel cosmic. Almost like a god. I feel like magic. I always do. But tonight, I don't feel like it's the good kind.

JOE It's like there's not enough room in the world for her arm unless I help her carry it.

MISSY I shot him, and he bled. Yes, he was a criminal. Yes, he was a thug, an animal, a threat. I shot him, all the way down to the blood, and the blood came spurting out, and it ran all the way across him, spreading across him from the side like a big wet shadow. Never done it before. Never want to do that again.

LETO It was a good shoot.

JOE She barely winged him, probably. I mean… he got away!

LETO You'd rather he was dead?

JOE I just… I'd rather not be working with a partner who's hysterical.

Who shoots when she ain't got to and who leans on me all the way back to the car like a cripple. She's a liability, she doesn't know how to handle herself.

LETO It was a good shoot, Joe.

JOE A good shoot would've gotten us a suspect to question. Shoot him in the leg so he can't get away, shoot him in the head and then cuff the junkie bystander, shoot the junkie and then throw him at the big guy like you're playing dodgeball, I don't care, just if you're gonna shoot, then shoot someone in a way that fucking gets us something!

LETO I can see that you're upset.

JOE Congratulations, you're reading my mind.

LETO I see it, and I can understand why you're upset. That said, don't expect me to do you any special favors. Don't expect me to cut you any slack, Joe, even though you're my favorite. This is a job, and it's about the job, and it has to stay about the job, even though I happen to be someone who cares about you, who's rooting for you, who wants you to catch these guys, who wants you to win, and win big, at this game.

JOE It's not a game.

LETO Oh, sure it is, as much as checkers or backgammon or Pin the Tail on the Donkey, but it's a game that's a lot harder to play. Part of playing it, you don't always get what you want right when you want it. That isn't how justice works, you know that, Joe. Justice is not ordering a pizza, Ryan, justice requires patience and compromises, because a lot of the time, it takes a while and isn't quite as good as you'd hoped. So, getting frustrated? That just tells me you can't see the big picture.

JOE I know, I'm sorry, I'll pull it together. I'll be fine.

LETO Good. 'Cause even though I like you, Ryan, remember: you work for me. That's why you're here. And she's here to help you. And that's how it's going right now, and that's how it's going to go until it's done.

JOE I know.

LETO And even though you're my favorite, no matter how good a job you do I'm not going to be baking you any cookies out of gratitude, or singing you any lullabies to calm your sorry ass down at the end of the day.

JOE Good, I hate lullabies.

LETO Now, it's been a long shift for everyone, but at least it's still only the middle of the night, and not the early morning yet. So get out of my office and get yourself home, before the sunrise comes in here and reminds us how ugly we're getting.

RABBIT Just keep breathing, keep breathing.

BULL I know… I know what to do.

RABBIT I'll keep pressing on it, keep pressure on it—helping you—but you have to—

BULL I know what to do. Ain't like I never been shot before. Little buddy. I'm… fine… just a little…

RABBIT You ain't fine, big man, you're bleeding like a crazy waterfall over here. You just gotta hang in till I got you fixed up.

BULL Don't need you doing anything… I'm just a little tired.

RABBIT Just keep talking.

BULL Don't feel like talking. It hurts to talk—like if I just—

RABBIT I gotta do some stuff to you, OK, and it's gonna hurt, OK, but if we don't get this bullet out, get you fixed up, it's gonna be real bad. I gotta get this shoulder of yours all fixed up, OK, but you can't pass, here, you gotta stay awake, OK?

BULL Yeah, I'll try to… aw, fuck, ow—

RABBIT Keep talking to me. Tell me funny jokes, huh? Just keep talking.

BULL Just be quiet, if I can just—for a minute, just maybe a little—just a little snooze and I'll—

RABBIT No, no, you just gotta stay awake till you're fixed up, that's all—won't be long now, just—I know you're losing lots of blood, you can't let it—if you let it shut you up, quiet you down, get you passed out, you don't know what'll—it could be so bad, real bad, so you gotta keep—ARE YOU LISTENING TO ME?

BULL Huh? Yeah, yeah.

RABBIT Talk to me. Tell me everything about yourself, about your life.

BULL I don't wanna… you don't wanna know from… you already know all about me.

RABBIT Well, I forget, OK? Just… talk about something! What'd you have for breakfast?

BULL I don't eat breakfast.

RABBIT You don't eat breakfast? You're a nutbag, how are you gonna expect to keep your strength up with no breakfast?

BULL Breakfast is for housewives.

RABBIT Yeah? Tell me. Tell me everything about it.

BULL Gimme a glass of water.

RABBIT No water till you're all sewed up, you gotta—

BULL Aw man, I don't want you sewing me up like some fucking quilt, I'm gonna be—

RABBIT STOP STOP you can't stand up you gotta—

BULL Aw. Oh, whoa, OK. Aw, man—

RABBIT Yeah, sit back down, just back down right here, now, OK, you cannot have water right now, OK, it's not good for a shooting, you can't—

BULL I'm gonna die of thirst.

RABBIT You can't eat or drink anything safely till you're stabilized, you can't have water till you have medical attention—I know, I had a buddy that taught me all about it.

BULL Die of thirst if you don't… accidentally kill me… with those scissors… aw geez, I can't look at what you're—aw—

RABBIT Don't look, look away, look at the wall, look over there at the wall.

BULL Looking at the wall with the—Christ, this place is a shithole—

RABBIT Now, listen, OK, just look at the wall and listen to my voice, and then I'll tell you about—it helps if you don't think about, try not to think about—OK, just listen, here's why I won't give you water, OK, see, I had a buddy, not a big guy like you, or a little wiry guy like me, he was like an average, normal-size guy, Jewish guy, little bit of a beard, he was a doctor, used to deal me pills, we did a little business back in Chicago before I got out here, he was real nice to me and he always told me, I don't want my people dying, I don't want my good customers dying, leave me with no business, so I'm gonna be a good doctor to you if you need one, and so if you get in trouble, you call me, OK, and I knew I could trust him, right, 'cause what's he gonna do, call the cops on me?

BULL Haha, uh-huh.

RABBIT And so I know I can trust him, this is a good guy. Once we got to be friends, doing business for a while you get to be friends, one day I knew we were real pals because he said to me every time I see you, I'm gonna teach you something, help you stay alive. Like he wants me to stay alive. That's what friends want for each other, we try to help each other with that however we—OK you're gonna wanna hold your breath for a minute so you don't scream, this is gonna hurt a lot and we can't have the neighbors hearing screaming, OK? You ready?

BULL I—yeah—

RABBIT I'm gonna count to five, then I'm gonna do this, OK? So, hold your breath and wait for five, brace yourself. 1, 2, 3, 4—

> *The BULL makes a muffled moan.*

They say it hurts less if you're not expecting it.

BULL I heard that, too.

RABBIT Hey, there you go, you're listening, listening real good. Right. You wanna hear about the doctor?

BULL Yeah, OK. Just… there gonna be more like that?

RABBIT No, no, that was the worst, that hurt the most it's gonna hurt. See, it's all all right now, actually, you're already getting better!

BULL Don't feel better, haha, don't feel good about—ohhhh man.

RABBIT You wanna hear about the doctor in Chicago?

BULL Yeah, sure.

RABBIT So for example one delivery, my guy, my doc, he comes by with my stuff and he gives me a talk, it's all about what to do if you're choking. The next time it's how you tape up a broken finger if you get in a fight, he's telling me good stuff, useful stuff. Then, one day he tells me what to do if I get shot and—you listening?

BULL Yeah, yeah.

RABBIT You listening? What am I talking about.

BULL Some… crap about Chicago.

RABBIT He tells me all about what to do if I get shot, and it's keep yourself sat up, keep talking, and don't drink or eat anything, and make sure you get someone—anyone—a friend, a bus driver, whoever is around— maybe even the guy who shot you if you beg hard enough, and if he's freaked out enough by watching you die—you get someone to call a doc for you, don't try to do it yourself—you know why, you listening to this, you know why not to call yourself, why you need someone to help you out, do it for you?

BULL Naw. Go on, naw, I dunno.

RABBIT You gotta get someone else to call for you, 'cause you might pass out before you get done with the call, and you gotta try not to move too much when you're losing blood, and you gotta keep pressure on the… on the wound, and… it's gonna be squishy and it's gonna gross you out and it's gonna hurt like crazy, but you gotta… keep pressure on it. And keep talking, get someone to keep you awake, keep you thinking, so you don't go out. 'Cause if you go out, it can mess up your brain. Even if the brain is not where you got shot, if you go to sleep before you're fixed up, that's where you'll end up getting hurt the most, in the brain. Isn't that funny?

BULL Can I have some water?

RABBIT So, that's why you gotta stay awake, you gotta stay lucid with me. That's your whole job right now, that's everything you gotta do, just stay awake. We're almost done. Just—you gotta talk to me now.

BULL My little buddy. Tryin' to keep me alive.

RABBIT You keep me alive.

BULL I do sometimes, I do… at that…

RABBIT That's what a gang's all about. It's about tryin' to keep each other alive.

BULL You're… the best friend I ever had, and I…

RABBIT No, now, don't go talking like that—

BULL I just want you to know it, you know.

RABBIT I know. Now, you know what friends do? They tell each other jokes, funny jokes, tell me jokes till you're all fixed up, we're almost done, you're gonna be fine, you just gotta tell me… just two, maybe two jokes, then you're good, OK?

BULL Well… a dog walks into a bar, a girl dog, and, uh…

RABBIT Yeah? What happens, I never heard this one.

BULL And the bartender goes "Whatchu want, little doggie?" and the dog is like "Gimme a martini."

RABBIT Ha, dogs don't drink martinis!

BULL …and the… and the…

RABBIT What's the bartender say, c'mon, the suspense is killing me.

BULL The barkeep, he goes, "How you like it, wet or dry? How do you like it?"

RABBIT Ha!

BULL And the dog goes "Ruff."

RABBIT Hey, I don't get it, what's a rough martini?

BULL No, like, the bartender, he's asking about the drink, but the little girl dog, the dog thinks he's asking about how she likes to get fucked.

RABBIT Ha! Haha, oh, oh that's a nasty one. Tell me another, you gotta tell me another, just—talk, keep talking, you gotta tell me another—

BULL Well, this dog goes into a church—

RABBIT Are all your jokes about dogs?

BULL What, you got something against dogs?

RABBIT No, no, they're great, dogs are great, they're the greatest animal. These are the greatest jokes I've ever heard, the greatest anyone's ever told, you just gotta tell me one more. You have to tell me another.

BULL The other ain't so funny.

RABBIT Tell me anyway, you go ahead, you tell me about the dog and the church and I'll see how funny it is.

BULL OK, so this dog goes into this church, and he says "I gotta talk to a priest, gimme the priest," so the priest goes "What's up, doggie, what do you need?" and the dog goes "Spiritual advisement." And the priest is thinking, well, tall order for a dog, but, you know, that is my job, so, I guess I'll try to help him out, and so the priest goes, "What do you, as a dog, need spiritual advisement about?" and the dog is like "I have sinned, and I need forgiveness." And the priest goes "Well... what is sinful for a dog?" and the dog goes "I don't know, you're supposed to tell me!"

RABBIT I don't get it.

BULL It's not... it's not funny "ha-ha," it's funny like "huh." Like it makes you think, you know, do dogs got a Bible of their own? Like, thou shalt not bury thy neighbor's squeak toy, and shit like that?

RABBIT Huh. I never thought about that.

BULL I mean, they gotta, kind of. Everyone's got a moral code. Even you and me, we got a code, the gang's got a code, and we do all kinds of awful shit to innocent people, so, you know, if we got rules, if we got laws, even if they are not the same laws as lawyers and cops have, if we got a code, then dogs probably got a Bible.

RABBIT OK. You gotta take it easy for a while, still, but you're all fixed up now.

BULL Huh?

RABBIT I stopped stitching you up a while ago, you didn't even notice did you, probably the adrenaline, bodies are funny things, they try their best to take care of themselves, help you out when you're getting hurt, that kind of thing.

BULL Adrena-what? You know a lot about this stuff, huh.

RABBIT Yeah. I used to be a doctor. Back in Chicago.

BULL Nobody told me about that, I bet you never tell anyone.

RABBIT I guess I don't.

BULL Why'd you never tell anyone that?

RABBIT Oh, I dunno, kind of embarrassing I guess, don't like to think about it much, you know, first it's pills always starts with pills and who deals with more pills than a doctor, of course you're gonna try a pill some time or other, and then if you like it, you're gonna have a… you're gonna have to make some changes in your lifestyle, you know? Hahaha, yeah, so, but, I don't tell people about it, I don't want anyone thinking that I think I'm better than anyone else, people think like that about educated people sometimes but it's just how things turned out for me, it's just the roll of the dice, you know how things are.

BULL Yeah, nobody was born for this life. I was s'posed to be a farmer, ha, can you imagine that?

RABBIT Ha! Hahahaha, you'd be an awful farmer.

BULL Walking through the fields, beating up the corn.

The RABBIT laughs hysterically.

I'm glad you was a doctor though. I'm glad you knew to fix me up like that.

RABBIT We take care of each other.

BULL Take care of each other. I'll always look out for you.

RABBIT I know. You do look out for me, you're looking out for me all the time. You're gonna be okay, you know, you know that, right?

BULL Yeah. I ain't OK now, but I'm gonna be. *(laughs)* But I ain't OK now!

RABBIT Haha, I know, it hurts like hell, right?

BULL Haha, yeah, it hurts like a motherfucker!

> *The atmosphere of the stage changes; the lights shift, so that the BULL and RABBIT vanish together. We see JOE and MISSY, visible but separate, each in their own space.*

MISSY *(to us)* There's something about getting home at the end of a tough shift, like tonight's shift.

JOE *(to us)* The Lieutenant tells me to go home, but I don't.

MISSY You get so close, and you want to be home so badly, and then it's down to like the last half-mile, and you're thinking, this is the longest half-mile in the world.

JOE I just walk. Me again, same guy, same city, just me spending another night wandering the streets, hoping I'll see something that'll change my thinking. Something that'll blow the case open. Maybe I'll see a deal on a corner, see a familiar face talking to another face half-lit in the shadows and overhear something I can use; maybe I'll find that little nudge that shoves me right back into the heat of the chase, back onto the Scorpio trail.

MISSY It's like the city shifts around you, like the concrete is some kind of quicksand. The closer you get to your front door, the farther away it feels, and the more tired every step makes you, and the longer every inch, every second gets, and it wears you out like that until you have this moment, just before the finish line, just before the victory lap where you turn your key in the lock of your front door, you think, God, I'm so exhausted—what if I never quite make it home? What if I just… give up? What if I just give up and sleep here in the doorway?

JOE Same streets, night after night, what am I really hoping to see, anyhow? Maybe what I'm hoping for, tonight and every night, maybe what I'm looking for isn't something that I'll see exactly. I think maybe what I want, what I'm really after, is just something that'll break my brain wide open. Like maybe I know the truth already. I've got it all, I've got the answers in there, I just can't shake them out. Let them out into the open. Let them out free. It's like there's something inside me, hiding in there, and it knows everything but it's trapped. It's keeping the secret from me, stopping me from seeing what's right in front of my face. I gotta keep moving till I break open.

MISSY I stand there, at the end of a long shift, at the end of a long day, and I think, what if this is it for me? What if I'm just… what if, when I put away the steel I've been wearing all day, put away the gun and the grimace, just stand here and breathe for a second… what if I'm actually the kind of person who falls asleep in the doorway, never makes it into the house?

JOE Something's gotta break this open.

MISSY I really stand there, with the front door key in my hand, and I know I'll be in the apartment in a minute, but I still—I stop and I… sometimes you think—and this is not just about the doorway to my apartment, of course it's not, I'm not stupid enough to think that I—it's just, you think, what if it's—what if, secretly, I'm just a quitter? I act like I have it, but what if I don't have it, don't have the drive to get through the door? I have this life, but what if this is all the life I ever get to have? This bad coffee, not enough sleep, too many arguments, wrinkled-skirt tired-shoulders life. This shithole life, is this really my life, is it going to be like this forever, is everything going to be uphill both ways, and be like that until it's done? It can't be. It's like there must be this other life, a secret life that's new and better, there's got to be this other, better, undiscovered life that I'm keeping from myself, that I'm pretending isn't out there. It must be there, my perfect life, running side by side with this shithole life, running like an artery next to every vein I have. And I can't be a quitter, because I need to get to it, to that perfect place, where I can have my real life. I just need to push a little harder, go just a few steps a few miles a few minutes further, and it'll all finally break wide open. There's got to be a door, a real door, and I can't stop until I map my way there, until I find it.

LETO *(to us)* I worry. About everyone. Young and old, good and bad. I do. I worry about everyone but me. 'Cause I… I am going to be fine. No matter what happens, I am going to be fine. Now, listen, we all know this already, but listen: when things are rocky, you need to sack up. So, you don't raise any fanfare about it you just… sack up! When you don't have a choice, you just sack up, do what needs doing, and then you take care of yourself. Cup of tea, bottle of rye, whatever you need to do to get to sleep after the day, you do it, because taking care of yourself, getting yourself to sleep, is part of what needs doing. I do what I need to do. I sleep like a dead man every night, I work like a dog every day. No matter what I see, what I hear, what I deal with, who I deal with, what I have to watch happen, what I have to do, I know how to be fine at the end of the day. And at the start of the next one.

BULL New orders, change the routes again? Aw man, I can't remember all this stuff.

RABBIT Change the routes, I love it, terra incognito, carpe diem!

JOE The next few days are quiet. Too quiet. I hate quiet.

MISSY What's going on right now, Joe, is this normal?

JOE Oh, now you're asking me for advice? For my expertise? All that "I know everything" and now you're coming to me to eat some shit?

MISSY I just mean… you've been on this case a long time, do they work like this? Lots of activity, and then suddenly… nothing.

JOE Oh, there's something. We're just not seeing it.

MISSY So this isn't normal?

JOE Aw, it's normal. We don't see everything. Don't you worry, they're up to something out there right now, we just don't know where to look.

MISSY Well shit, let's go look.

JOE You don't want to… sit around, maybe put some dots on omething?

MISSY There's nothing left to put dots on. They've changed patterns.

JOE You're saying the stakeouts were a wash?

MISSY I'm saying they've changed patterns.

JOE So…

MISSY So… let's go look for trouble.

JOE Look anywhere.

MISSY Look everywhere.

JOE So we do. Start at the base of the city.

MISSY Start at the water, down where the city is low and flat, in the Marina.

JOE Work our way up over the first hills.

MISSY Past the mansions of Pac Heights, gotta get back on those roads, gotta get back on those sidewalks and show them I'm not afraid, even after what happened last time I was on this corner… or was it that corner?

JOE Nothing going on here, gotta head even further in, twisting around Polk Street, up and down the side streets of Russian Hill, dipping down into the Tenderloin.

MISSY Still learning my way around, it's not like D.C. where everything has signs telling you how to get to all the important shit. San Francisco has so few signs, nothing points you away from anything else. It's like it's all important shit. In its own way.

JOE Up and down Market for a minute, watching the streetcars, peering into the streetcar windows trying to find a reason to look closer.

MISSY Let's ride a cable car.

JOE Nobody rides cable cars.

MISSY Just once. Just to see.

JOE So we do.

MISSY Up to the top of Nob Hill.

JOE We go all the way to the top of the hill.

MISSY Do you know what they keep on top of the highest hills in San Francisco?

JOE Yeah, I know what they keep here. A lot of rich guys in fancy cars, and a real old church where nobody prays, 'cause they've all already been blessed.

MISSY In San Francisco, on the top of the highest hills, that's where they keep all their tallest buildings. That's no way to organize a city! It's all out of balance, doesn't make any sense. This city doesn't make any sense.

JOE You want to see what's at the very top?

MISSY We take the elevator all the way to the top of the Fairmont.

JOE You know what's at the top of the Fairmont? The richest people in this town.

MISSY With these views, it's no wonder.

JOE I guess you can't blame them, at that.

MISSY You look around up here, look out the windows from the hallway, and it's like being smack in the middle of the sky.

JOE She's right, of course. For once. She's right about that.

MISSY You really think Scorpio is everywhere? Even here?

JOE Don't see why not. Hell, I don't see how it could be any other way.

MISSY Well, that isn't proof of anything. You "don't see" a lot of things.

JOE A gang this powerful has got to have some big friends, otherwise they can't live and work the way they do, with almost no trouble coming to them. Some big people must be looking out for them, protecting them.

MISSY *(to us)* Then we're in the garden on the roof.

JOE The garden's really... it. The very top of the city. It's the closest you can be to being yourself a star or a sun, to being up in the sky, living there, so far from the problems of this world. You get up to the garden and it's just like there's nothing between you and the gods, between you and the heavens, there's no windows, no metal roof between you and the stars, nothing, just you and sky, and the stars, and the clouds.

MISSY I guess you're not supposed to be up here unless you're a guest. Of the hotel I mean.

JOE Yeah, I expect not, they don't want every Tom Dick and Harry up here mingling with the gods, with the sky and with the wealthy. It'd give the hotel a bad reputation.

MISSY We shouldn't be here, really. There's no reason to be, except that it's been a long week, and we don't know where to go. One of the perks of the job is that, if you can find the time, you can go anywhere you like. You can look for trouble, or for beauty, pretty much anywhere on earth.

LETO *(to us)* I tell my boys, my girls, my team, I tell them "Look anywhere. Look everywhere." Nowhere's too high, and no one's too big, to be out of your reach.

MISSY *(to us)* I can be anywhere, and nobody can keep me from their secrets. That's the power of the badge, opening doors to anywhere; sometimes, it opens doors to the sky. Or at least, to the playground of the gods, to the rooftop garden on the edge of the sky. After all, there's no point in having an FBI badge unless you—

JOE *(to us)* And that's when we see him.

MISSY I'm not sure if I hear the panting first, or see the silhouette against the ground—

JOE His tremendous shape, unmistakeable, and snorting, angry—

BULL I got you guys. I see you. You see me? Maybe you think you do.

JOE What is he doing here?

MISSY What is he, the scum of the earth, doing up here, in the garden at the edge of paradise?

BULL What are they doing up here, they ain't supposed to be here, this place is supposed to be protected, the Boss promised us we could be protected here.

JOE We're after him before we're even sure it's him.

BULL How are we supposed to do business here without any protection? Shit.

MISSY We're doing this like we were born for it, Joe goes left, I go right, he goes forward and I rush back, it's like we've been practicing for how to cover this little square of sky.

BULL Aw, shit.

MISSY I'm behind a tree ready to bolt for him as Joe chases the big lunk right towards me—

BULL AW, SHIT.

JOE It doesn't hurt that he's moving slower than normal—

BULL Still hurt, still a little hurt but I'm making time, making time as good as I can—

MISSY He ducks the other way, but Joe is ready for him—

JOE It's like watching chess on fast forward—

MISSY Joe seems to be around every corner, just on the other side of every hedge, running through every gate—

BULL It's like they're everywhere, how many guys they got up here, how many cops are up here?

JOE It's like she's everywhere at once, leaving a footprint in every open space between the plants—

BULL How many guys they got up in this garden, anyhow? Aw, shit.

MISSY We've almost got him—

JOE I can almost touch him—

MISSY I can smell the sweat, the fear, and I know before he turns—

BULL I gotta get outta here!

MISSY I know he's heading for the door, heading back inside.

JOE Missy's through the door a step behind him—

MISSY Elevator door closing, I see his face, it's like he's grinning, I know he's grinning at me all the way down from his teeth to his fingernails, every inch grinning at me as he gets away—

BULL Buh-bye sweetheart.

JOE STAIRS! Take the stairs! You take these down, I'll take the ones at the other end, go!

MISSY Joe runs for the stairs on the other end of the long hall, I hear him disappearing, footsteps so fast they're just a blur of noise, like a rumble of thunder.

JOE And we're both headed down—

MISSY Now we're all headed down, racing for the bottom—

JOE Faster than I've ever run before, running down the stairs like water running through a hose, I was built for this—

MISSY Jumping two, three steps at a time, swinging big corners, making the banister my friend, my ally, get me to the bottom, help me take the corners—

JOE Another floor down—

MISSY Two more floors—

JOE Hotel guests going to and fro on every hall, hear them laughing, it's like another world in here, in the stairwell, all alone—

MISSY All these people, going about their night in their fancy hotel, in their plush bathrobes and travel slippers, a couple inches through the wall they have no idea what tonight is really about.

JOE One more floor to the lobby—

MISSY One more flight of stairs and I'll hit the lobby, and he better be waiting—

JOE He better be waiting—

MISSY Please let me beat the elevator, let me get there first, let me beat it, let me get him, I want this so much, I need to make this collar—

JOE Burst through the lobby door like a hurricane, elevator door's just about to open—

MISSY Leaping through the lobby, skirting around suitcases and luggage carts, baffled uniformed luggage boys stepping aside, wondering what the hell—no time to flash the badge, just time to get to the elevator door as it starts to open—

JOE Ding!

MISSY We beat it, we made it.

JOE We're waiting, waiting when they open, and then I see the eyes—

RABBIT Hi, Joe.

JOE How did they—when did they—

MISSY Aw, shit.

JOE Where is he, where'd he go, how'd he get away? Where's the fucking Bull?

MISSY In the second it takes me to realize the Bull isn't waiting there for us, the Rabbit is already gone—

JOE Damn, he's fast.

MISSY The Bull is long gone, and now the Rabbit's gone in the crowd, lost in the people, maybe he went out the front—

JOE He could've jumped out a side door, already be on the street—

MISSY Rabbit could be anywhere by now.

JOE I barely blinked, how'd he get so far so fast?

MISSY We're ready to run, but we don't even know where to go. We don't even know which way to chase him.

JOE Might as well go back to the precinct.

MISSY Back to the desks, the maps. Back to the drawing board.

LETO I'm sorry, kids, sounds like a rough chase.

JOE Did you see anything?

MISSY I didn't see anything you didn't see.

JOE What'd you hear? In the stairwell?

MISSY You know, hotel stuff. I don't know.

JOE Hotel stuff?

MISSY Why, did you hear something, are you holding something back?

JOE No, I didn't hear shit.

MISSY Well me neither, why should I have something to tell you when you have nothing to tell me?

JOE I don't know. I'm sorry. I'm edgy.

MISSY Oh, sorry baby, let me sing you a lullaby.

JOE Stop it, just stop it.

MISSY So, what now?

JOE Go back out. Look for something else.

MISSY No. No, we gotta make a plan.

JOE Not another fucking—I can't deal with any more dots right now—

MISSY No, OK, no dots. But we gotta do something different.

JOE OK. We'll do a plan together.

MISSY OK. A plan. Well—

JOE Nope, changed my mind, already hate this.

MISSY Joe. Stop. Let's think. Why do we keep losing them. What didn't work today.

JOE We had the Bull… then he was the Rabbit.

MISSY We have one, then he's the other. That's happened before. It always happens.

JOE So we can't keep letting them pull this bait-and-switch stuff. We've got to split them up somehow.

MISSY We've got to get the Rabbit. He's the tricky one. The big guy, we'll get him easily, if we can get him alone.

JOE We almost got him in that garden.

MISSY Because he was alone. If he hadn't had that little shit to bail him out, he'd be ours.

JOE OK, so first we get the Rabbit.

MISSY The Rabbit, the quick one, he's the tricky one. But we can get him.

JOE We can't get him in a chase. He's just too fast. That kid's like magic.

MISSY No, a chase isn't going to do it. Fuck.

JOE So what else can we do?

MISSY Shit. I don't… I don't know. Shit.

JOE Are you saying we should give up, quit? We can't get the Bull if we don't get the Rabbit first, but we can't get the Rabbit because he's too fast, are you saying we should just walk away, leave it, leave this city sick and polluted, the streets thick with crime, infested with all this scum, are you saying we can't do it?

MISSY No, not at all.

JOE Well, what then?

MISSY We'll get the Rabbit. We can get him with a… trap.

JOE Ha! Like what, how's that going to work?

MISSY That's what we need to figure out. You go through these reports, I'll go through these ones.

JOE I've been through these a hundred times.

MISSY Sure, looking for proof, or looking for names, for clues… but were you looking for traps?

JOE Of course not. *(beat)* OK. OK, we'll try it.

MISSY *(to us)* So we did.

LETO Sounds like you've got yourselves a real plan. It's almost like listening to real police.

MISSY Thank you.

LETO Let me know if there's anything you need. Manpower, extra cars, just let me know. And remember, this gang is dangerous. They're crazy, they're insane, and they're not afraid to kill. And they do what it takes to protect their own. So keep me posted. I want to know what you're doing, and I want to know where you're going when you are ready to go after this guy, so that when your radios go quiet, I know where to go look for your bodies.

JOE We'll let you know.

LETO Thank you. I'll hold you to that. And, Joe, Missy…

MISSY What, Mom?

LETO Good luck.

JOE She's your mother?

MISSY It doesn't matter.

JOE Ha! Now at least I see where you get it from.

MISSY Get what from?

JOE Oh, it doesn't matter…

MISSY We better put on another pot of coffee.

JOE We drink another pot of coffee, then another. Then we go for a ride through the streets, double-checking intersections, double-checking the time it takes to drive from point A to point B, figure out whether we need a lookout at point C and whether we need to cover both sides of the block.

MISSY Edge of the park, edge of the green and the gray.

JOE The edge of Golden Gate Park, where the green grass meets the cement sidewalk, the end of one thing and the start of another.

MISSY The most Rabbit sightings we've had anywhere in the city, the highest concentration, are here. You've seen the Rabbit more in this square mile than in the rest of the city combined.

JOE I guess I have at that, I never counted it up like that. I got no time to sit around doing accounting like a stooge.

MISSY Trust me, this is where we need to set the trap.

JOE Streetlights, find the place with the least streetlights, pull over. Does this feel like the right spot to you?

MISSY I like this spot. Yeah, I like this spot.

JOE Right at the end of the Haight-Ashbury district, on the edge of Cole Valley, not far from the hospital on the hill, not far from Golden Gate Park. Not far from the thousand places he's disappeared to before.

MISSY I like this spot. It's quiet. We'll see him easy.

JOE *(to us)* We head back to the precinct, give Leto the details. We need a car here, a car here. A guy on the street, plainclothes, planted over here, so he can radio the team if the Bunny hops in from the west, and another guy over here, keeping his eyes peeled towards the east. And Missy and me, we'll be in the car, right in the middle of it all, in the heart of the trap, just sitting and waiting in the dark, waiting to pounce. We're making a net, and we're gonna trap that little junkie, we're gonna trap that son of a bitch, we're going to catch his scent like a bloodhound and then the San Francisco Police Department is going to tear into his neck like a rabid bulldog, and we are going to make him bleed information. He is going to tell us everything. Everything there is to tell about the gang. What their methods are. What they're planning next. Mostly, he'll tell us where their hideout is. Where we can catch the rest of them.

MISSY This is going to make my career.

JOE *(to us)* This is going to be the greatest collar of my life. This is the case of a lifetime, the kind of case that gives a cop a reason to be alive. I've caught plenty of criminals already. Plenty of junkies before this one, plenty of killers and thugs. I've jailed dealers aplenty, and I've built cases against bookies and blackmailers, against big-shot people who use their power wrong and against crazy nobodies, wacked-out people who use knives against the innocent. I've chased and I've caught lots of people, and most of them are people who are really more like animals, they're barely people at all. I've done all that, and that's why I have the power I do, the freedom to chase who I want, the trust of the Lieutenant. I earned all that, and I earned it the tough way, on the streets, fist to fist with the scariest bad guys in this dingy town. But this collar. This Rabbit. This little man with the secret to breaking the big case, this is going to be the greatest collar of my life.

MISSY *(to us)* This one arrest, the arrest that leads to everything that is going to come after it… this one night is going to make my entire career. I've worked my way up the ladder so far, hand over hand, racing for the top, playing the game in D.C., but this… this is the real thing. If I get this guy, if I get this gang? It's going to make my career. I'll be untouchable. Like a god.

LETO The plan is good. It's smart.

MISSY Thank you.

LETO It's strong, it's tight. You did a good job, you're doing good work together. Now get out of my office, if you want this happening tomorrow night, I got to make calls starting right this second. So get out. Get some sleep. You're going to need it.

JOE Go home. For once. I go home. I don't sleep.

MISSY I can't sleep. How the hell are you supposed to sleep the night before the first day of the rest of your life?

LETO Making calls, putting everything in motion, telling everyone who needs to know, and telling nobody, but nobody, who doesn't. It's a long night, a late night, making sure we've got the best people for the job in place, in all the right places, so careful, so sure. If we're going to do this, we've got to do it the best we can.

MISSY and JOE sit together in the cop car.

MISSY I can't believe we're doing this.

JOE Right now, we're doing a whole lot of nothing.

MISSY Waiting.

JOE Waiting for a lookout to spot him. Whole lot of nothing.

MISSY Are you nervous?

JOE No. Yeah.

MISSY Me too.

JOE Then, she—

MISSY *(to us)* I don't know why I took his hand, it just seemed like what I had to do.

JOE *(to us)* Her palm was freezing, and a little damp, like she'd just put down a carton of ice cream. But I liked it.

MISSY *(to us)* His palm was warm, red with pulsing blood, a little sweaty, like he'd just come in from an August night in the South. It was awkward.

JOE *(to us)* It was awkward.

MISSY *(to us)* But I liked it. It was comforting. And strange, exciting, so… different. So different from how I feel, from how my own hands, my own life, from how everything feels to me. So… awake.

LETO Do you hear it?

JOE The radios, suddenly—

MISSY They've got him, they've got him, he's on the way—

JOE One on each side of him, front and back, they're pushing him this way, like dogs flushing out their prey in the hunting field, a whole pack of cops closing in from all sides, they're bringing him here—

MISSY Bringing him right to us, might as well be carrying him here on a silver platter—

JOE Bring him here, good doggies, bring him to the master, bring him around the corner—

MISSY He's almost to the corner, this is it, this is IT—

JOE OUT OF THE CAR, we're on the street, on the street waiting, and this is it, this is—

MISSY We see him before we hear him, smell him before we see him, the sweat and the fear, the yearning and the terror—

RABBIT Get me home. Just wanna get home.

JOE We're on him, on either side of him, on all sides—

MISSY We've got him, we've got him, where the fuck's he going?

JOE Golden Gate Park, he's heading for the park, all cars, calling all cars—everyone on foot—get to the—aw, shit—

RABBIT I just want safety, all I want is to be safe—home—home safe—aw, shit, aw God—

LETO He won't get away.

MISSY He won't get away, we're on him.

JOE We're right on his heels, and there are lights in front, cop car lights, and sirens howling like wolves howling at the moon—

MISSY Where the fuck's he going?

JOE He's heading for the stadium—

LETO A.P.B., A.P.B., Rabbit heading for the stadium, everyone head for

Kezar, stay on him, cut him off if you can, head for the stadium.

MISSY Why the fuck is he going for open ground?

JOE He's a psycho, he's nuts, unpredictable, don't ask questions just STAY ON HIM.

MISSY I'll cut him off—

JOE Don't talk, just GO!

MISSY Then we're there. I'm there. Where did everyone go? I'm in the stadium, at Kezar, running down the stairs, towards the big open field. It's quiet, silent, eerie, a thin layer of fog on everything, hard to see the sky through the fog, there's nothing but gray and wet, and quiet, and bright, the bright stadium floodlights shining through the mist. I'm already there, running down the steps, running towards the field when the Rabbit shows up, Joe close behind him. Joe Ryan, gun gleaming under the bright stadium floodlights, chest heaving, the cop breathing heavy, breathing the dirt that the junkie kicks up with his frantic scramblings—they run across the field, run around the circular stadium in a lap, the junkie's shoulders quivering, the cop with footsteps like thunderclaps, the little guy screaming and howling in gasps of fear, and Joe Ryan on his heels, weirdly calm, his face like stone, his shoulders steady, his body coursing with certainty, with power. I'm seeing it all in panorama, running towards it, running towards the field, almost down the steps when—

The RABBIT squeals in laughter.

JOE What the—

MISSY Where did—

JOE WHERE THE FUCK DID HE GO.

MISSY Where'd he go?

JOE HE WAS HERE. HE WAS HERE. YOU SAW. WE. HAD. HIM.

MISSY You had him.

JOE I... I had him. I had him.

MISSY Then the cop is on his knees, in the dirt, shaking with shock and anger. He's quiet, barely speaking, I have to get close down to hear him, he's whispering, fast and quiet—

JOE —I had him I had him we had him I had him we had him right here I was gonna get him this time I almost had him we had him I had him where'd he go how could he we had him I had him I had him—

MISSY Joe's eyes are closed, sweat is pouring off him, or maybe it's the fog all over his face, his clothes, and his uniform is covered in dirt and there's so much sadness, so much—disbelief. And then, suddenly—

JOE WHERE WERE YOU?

MISSY He's looking up at me and I don't know what to say.

JOE WHERE WERE—

MISSY I was here, Joe. I was right here. I saw the whole thing.

JOE Then where'd he... where did he go?

MISSY I don't know. I don't know. Into the fog. Into the ground. Into the... into the ground.

JOE Then there are sirens, flashlights, feels like a hundred cops, a million, but too late, of course, too late to be useful, too late to see anything, all they see is fog, and Missy pale and damp and baffled, and they see my failure. All they see is that.

LETO What the hell happened, Joe.

MISSY He was right here.

LETO I know he *was* right here, where is he now?

MISSY He must have... I can't see how he... OK, everyone, everybody!

JOE Why's she shouting, what is there to shout about?

MISSY Everyone, EVERYONE, look over every inch of the stadium, every inch of the field. There has to be a secret door, a tunnel, a hole, he went down into something, he got out of here somehow, there must be a place he ran to, we're probably right on the doorstep of their hideout, we're probably just a few inches from the doorway that'll take us right to their headquarters, right deep into the heart of this whole gang. Spread out, look close, look between every blade of fucking grass, between every bit of grit in the concrete, look everywhere, and if you don't see anything, look again. There's a door here, right here, and he went through it, and we're going through it after him.

LETO Don't just stand there, people, you heard the woman, now look!

MISSY *(to us)* They're looking everywhere, all of them, and it's some pipsqueak, some rookie cop I've never even met—

JOE *(to us)* It's the new guy, the rookie, the Italian kid who finds it—

MISSY This little handle by the edge of the grass—

JOE There's not even a lock, just this little handle you pull and—

MISSY And it's dark in there, but once you get through the opening it's big, it's a big old tunnel, feels ancient, like it's been there forever, running under the field since God knows when—

JOE Musty and bleak, the dirt trodden down to a hard mass, weathered and worn—

MISSY Probably built when the stadium was built, this has to have been here forever—

JOE Then an open space, a big open space, like a big dark ballroom, with wooden beams, tree trunks holding up the ceiling, holding it open for God knows who—

MISSY It's huge. Huge and empty.

JOE Tunnels leading everywhere, three going this way and two heading off in that direction, who knows where they lead to—

MISSY Probably lead all over the city.

LETO We'll have to get a team down here to map this all out. I don't want you taking any more risks tonight.

MISSY It'll take a ton of people hundreds of hours, probably, there's so much to map—

JOE We don't have time.

MISSY This is a big job, we don't have time to—

LETO I will not stand here and watch you run willy-nilly through the dark getting yourselves killed. My job is to keep my team alive. So, listen up, all of you. We'll take the entrance, we'll watch the entrance in shifts. We'll plant a lookout in the stadium, twenty-four hours a day, until we see someone coming or going, and then whoever it is, whoever we see, I don't care if it's the Rabbit or the Bull or a state Senator or a three-year-old kid, whoever comes out of this door, comes up into the stadium, when we see someone, we grab him. Or her. We grab that person, and we interrogate that person in the station, like real cops, and we don't come down here and do anything stupid, we don't get ourselves shot in the dark, on their turf, like we're a bunch of imbeciles. They know this ground. They know the escape routes, the hiding places, they know the terrain. We don't know shit down here, we might as well be wandering blind, deaf, and dumb, so we are pulling out now, and we are watching that entrance for as long as it takes. And Joe, Missy, you are doing none of this. You are both going home. Now.

JOE Let me finish this, Lieutenant.

LETO No. You're exhausted, you're shook up, you're emotional. You're in good shape to make a lot of mistakes right now, and I don't want that on my shoulders, so you are off for the night. I'll see you at the precinct tomorrow.

MISSY But, Mom—I'm fine. I just need to be here, to see this through. Let me finish this.

LETO I'll see you tomorrow. At the precinct.

JOE *(to us)* So we leave.

MISSY You don't always have a choice, sometimes you just have to do what you're told.

JOE My gun feels like a thousand-pound weight, every step hurts.

MISSY *(to us)* We get back above ground, and the fog, the floodlights, it's all still there, untouched, like nothing happened.

JOE Every breath is like a slap in the face. We should have these guys in cuffs right now.

MISSY Let me drive you home.

JOE I'm fine.

MISSY You're in no shape to drive.

JOE I'll walk.

MISSY You can barely stand up. Let me drive you home.

JOE We walk back to the car. Not even close to touching. Two feet apart, maybe a foot and a half, feels like a million miles, a thousand years. I feel like the only guy in the world.

MISSY I've never been so tired. Turning the key in the ignition is like lifting a thousand-pound weight.

JOE We sit in the car, we're not even close to touching.

MISSY Stoplights take forever, every red light feels a thousand years long.

JOE I need a drink.

MISSY I need a thousand drinks.

JOE We're not even close to touching until we're already in bed, then suddenly everything is so fast, we're so close together and it's like we've never been any other way, like we've just met each other for the first time right that second.

MISSY It feels like the first breath I've taken in days.

JOE I don't even remember the last time I was with a woman.

MISSY It's not even that I want it, and I don't think he does either, it's not about wanting anything; it's about not knowing anything else to do, not remembering how anything else works in the whole world, except for this. The oldest boy-girl dance in the book. It's the thing you know how to do when nothing else can happen, when nothing else works, the thing you never forget how to do, that you never learned how to do. The thing you were born knowing how to do. The oldest dance in the book.

JOE There's no difference between people and animals and gods. I've seen enough people get confused about what they are, I've seen people piss like dogs on the street and whinny like wounded horses when they're shot. I've seen people strut like gods, think they're untouchable, think they can't be hurt, can't die. There's no difference between us and them, between gods and animals and us. If there is a difference, any difference at all, it's this. If there's anything that makes us people, it's what we're doing in this bed tonight; no, it's the reasons why we do it, those are what make us human. We do it to hide our sadness, to erase our memories, get past our failures, our doubts; to get lost for a minute, for a moment; to step away from "I don't know" and to just feel, for a moment, just for a moment, that we know what we're built for. That we're sure about something. About anything.

MISSY It feels like the first real breath I've taken in years.

JOE I don't even remember falling asleep, but when I wake up, she's already getting dressed. I've slept without dreaming. Don't know for how long. She's zipping up her skirt.

MISSY I can't stay here. This isn't my house, isn't my place. I can't be here in the morning.

JOE *(to us)* I can't be here either. I need to get out of here, out of this shithole apartment. I feel like I can't breathe in here.

MISSY You want breakfast? Some pancakes or something?

JOE No.

MISSY Me neither.

JOE What time is it?

MISSY It's only about eleven.

JOE At night? Jesus.

MISSY You know what I want to do?

JOE What.

MISSY I wanna go to the movies. You wanna go to the movies?

JOE *(to us)* We go to the movies. The late show. Popcorn and velvet seats. Half-empty theater, full of drunks and losers, people with nothing better to be doing, nobody waiting up for them at home. Guy playing the organ before the show. Velvet curtains open in front of the screen. The 5-4-3-2-1 countdown before the picture starts. She rests her head on my shoulder, and I feel it. Really feel it. The exact weight of her, the warmth and pressure of her neck, her shoulder against me, the scent of her hair. I sit, and I'm so still. I can't remember the last time I sat this still. I breathe; it feels like the first real breath I've taken in years.

LETO stands, holding a gift-wrapped box.

LETO Boy, I'm really disappointed in you.

RABBIT I'm sorry, Boss.

LETO I gave you all the warning in the world, told you where everyone would be, and when, and why, and you still got your ass spotted by those cops.

RABBIT I'm sorry, I'm sorry, it was an accident! I needed—

LETO I know what you needed.

RABBIT I know you said to stay, to stay down here, but I needed my fix, I needed my stuff, I would—I felt like I was gonna die, I wasn't gonna make it, you should've seen me, I was in a bad way, it was real bad—the worst I've ever—and I was all alone down here, and I—Boss, I held out as long as I could, but I needed—I NEEDED IT.

LETO You junkies are all alike, you're all useless.

RABBIT If you hadn't sent the Bull away—why'd you send him away, where'd you send him, huh? We're supposed to look out for each other, he's supposed to look out for me, and—we would've, I would've been fine—I needed to get my stuff, I would've gotten it and he would've protected me, but—why'd you send him away?

LETO He had a job to do. He had to send a very important message to some people tonight, some big-deal people down in Sacramento. Sometimes you need to make a house call. I had to send him on a house call.

RABBIT I'm sorry.

LETO I don't want to hear your excuses. You can't work by yourself, you need a bodyguard? You need a shepherd, you need someone keeping tabs on you, keeping you safe, you need a babysitter? Then you are useless to me.

RABBIT Don't say that, don't—I'm not useless—I'm useful, I'll be useful, I'll try harder, I'll be better, I'll be—

LETO It's too late. You've let me down. You've let me down before, and I've been kind to you. I've been lenient.

RABBIT Please, ma'am, just one more chance, just another chance, one more, and I'll—you'll see.

LETO I don't want to see anything more from you. I don't want to hear anything more from you.

RABBIT Aw, God.

LETO You know what happens now.

RABBIT I don't—I don't want to die! I don't want to, I don't have to die now, I don't want this to—please, please!

LETO It's not a choice I can make, little Rabbit. My little doctor. You made the choice. You made the choice when you fucked up.

RABBIT Aw, God, aw shit.

LETO But, still, I am not without mercy. I'm fond of you, little guy. You've always been one of my favorites.

RABBIT Aw, thank you, Boss, thank you.

LETO So, we don't have to do this the tough way. We don't have to do this with a baseball bat, in an alley, like you're some common nobody. You're special to me, so I want it to be nice for you.

RABBIT Thank you, thank you.

LETO I'm going to let you do it. You can do it yourself.

RABBIT Aw, Jesus. Aw, shit.

LETO This is a present.

RABBIT Aw, with a little bow and everything!

LETO Yeah. In the box, it has a needle, and it has a little bag, and in that bag is a lot of heroin.

RABBIT Yeah, yeah.

LETO This present has everything you've ever wanted. It has three times what you've ever had.

RABBIT Awwwww… oh, wow.

LETO It's going to be beautiful, and then it's going to be over. You just sit here. You just sit here, sit tight, and when you want something… you can have this. But you have to take it all. All of it, the whole thing, all at once. You do that tonight, you understand?

RABBIT Yes, ma'am.

LETO You do that tonight, or it's going to be so bad for you. So bad. The worst. You remember what happened to Robert? After he talked to the cops?

RABBIT Yes, yes, I remember what happened to McCoy, oh Christ I don't want to remember that, I wish I'd never seen that, I wish I'd never seen Bobby like that, I never wanted to see so much… more blood outside of him than in… oh, God.

LETO If you don't want that… if you don't want worse than that… you do this the easy way. Tonight.

RABBIT Yes, ma'am.

LETO I wish I could let you go, just send you to another town where they don't know your face, don't know your routes, your habits, but it can't be like that. I need the rest of the gang to understand, I need them to see that I've punished you. If they don't see you die, they will think they can go against my wishes, against my advice and my orders, any time they feel like it. And we can't have that, right?

RABBIT No. No, we can't.

LETO I didn't get to be the boss of this gang by letting animals like you get away with doing whatever they feel like doing.

RABBIT I know. I know. I'm sorry.

LETO I'm sorry, too. Now, I'm going to leave this here, I'm going to leave you this present. And you, you take care of this tonight. You understand?

RABBIT I understand, Boss.

LETO Good. I'm sorry, little man.

RABBIT I'm sorry. I'm sorry, too. I'm sorry thank you I love you I'm sorry! Tell the Bull… tell him I'm sorry and thank him, I love him, tell him I'm sorry.

LETO I'll tell him. Goodnight, Doc.

LETO gives him the gift-wrapped box.

RABBIT Goodnight, ma'am. Goodbye.

JOE *(to us)* She goes home, I go home, we shower in our own homes, dress in our own homes, drink our first cup of coffee of the day separately, in our own homes, then we go to work.

MISSY Is this going to be weird?

JOE Doesn't have to be.

MISSY I don't want it to be. Last night was…

JOE When we're here it's about the job.

MISSY It's all about the job.

JOE That's what matters.

MISSY I'm glad. Don't…

JOE What?

MISSY Don't tell my mom.

JOE Ha!

LETO Good morning, kids. No action at the stadium yet. I don't expect they'll try anything in the daytime, but keep your radios on just in case.

MISSY Of course.

JOE Always.

MISSY We should go down there. Just in case.

LETO Sure. Go ahead.

JOE So we do.

> *The RABBIT opens the gift from LETO, looks through the box.*

RABBIT Just want to get home. Gotta get home.

MISSY In the car, on the way to the stadium, we don't even come close to touching.

> *As the RABBIT speaks, he ties off, getting ready to shoot up. By the end of the speech, the drugs have kicked in.*

RABBIT Gotta be… safe. All I ever wanted was to be safe. Nowhere is safe, nothing feels safe, except when I'm… when I have my stuff. I need to have what I need. Then, it's like nothing can touch me. It's like I'm the only guy in the world, and there's this glow, like a shield, all around me, and nothing can get through it, nothing can get to me. Just want to get to there, just want to get home. When I'm on the stuff, when I'm feeling it, I can breathe, feels like the only time I can breathe. Only time I can rest. Then, it's so good, it's like it's just me alone in this tunnel of light, just me and nobody and nothing can hurt me. It's the only time I'm safe. Only time I'm home. My mind is free, running through all the tunnels, the heroin going so fast through me, through my veins to my heart, back down the arteries, running all through me like I run through this town, maybe even faster, making me safe. Taking me home. Just wanna get home.

> *The RABBIT stares ahead. The light stays on him for a minute as he is quiet, breathing slowly.*

JOE In the car on the way, we barely look at each other. We don't look at each other. Look out the window, look down at your shoes, don't look at her. What if she's looking at you, making a face you don't want to see. What would you want to see? A welcome, a smile, a welcoming home to a home you never knew you needed to come home to? Is that what you'd want to see on her face? Or would you want to see a steel-door frown snapped shut, a face like there's nothing up for discussion, no changes that need making or might need making? Which of those is the right thing? I don't know.

The RABBIT twitches, he is dying. Maybe moaning softly.

BULL Little buddy, I'm back! Gawd, I hate making house calls, I know she needs me to do it, I know it needs doing, and I don't mind making a point, sending a message, I don't mind roughin' a guy up from time to time if he's stepped out of his boundaries, you know, I don't mind doin' what I'm good at, ha, but these house calls… geez. OK you gotta hear this, don't even say anything till I'm done telling you, you gotta hear this—

JOE Worst of all maybe you look at her and she's looking back and there's nothing. It's not a beckoning or a refusal, it's just… nothing. Like she doesn't even care. Like you are nothing to her, not even worth saying "no" to, never mind "yes." That's what you don't want to see, if it's there. Don't look at her. Don't find out.

BULL I'm whalin' on this guy, and—and I'm not feeling bad, because believe me, he deserves it—but, get this—and this has never happened to me before—get this, I'm doing my thing, and the whole time, his DOG is watching. Ha, this fucking DOG. Just sitting there, watching. All curious-like. And it's this cute, fluffy little piece of shit, floppy ears, real big eyes. It's so cute, it's like a fucking… cartoon of a dog. Just sittin' there, looking at me, like "What are you doing, guy? Is that a game you guys are playing? What are you doing?" The fucking DOG. *(beat)* Geez. *(beat)* I wish the Boss would stop sending me on these… OK, fucking errands I don't mind—house calls, though, that I mind. You know?

RABBIT Uh… uh-huh.

MISSY *(to us)* Pulling into the parking space, getting out of the car, we haven't said anything the whole ride over, I mean we've been talking, talking like crazy, about the case the news the weather, about why Leto buys bad coffee, what it's like working for your mother, about whether there's a God or not, I don't know what we're about, we're talking non-stop, and never looking at each other, and not listening to a single word.

BULL I don't mind most of it, you know, it's just business. There are only two things I mind that I gotta do—One, I mind the house calls, 'cause you gotta look around the house and you see all the guy's stuff, and his photos and everything, you get to know the guy too much, and then you feel bad. Two, the other thing I mind is… I got a tough stomach, but the really rough stuff, the really bad stuff, like what we hadda do to Bobby, I mind that. I mind that plenty. Ah, you're not even listening, you're just sitting there tripping balls.

JOE We're almost there.

MISSY Yeah, I know.

JOE So shhh!

MISSY *(whispering)* Yeah, I know!

BULL Little buddy, say something. Don't you think the dog was funny? You ever had a dog? *(beat)* Hey, what is up with you? *(beat)* Hey, did you take too much or something? *(beat)* Oh, hey, hey little guy. You had too much, you're not good, this is… oh man, oh man. I never should've left you, even if she said I hadda, I shouldn't have said OK, I shoulda stayed, looked after you, we're supposed to—I'm supposed to have your back, and—oh, man, this is not good, this is not—this ain't good at all, not at all, what'm I…

MISSY The stadium in the daylight, no fog this time, no floodlights, just… sun. Real sun on the grass. Like it's a place where kids could go play.

JOE Kezar's beautiful in the daylight. San Francisco breeze tickling the back of your neck. 1920s steps and seats growing up to the sky, like a big amphitheater, almost like a place of worship.

BULL What am I s'posed to do? I don't know what to do, you're the doc. You gotta tell me what to do, Doc, tell me what to do, what do I do? I gotta get you outta here, maybe you just need some air. Maybe you need a doc, a real doc.

JOE *(to us)* A stadium is a place of worship. It's where we worship the fight, the feeling of a fight, the beauty of a battle. Two teams against each other to make a goal or a shot. One man running hard against his own record for speed. Our stadiums are our temples. The places where we thank the gods for all the gifts they give us. For our ability to fight, to run, to plan and to jump. We thank the gods here, in our fights. Our battlegrounds are how we pray.

MISSY The sunlight. The breeze. Joe next to me. I'm thinking, what do I say to him? Do I say anything?

JOE I don't have anything to say to her.

MISSY Then suddenly—

JOE What the HELL—

MISSY The earth splits wide open, with such a big noise, and the Bull is coming up out of the ground—

JOE He's got the Rabbit over his shoulder like a sack of potatoes—

MISSY Looks like the little guy's dead, his head rolling back and forth, loose and floppy at the end of his neck as the Bull shakes with rage—

JOE The Bull coming up out of the doorway in the ground, coming out of the hideout into the sun—

BULL YOU FUCKERS. YOU FUCKING GODS, YOU FUCKS. YOU DON'T TAKE HIM. YOU DON'T TAKE MY FRIEND.

JOE We're close, too close—

MISSY The Bull's like a volcano, coming up outta the ground like angry lava, out of control—

JOE We shouldn't be so close—

BULL I loved this guy. I loved this little guy, we were pals, he looked out for me, he was the only guy who looked out for me, and he's—YOU DON'T TAKE HIM. HOW COULD YOU TAKE HIM.

MISSY Leto, Leto, we've got him, the Bull and the Rabbit, we've got them coming out of the door—

LETO On my way. It's on. I'm sending the team in. Let's get these guys.

JOE Missy, back up.

MISSY Joe, we can't lose him.

JOE Missy, I said, get back!

The BULL snorts and bellows.

I'm gonna have to put him down.

MISSY No, we've gotta talk to him, we've got to get him to the station, find out what he knows.

JOE That man, that thing, he's not going to talk to us, look at that, he doesn't even know where he is, doesn't even know that guy is dead, he's carrying a corpse like it's a handbag—

MISSY There are rules—

JOE You know how many guys that thug has killed? Bare hands, no remorse, you know how many bones he's broken, how many skulls he's popped in his hands like balloons?

MISSY Joe, we can't just—

JOE And you want to talk with him, like he's civilized, you want to what, have a tea party with this psycho?

MISSY I just—it's procedure, people have rights.

The BULL sobs and bellows.

JOE We're too close, we gotta stay back. I'll put him down if I have to. If I do it, you gotta know it's because I have to.

MISSY OK, Joe.

JOE OK.

MISSY Then Joe has his gun out, has it trained on the Bull, just in case, but when the shot rings out, Joe's the one who falls.

A gunshot. JOE collapses. Another gunshot. The BULL bellows and collapses. MISSY whispers:

—two shots, who shot who, they shot each other, no, Joe was already

LETO enters.

JOE Lieutenant…

MISSY And that's it, he's gone.

LETO Baby.

MISSY My mother, her arms around me, my face against her warm beating heart, she is all around me right away. He's gone, and I never told him. She holds me, I never told him how I feel, I didn't know, and then I saw him fall and now I'll never—

LETO Baby, it's OK, it's going to be OK.

MISSY It's when my mother's shirt feels wet against my face that I realize I am crying, no words, no talking, I am just crying. My arms around her, she is breathing slow and steady and calm, she says "Baby, it's OK, it's going to be OK." He is gone. I didn't look at him enough, I didn't tell him, I didn't tell him in time, he'll never look at me again.

LETO Baby, I'm sorry you had to see that.

BULL Boss…

MISSY The Bull still gasping a little, suffering, reaching out to us.

BULL Boss…

LETO shoots the BULL. He dies instantly.

MISSY Mom.

LETO I wish you hadn't seen that. I don't like to upset you.

MISSY Dead bodies on the grass. Dead thug. Dead junkie. Dead cop. My mother's arms around me, but where did she come from, where was she a minute ago?

LETO I tried to make it quick, for both of them, but I guess my aim isn't always perfect. I try to make it quick. I don't want anyone to suffer when I put them down.

MISSY The back of my neck turns to ice. I put my hand on my gun, in case she's broken, in case her mind crumbled inside her body, she might not know what she's doing? I don't have to hurt her, maybe I can just scare her, if she tries to do anything to me I'll just scare her, that's all. She doesn't know what she's doing.

LETO I'm sorry you had to watch.

MISSY People are coming, backup is coming. Pull away slow, my arms at my sides now, distance, put a few feet between us.

LETO I didn't want to kill either one, but if one of them was going, both of them had to. You have to keep things even, on both sides, or the whole thing gets out of whack.

    MISSY pulls out her gun, points it at LETO.

MISSY Let me see your hands. I don't want to hurt you, so I'm gonna need you to put the gun down, and then put your hands over your head now, slowly.

LETO OK.

MISSY She does, and then we're still for a minute, but I have to ask her why.

LETO Why? 'Cause I have to see the big picture, I have to see both sides. Baby, I'm the one in charge. Nobody was as good a cop as me, so now I am a Lieutenant. Nobody could run the gang as well as I can, so now I am the boss there, too. I am the best person for both jobs.

MISSY Look her in the face, she is calm. She is sympathetic.

LETO I'm sorry about Joe.

MISSY She knows exactly what she's doing.

LETO One from each side. Gotta keep the fight fair. Always trying to keep it fair. Why do you think Robert McCoy got caught?

MISSY Who?

LETO The squealer. That first squealer. Why do you think a little teenaged bullshit twerp had all those documents, had all those paper alarm clocks to wake Joe up to what was going on? Why do you think that little McCoy punk showed up and got collared, dripping with evidence and ready to squeal? You think that was an accident, an oversight? That was no accident. That was… a corrective measure. I plan corrective measures all the time, on both sides. Got to keep it all humming.

MISSY This is humming?

LETO I see that you're angry, I understand, but before you do anything, you need to know there's nobody above me anymore, nobody of consequence is left above me. On either side. That could mean big things for you.

MISSY But, Mom, how can you do it? How can you set your children up against each other, watch us fight each other, make us kill each other?

LETO I don't make you do anything, you like it this way.

MISSY The fuck I do.

LETO Hell, you got something better?

MISSY It's sunny. The smell of the grass. A day in the park. This is just a moment, in a beautiful open-air stadium in San Francisco on a nice day, looking at the soft hair of the woman who loved me, raised me. For a moment, I forget the gun, I forget the bodies, I just listen to her voice.

LETO You can see the beauty of it, can't you? Without two teams, there's no game. Without a game, without two teams, there's no society. As the boss, it's not my job to end society. It's my job to keep things going, to keep it all going the way all you people, all you cops and robbers, you all like it this way, you love the hunt, the chase, the beauty of the battle. I'm just trying to help you keep it up, give you what you've decided you want, let you have what you've decided life on earth should look like. You love it this way, all of you, you love it.

MISSY I don't.

LETO Really.

MISSY Really.

LETO Missy, take me down if you want. Self-defense, if you want to tell them that. Take me down. But if my run ends here, it won't stop the fight, the game you've all decided to play with each other. I'm just one person, getting rid of me won't change people always wanting to chase each other, hurt each other; at least I run things pretty clean.

MISSY She moves down slowly, like the sun setting, she gets down on her knees, in front of me, her arms out, chest open, waiting for me to decide.

LETO I run the show for now, but I've always known my time won't go forever. Take me down. If it isn't you, it'll be someone else. Maybe someone I don't love. I love you, Missy, I raised you with love. I raised you to be able to do anything, now what do you want to do?

MISSY I don't know. Maybe she's right. Maybe the blood, the fighting, maybe it needs to happen, maybe people need this, and it's all gonna happen, it's just a question of how.

LETO I raised you to be able to do anything, you're as good as I am, and now, if you want, we could do this together. One running each side. You wanna take good? I'll be evil. Or maybe you wanna mix it up, you wanna be evil? I'll handle good. We can fight each other, cops and robbers, the beauty of the battle, make a fight that shows our power and our strength to the gods. Or you want the whole thing? Take it. Kill me and take it all, take over both sides, if you want. A good man always knows his limitations. How well do you know yours?

MISSY The worst part somehow, is this: it's not the bodies on the grass. It's not even the fact I'll never hear Joe's voice again. And the fact that Leto who runs it all, she runs both sides, both sides like they're equal? Somehow, the worst part is, that doesn't bother me. And it should. It really should.

LETO Sirens in the background now. Everyone's coming. *(beat)* So. What are you going to do, sweetheart?

End of play.

Cassiopeia

by Christian Simonsen

Cassiopeia

The first public reading of *Cassiopeia* was on October 8, 2011 at EXIT Theatre, as part of San Francisco Olympians Festival II: Heavenly Bodies. It was directed by Stuart Bousel and featured the following cast:

Michelle Jasso	CASSIOPEIA
Vahishta Vafadari	ANDROMEDA
Shane Rhoades	PERSEUS
Keshuv Prasad	CETUS
Maro Guevara	PEGASUS
Travis Howse	STAGE DIRECTIONS

Characters

CASSIOPEIA, the Queen

ANDROMEDA, the Princess

PERSEUS, the Hero

CETUS, the Sea Monster (portrayed by offstage growls and shrieks)

PEGASUS, the Winged Horse (portrayed by offstage horse whinnies)

Setting

A rocky outcropping at the ocean's shore.

Lights up.

ANDROMEDA, young and beautiful, stands center stage, chained at both wrists to the rock. She is dressed in a skimpy ceremonial toga. Her mother CASSIOPEIA stands next to her. She is an older but still beautiful version of her daughter, without the chains.

CASSIOPEIA Now, Andromeda, dear, I don't want you to get too excited, but I really think this night could work out for you.

ANDROMEDA Mother.

CASSIOPEIA Now, his name is Cetus.

ANDROMEDA Mother.

CASSIOPEIA I hope I'm pronouncing that right.

ANDROMEDA Mother.

CASSIOPEIA He's a seafarer, so we're really quite lucky he can make it to shore for you.

ANDROMEDA Mother.

CASSIOPEIA Now, I confess, I haven't met him myself, but I've heard just wonderful legends about him.

ANDROMEDA Mother.

CASSIOPEIA Try not to think of this as "a date"—

ANDROMEDA Mother.

CASSIOPEIA —because knowing you, you'll just get nervous and make a big production out of it.

ANDROMEDA This is not a date.

CASSIOPEIA That's the spirit, dear.

ANDROMEDA This is not a date, Mother.

CASSIOPEIA Exactly. Just relax, and be your bright, cheerful self. Don't talk about politics, unless of course he brings the subject—

ANDROMEDA —Mother! This is not a date! This is not a festivity. This is not a soiree. This is a Sacrifice.

CASSIOPEIA Here we go. How many times have I heard that from you?

ANDROMEDA No, Mother. I don't mean, "This is an inconvenient chore I'm putting up with to please you, and you'll owe me back later big time." I mean, this is a Sacrifice. A real live Sacrifice. In fact, I am the real live Sacrifice, and Cetus is a real live monster.

CASSIOPEIA Dear, you should really give him a chance before judging him.

> CETUS *the sea monster growls offstage, far off in the ocean. Terrified, both women snap their heads towards it. Slowly,* CASSIOPEIA *regains her regal game face.*

ANDROMEDA Oh, Gods.

CASSIOPEIA That… that must be him now, Sweetie.

ANDROMEDA Please be honest with me—

CASSIOPEIA —He's punctual. That's always a good sign—

ANDROMEDA —just this once.

> CASSIOPEIA *turns to* ANDROMEDA.

CASSIOPEIA You look really nice.

ANDROMEDA I just want to hear you say why I ended up here.

CASSIOPEIA More than nice. Beautiful. You must get your looks from me. *(beat)* We all have our responsibilities, dear.

> CETUS *growls offstage.*

Ever since you were a little girl, your father and I warned you that something like this might happen.

ANDROMEDA Mother, I know the setup. It's pretty darn Classical, and I get it. I'm a princess. I've never had to do a day of work in my life. I've eaten better, dressed better, and slept better than anyone else in the entire kingdom. But the catch is, there might come a day when a sacrifice to the gods is required to save that kingdom… and that's the one job posting I'm qualified for. I get it. And I accept it. Willingly. Our kingdom is glorious. Our subjects are good, decent people. There is just one thing I hate about this, and that's the lame-ass cause of it all. And I want you to explain it to me.

CASSIOPEIA You know why, dear.

ANDROMEDA Yes, but I want to hear it from you. *(beat)* It's my dying request.

> *CETUS growls offstage.*

CASSIOPEIA *(beat)* Poseidon, and possibly some of the other gods, was offended by me. And to restore their honor, they demanded that I either sacrifice my only daughter to the sea mon—to Cetus, or watch them destroy my entire kingdom. *(beat)* A bit bratty of them, if you ask me.

ANDROMEDA And what crime did you commit to offend them?

CASSIOPEIA I'm guilty of being more beautiful than the sea nymphs.

> *ANDROMEDA stares at her.*

All right, I said I was more beautiful than the sea nymphs.

ANDROMEDA Do you think that might have been just a little bit vain?

CASSIOPEIA Well, it's a true statement.

ANDROMEDA True, who cares?

CASSIOPEIA It's a matter of principle.

ANDROMEDA Nobody cares, Mother.

CASSIOPEIA Granted, I'm not saying the sea nymphs aren't attractive, in their own way.

ANDROMEDA Father doesn't care.

CASSIOPEIA Of course, when you're forced to look at them through the ocean depths, the layers of shimmering water do wonders in hiding complexion defects.

ANDROMEDA Our terrified citizenry doesn't care.

CASSIOPEIA And don't get me started on that one skanky nymph with the huge gills.

ANDROMEDA And I certainly do not care.

CASSIOPEIA She's clearly had work done.

ANDROMEDA Mother, for Poseidon's sake, can't you admit how stupid this is?

CASSIOPEIA Well, the gods certainly overreacted, I must say.

ANDROMEDA Yes, they did, and do you know why? Because they're the frigging Gods, and they get to. You have no control over their actions. All you have control over is your own actions. And you blew it. Yes, you are still very beautiful. So what? It doesn't matter.

CASSIOPEIA That's easy for you to say, dear. You're still young. When you get to be my age—

> *CETUS growls offstage.*

ANDROMEDA What's that, Mother, when I get to be your age? Judging from how loud those ferocious growls are getting, I think I'll be spared the dread of any future midlife crisis. I'll get what you always wanted… to die young and beautiful.

CASSIOPEIA You… you have no idea what I'm going through right now. This is killing me.

ANDROMEDA No, Mother… it's killing me. I'm half-naked, chained to a rock, waiting to be devoured by a sea monster. You are not the victim here.

> *CETUS growls louder offstage. Both women turn towards the sound and stare.*

CASSIOPEIA Oh, no.

ANDROMEDA It's… Mother… Mother… It's a… it's a monster… a real monster.

> *CETUS growls again offstage.*

CASSIOPEIA Well, dear, he's—he's here.

ANDROMEDA Oh dear Gods, it's huge. The teeth look so… so sharp.

CASSIOPEIA Greetings, Cetus. I am Queen Cassiopeia. May I introduce my daughter, Princess Androm—

ANDROMEDA —I'm scared, Mother.

CASSIOPEIA No… no need to be, dear.

ANDROMEDA I'm scared, do you hear me! I'm terrified! Let me please express at least one real emotion before I die, you cold, shallow bitch!

CASSIOPEIA You did not just say that.

ANDROMEDA I'll say anything I want!

> *CETUS growls offstage. CASSIOPEIA looks out towards him.*

CASSIOPEIA Cetus, I'm sorry you had to hear that. She's usually much more gracious.

> *A brown substance plops down from above and lands between the two women.*

ANDROMEDA Horse shit.

CASSIOPEIA *(to ANDROMEDA)* All right, now you're just being juvenile.

ANDROMEDA No, I mean, look what just fell at our feet… It's horse shit.

> *A HORSE whinnies offstage.*

CASSIOPEIA Don't talk nonsense. A horse could never get out on these narrow rocks.

> *The HORSE whinnies again offstage. More brown substance plops down, this time right on CASSIOPEIA's head.*

Oh Gods, that's disgusting.

> *The HORSE whinnies offstage. CASSIOPEIA grabs her head and shakes the offensive substance out of her hair as ANDROMEDA squints and looks up at the sky.*

ANDROMEDA Praise the Gods, my prayers are answered!

CASSIOPEIA shakes her hands clean.

CASSIOPEIA You don't ask for much, do you?

The HORSE whinnies offstage.

ANDROMEDA Look, Mother, a brave young man on a magnificent winged stallion!

CASSIOPEIA looks up.

PERSEUS *(offstage)* Hail, young maiden!

CASSIOPEIA and ANDROMEDA Hail noble, handsome—

Mother and daughter glare at each other.

ANDROMEDA I think this one's for me.

CASSIOPEIA Don't be so sure. The Oracle at Delphi mistook us for sisters.

ANDROMEDA The Oracle at Delphi was being polite. *(looking up)* Oh noble, handsome stranger, take pity on me!

PERSEUS *(offstage)* I am Perseus, son of Zeus. Beautiful maiden, are you in distress?

CETUS growls offstage. ANDROMEDA looks out towards CETUS, looks down at her chained left wrist, looks over at her chained right wrist, and then looks back up towards PERSEUS.

ANDROMEDA How could you tell?

CASSIOPEIA That's right, dear… men just love sarcasm.

ANDROMEDA *(to CASSIOPEIA)* Oh. Yeah, right. *(to PERSEUS)* Sorry, bad day. Yes, hell, fuck yes. This damsel needs rescuing.

PERSEUS *(offstage)* It would be an honor to be of service to such a fair maiden.

CASSIOPEIA That's quite a line. He's not the kind of man you can trust, dear.

ANDROMEDA He's riding a winged horse. Right now, he seems like a good option.

CASSIOPEIA It's probably just a rental. And don't fall for that "Son of Zeus" bit either. If I had a gold piece for every time a boy tried that line on—

CETUS growls offstage.

ANDROMEDA Oh noble Perseus, can you slay the horror from the sea that is almost upon me?

PERSEUS *(offstage)* Fair maiden, I have just returned from a harrowing journey where I killed Medusa the Gorgon, the most feared, the most hideous creature on Earth. Many brave warriors have entered her dark, cavernous lair, only to fall victim to her wretched—

ANDROMEDA —so "yes." The answer to that question would be "yes."

PERSEUS *(offstage)* I can handle it.

ANDROMEDA Great, you're hired.

PERSEUS *(offstage)* I ask only one favor.

CASSIOPEIA My my, there's a catch. Who knew?

ANDROMEDA Name it.

PERSEUS *(offstage)* That you marry me.

ANDROMEDA *(beat)* That's a pretty big favor.

PERSEUS *(offstage)* It's a pretty big monster.

ANDROMEDA Still, marriage?

PERSEUS *(offstage)* I just feel we have chemistry.

CASSIOPEIA Meaning, he likes the way you look in a wet, clinging toga. Have you noticed he hasn't even bothered to ask what your name is?

ANDROMEDA *(Beat. To CASSIOPEIA)* I hate it when you're right.

> *CETUS growls offstage. ANDROMEDA addresses PERSEUS.*

OK, OK, sickness and health, death do us part. Deal.

PERSEUS *(offstage)* Yippee!

CASSIOPEIA "Yippee?" Really?

ANDROMEDA Now grab your sword and get your ass down here.

PERSEUS *(offstage)* I possess an even greater weapon. I vanquished Medusa by decapitating the fiendish hag. Behold, inside this cloth is the trophy that proves my bravery.

ANDROMEDA You mean—

CASSIOPEIA —Dear, you must admit, any man that carries around a woman's severed head in a sack probably has some intimacy issues to work out.

> *CETUS growls offstage.*

ANDROMEDA Please hurry!

> *The HORSE whinnies offstage.*

PERSEUS *(offstage)* Whoa, Pegasus! He has a problem with hovering.

> *CETUS growls louder offstage. ANDROMEDA and CASSIOPEIA look out toward the monster, and cower back against the rock.*

CASSIOPEIA His breath is horrible.

ANDROMEDA Mother, please, always remember, I never wanted—

PERSEUS *(offstage)* —Foul creature of the deep!

> *PERSEUS enters with a heroic leap, carrying a cloth sack. He steps in front of the two women, looks out towards CETUS, and raises the sack up and out in front of him.*

In the name of my father Zeus, I prove my undying devotion to my true love… my true love…

ANDROMEDA Andromeda.

PERSEUS Andromeda!... Thank you.

CASSIOPEIA What did I tell you?

ANDROMEDA Shh! He's working.

PERSEUS Loathsome beast from the ocean depths!

CASSIOPEIA What exactly is your plan, young man?

PERSEUS *(to CASSIOPEIA)* Turn him into stone. *(to CETUS)* Witness an evil even more repulsive than yours!

CASSIOPEIA You have got to be kidding.

ANDROMEDA Mother.

PERSEUS *(to CASSIOPEIA)* Please, if I could just focus for a moment. *(to CETUS)* Behold, in all her ugliness, the deadly face of the Gorgon, Medusa!

> *PERSEUS whips the sack open, revealing Medusa's grotesque, snake-haired head. CETUS growls offstage. Then CETUS shrieks offstage. Then... silence. CASSIOPEIA and ANDROMEDA straighten up and look out toward CETUS.*

CASSIOPEIA Cetus... he, he looks like a statue.

ANDROMEDA Yes, a statue of stone. You did it, Perseus!

PERSEUS I did it... yes, I really did it! Frankly, I wasn't sure if it was going to work.

CASSIOPEIA I'm... I'm impressed.

ANDROMEDA Congratulations, brave Perseus.

> *PERSEUS jumps up and down, waving Medusa's head.*

PERSEUS I did it, I did it! Yippee!

CASSIOPEIA He may be a little dorky, but I have to admit, he's a cut above your past boyfriends.

PERSEUS turns to CASSIOPEIA.

PERSEUS Thank you!

CASSIOPEIA Noble Perseus, may I be the first to welcome you to our fam—

CASSIOPEIA freezes into a statue of stone.

PERSEUS Oh thank you, thank you! Can I call you Ma—

PERSEUS looks at CASSIOPEIA, and stops jumping.

Fuck.

ANDROMEDA Perseus, you have conquered a Gorgon, a sea monster, and my mother's mistrust.

PERSEUS Yeah… sure did.

PERSEUS taps CASSIOPEIA's stone arm.

ANDROMEDA Those are three miraculous victories in one day.

PERSEUS Yep.

ANDROMEDA Don't you find it amusing, Mother, that despite all your lectures on the power of beauty, it was the face of the ugliest woman in the world that saved me?

PERSEUS Yeah, dramatic irony, what a hoot. Look, about your mother…

ANDROMEDA I no longer have to be a prisoner to your standards, Mother. Your oppression all these years has bound me worse than these chains.

PERSEUS Nice metaphor, but the thing is, she can't hear you.

ANDROMEDA You are so right, Perseus. She never could, because she never wanted to.

PERSEUS Perhaps, but you see, she really can't hear you. *(beat)* She's dead.

ANDROMEDA What?

PERSEUS She saw Medusa's face. She's turned to stone. She's dead. Stone dead.

ANDROMEDA *(beat)* Fuck.

PERSEUS Yeah, that's what I said.

ANDROMEDA I was really beginning to like you.

PERSEUS You see, the thing is, this head of Medusa, I hadn't really had time to practice with it. The lethal sight lines around her face are a little tricky.

ANDROMEDA Just how clumsy are you?

PERSEUS Not to make excuses or anything, but I just came straight from the epic adventure of slaughtering Medusa the Gorgon, which was foretold as part of my destiny, and quite an accomplishment in and of itself for one day…

ANDROMEDA You know, it kind of does sound like you're making excuses.

PERSEUS …but then I saw you with your sea monster problem, and even though your situation wasn't part of my prophecy, I thought to myself, "There's a nice girl that I could—

ANDROMEDA —You killed my mother.

PERSEUS Yes, but it was an accident. And, frankly, it kind of sounded like you might be better off without her.

ANDROMEDA You did not just say that.

> *PERSEUS raises both his hands—and Medusa's head—in a "surrender" gesture.*

PERSEUS OK, OK, you're right. That was definitely crossing the line.

ANDROMEDA averts her eyes.

ANDROMEDA Will you put a sack on that thing?

PERSEUS Sorry.

PERSEUS covers up Medusa's head.

If there's anything I can do—

ANDROMEDA —Chains.

PERSEUS What?

ANDROMEDA Unbind me. Now.

PERSEUS unlatches both of her chains during the following:

PERSEUS Look, as first dates go, this one has been kind of hit and miss. We could drop the whole marriage obligation, if you want. You're free to go.

ANDROMEDA stares at her bare wrists.

ANDROMEDA Free…

PERSEUS And I think my winged horse might have pooped on your mother. I'll make sure she's clean.

ANDROMEDA Thank you.

ANDROMEDA rubs her swollen wrists, as PERSEUS looks over CASSIOPEIA.

PERSEUS The shit didn't stick to her.

ANDROMEDA It never does.

They both stare at CASSIOPEIA.

PERSEUS She is very beautiful.

ANDROMEDA Yes.

PERSEUS You look a lot like her.

ANDROMEDA Thanks.

PERSEUS Kind of sound like her, too.

ANDROMEDA Like when I'm pissed? I was afraid of that. *(beat)* She never said she loved me.

PERSEUS That's a shame. Really.

ANDROMEDA It's OK. *(beat)* Sorry I snapped at you.

PERSEUS That's all right.

ANDROMEDA You look very tired. You were right. Killing Medusa the Gorgon was enough of an epic for one day.

PERSEUS Still, I should have been more careful.

> *She reaches out her hand. He takes it in his.*

ANDROMEDA Will you promise me one thing?

PERSEUS Sure.

ANDROMEDA Whenever I sound like my mother, tell me.

PERSEUS You'll hate me when I do.

ANDROMEDA I know.

> *PERSEUS and ANDROMEDA exit hand in hand, leaving the statue of CASSIOPEIA all alone. The HORSE whinnies offstage.*
>
> *Lights fade to black.*
>
> *End of play.*

Pleiades

by Marissa Skudlarek

Pleiades

The first public reading of *Pleiades* was on October 22, 2011 at EXIT Theatre, as part of San Francisco Olympians Festival II: Heavenly Bodies. It was directed by Liz Anderson and featured the following cast:

Xanadu Bruggers	MOIRA
Rachel Ferensowicz	ELENA
Lily Yang	TERESA
Brianna Calabrese	ALISON
Alisha Ehrlich	KELLY
Sarah Rose Butler	SARAH
Megan Cohen	MEREDITH
Karen Offereins	MISSY
Brant Rotnem	BRUCE
Allison Payne	STAGE DIRECTIONS

The script of *Pleiades* was subsequently revised and received a staged reading on April 14, 2013, at the Atlantic Stage New Voices Play Festival in Myrtle Beach, South Carolina.

Pleiades will be staged in a full production at the Phoenix Theatre in San Francisco starting August 7, 2014. It will be directed by Katja Rivera with the following cast:

Susannah Lee	MOIRA
Amy Nowak	ELAINE
Monica Ammerman	TERESA
Annabelle King	ALISON
Miranda Hanrahan	KELLY
Emily Ludlow	SARAH
Kailah Cayou	MEREDITH
Erika Bakse	DIANE
Paul Rodrigues	BRUCE

Characters

MOIRA Attlee, 24, eldest of the seven Attlee sisters

ELAINE Attlee, her sister, 22

TERESA Attlee, their sister, 20

ALISON Attlee, their sister, 18

KELLY Attlee, *their sister, 17*

SARAH Attlee, *their sister, 15*

MEREDITH Attlee, *their sister, 14*

DIANE Archer, *cousin to the sisters, 26*

BRUCE Cronin, *friend of the family, 28*

Setting

Fourth of July weekend, 1971. The Attlees' beachfront summer home in the Hamptons. Two different playing areas: the back porch, and the beach itself.

The porch extends from stage right about two-thirds of the way across the stage. A door, stage right, leads to the kitchen. Stage left, sand, sky, and horizon can be seen, as well as the side of the house next door (the Cronins' summer house). The porch is elevated a few feet off the ground and has wooden steps at its downstage end. A path runs upstage from the steps to the Cronin house. The porch contains benches, Adirondack chairs, etc., sufficient to seat the seven Attlee sisters and their guests. Perhaps there is a porch swing. There is also a combination radio/record player in a cabinet.

For the beach scenes, the "fourth wall" represents the ocean. Upstage are low sand dunes, with the Attlee house visible in the background. A path leads from the house over the dunes and onto the beach downstage.

Act One

Scene One

Sunset, Friday, July 2, 1971. The porch. An ironing board protrudes halfway out from the kitchen door: SARAH has laid her head on the board and KELLY is ironing her hair. MOIRA sits upstage center, pensive. ELAINE sits near her, fidgety. ALISON is on the porch swing, reading a book; MEREDITH lies on the porch floor, reading Seventeen *magazine. TERESA, at the record player, puts on Judy Collins'* Wildflowers *album; the song "Both*

Sides Now" begins to play. Tableau: KELLY irons SARAH's hair; ALISON and MEREDITH read; the others listen to the music.

SARAH "Debutantes, like stars, come out at night." *(giggles)*

MOIRA Who told you that?

SARAH It's what they wrote about Elaine's debutante ball, remember? The stars are coming out, and I thought…

MEREDITH "Star light, star bright…"

ELAINE *(annoyed)* Nursery rhymes?

KELLY If we're too old this summer for our baby sister to say nursery rhymes—

TERESA "Debutantes, like stars, come out at night." What will they think of next?

SARAH We'll never know, will we, since *you* refused to make your debut—

TERESA Yes, because I didn't want them writing inane things about me!

ALISON I'm not having a debut either.

KELLY You are such party poopers. Sarah, it's up to us to maintain the family tradition.

SARAH If you're in college, who'll iron my hair for my debutante ball?

ELAINE Star light, star bright. Oh, I guess it won't do any harm—we all have things to wish for!

TERESA *(to ALISON)* You could thank me, you know.

ALISON Why?

TERESA I had to fight Daddy for months not to have a debut—all *you* had to do was ask.

MEREDITH *(to SARAH)* Elaine is going to get you a hair-straightener for your birthday. I think she's sick of you always stealing the iron.

ELAINE Meredith, that was supposed to be a surprise!

MEREDITH Since when has this family ever been able to keep a secret?

Inside the house, the phone rings.

KELLY I'll get it.

KELLY abandons the iron and runs into the kitchen.

SARAH *(lifting the iron off her hair)* Kelly! You could have burned me alive!

Inside the house, KELLY can be heard saying things like "Uh-huh… Sounds fun… I'll check." "Both Sides Now" has reached the second chorus; the record begins to skip and repeat the lyrics "Love's illusions."

TERESA OK, who scratched it?

Silence, except for the broken record.

Meredith?

MEREDITH No.

TERESA *(taking the needle off the record)* Sarah?

SARAH I hate Judy Collins.

MEREDITH Which is why she scratched it on purpose.

SARAH Shut up.

ALISON I really like this song!

TERESA Alison. Of course.

ALISON I'm sorry, I'm sorry! I really like this song! So I borrowed your record and I guess I listened to it too many times—

ELAINE "Love's illusions, love's illusions"—that's the last thing I need to hear!

ALISON Maybe everything is an illusion.

TERESA Look who took Philosophy 101.

MOIRA I don't think that's what she means.

KELLY reenters through the kitchen door.

KELLY That was Melanie Prewitt. *Love Story* is playing at the second-run theater… she says we should go see it with her!

SARAH Oh, *Love Story*!

MEREDITH I hope college is *just* like that.

SARAH Oh, but my hair—

KELLY What?

SARAH It's only half done—and if Trip Harris is there—

TERESA If Trip Harris is spending Friday night at *Love Story*, your hair is the least of your problems.

KELLY You joining us, Teresa?

TERESA To see *that*? No thanks.

ALISON Are we leaving now? Just let me get my sandals on—

A beat.

KELLY Alison—you're coming?

ALISON Yeah.

KELLY I don't know if it's your kind of movie.

ALISON I want to see it with you.

SARAH But if Trip Harris is there—

MOIRA So what if he's there? Let Alison get her shoes on—

ALISON Will you come too, Moira?

SARAH Oh, what do you think.

MOIRA No... It's all right... I'll stay in tonight.

SARAH And *every* night...

KELLY Elaine, what about you?

ELAINE No thanks, I'm good. You have fun with your *Love Story*. *(giggles)*

ALISON You are acting very strange.

ELAINE Takes one to know one.

KELLY Well, we'll see you later, then...

MOIRA Don't stay out too late—

MEREDITH See you later, alligators!

ELAINE In a while, crocodile!

> *ALISON, KELLY, SARAH, and MEREDITH exit through the kitchen door. ELAINE fidgets and looks at her watch.*

Is it really only eight-thirty?! Why can't it be tomorrow already?

TERESA What's happening tomorrow?

MOIRA Diane's coming for the weekend.

TERESA I didn't know you were so excited about seeing Diane.

ELAINE Maybe I'll see someone *else* tomorrow... "Star light, star bright..." no, I did that already...

MOIRA Why didn't you go to the movie?

ELAINE But why would I want to go see Love Story when— *(giggles)*

MOIRA Alison's right—you *are* acting mysterious.

ELAINE Am I?

MOIRA Oh, don't be like that.

ELAINE *(beat)* I guess you'd know soon enough. I have to tell somebody, I'm nearly bursting out of my skin. I'm in love, I have my own love story—don't give me that look, Teresa—

MOIRA All right, who is he?

ELAINE He's marvelous—he isn't like any other boy I've ever told you about! He's not a boy, in fact—he's a man.

MOIRA I see. So, do I know this man?

ELAINE Well, yes. We all do.

TERESA Is he here for the summer?

ELAINE No… and yes! So, can you guess? Can you guess why I'm so excited? *(beat)* Because his house is next door and he's coming tomorrow! *(beat)* Yes, that's right, it's Bruce! I can say his name if I want, we all know it!

MOIRA Bruce.

ELAINE You don't think it's weird, do you? That we've known him since we were kids? But I think Daddy always hoped one of us would marry Bruce…

TERESA You can't be *marrying*—

ELAINE Oh, I'm getting ahead of myself. But—say something! You can't disapprove! He's a war hero and he's ambitious and he's gorgeous—and that is not a matter of opinion, he is a *fox*, isn't he?

MOIRA So this is serious.

ELAINE I think I could be with him for the rest of my life.

MOIRA And does *he* feel that way—about you?

ELAINE He *will*.

MOIRA Please. Be careful.

TERESA Or what?

MOIRA Things can happen.

TERESA Like what? She'll end up in McLean like you?

ELAINE Teresa!

TERESA Admit it, you're curious too.

ELAINE Moira, I'm sorry, I should have thought, it was so different for you after you graduated college, and here I am going on and on about—

MOIRA It's in the past.

TERESA Yes, but what? *What* is in the past? *(beat)* Why do we always tiptoe around this? You went to a mental hospital for eight months, and we don't really know why. We're always thinking about it, but we never mention it. But, like you said. It *happened.*

ELAINE We always wondered if you had some tragic love affair that gave you a nervous breakdown… so I guess I'd like to know… Moira, *were* you in love when—

MOIRA Yes. But it's not how you think. *(beat)* It's funny. You said it's important to remember it happened. What if I told you it didn't happen that way at all? Well, most of the details are correct. My last semester at Wellesley, I had a love affair. Then I graduated and had a crisis. And I went to stay at a—a kind of hospital, in Massachusetts. But it wasn't a psychiatric facility.

ELAINE I—

MOIRA It was—it was a home for unwed mothers—

ELAINE No.

MOIRA I had the baby and then I went to fat camp to get the weight off and then I came back.

TERESA Oh my God.

ELAINE Moira—

MOIRA You're not the only one who can keep a secret around here.

ELAINE Moira—poor Moira… And of course that's why you've been different since you came back—quieter, and more subdued—but we never suspected, never—

MOIRA Good.

TERESA But—you had a baby—!

MOIRA Yes. A boy. I hardly even got to look at him…

ELAINE You could've kept him.

MOIRA I don't think so.

ELAINE We would have spoiled him rotten!

MOIRA Can you imagine the scandal? But—but I'm glad it was a boy. It made it easier to give him up. I couldn't imagine raising a boy, when all I know are sisters…

TERESA You could have gone to a doctor.

MOIRA I did.

TERESA I mean early on.

MOIRA Nice girls don't do that.

TERESA No, they hide, tell lies, pretend they've gone nuts, go off have a secret baby and never talk about it again. Well, maybe you *did* go nuts, you'd have to be nuts to come up with a plan like that…

MOIRA It's in the past.

ELAINE Moira, I'm glad you told me… I'm glad I know. So you *were* in love!

MOIRA That's one way to put it.

ELAINE And this means that nervous breakdowns *don't* run in the family! And babies can be prevented, right? I know what comes next: you tell me to go into the city and get a prescription for the Pill.

MOIRA Yes. Well, no. There's one more thing, I guess, so you know everything—

TERESA Something *else*?

ELAINE If you don't want to tell—

MOIRA I think—I think you should hear this. *(beat)* I was in love. Yes. But not in the abstract… You see, I was in love with… somebody specific.

ELAINE No.

MOIRA Yes.

> *ELAINE turns away, crumples.*

It was Bruce—Bruce was the father…

TERESA Oh my God!

ELAINE You're not still carrying on with him?

MOIRA No, it was over long ago. And it was very brief while it lasted.

ELAINE But I love him—I love him…

> *ELAINE cries. MOIRA strokes her hair.*

TERESA My God, why is this family so weird?

MOIRA There were times I wanted to tell you—all of you. It was very hard to keep this secret, when I was so used to telling you everything. I wondered if you would be shocked. I wondered if you would judge me. Sometimes I wanted to tell you just so I could see the looks on your faces when you found out… But I never wanted to see you like this…

ELAINE I'm not leaving him, I don't care what you say!

MOIRA *(soothingly)* Did I ask you to? You can think about it in the morning. I trust you'll do the right thing—

ELAINE Does Daddy know?

MOIRA Yes, about the baby, of course. But I refused to say Bruce was the father. I didn't want Daddy to be mad at him—

ELAINE Good Lord—you *are* still in love with him!

MOIRA No.

ELAINE Of course you are—how could you forget him—you don't just forget a man like Bruce—I *can't* break up with him, don't make me…

TERESA Get ahold of yourself!

MOIRA Elaine. I want you to be happy.

ELAINE Then you can't make me leave him—because *he* makes me happy—

MOIRA I know. I know. *(beat)* Now I want to cry and I hardly know why… Perhaps I'm relieved. To have finally told you…

ELAINE I couldn't have kept it secret this long. I don't know how you did—and Bruce right next door—

TERESA God, what a creep!

MOIRA Teresa, don't be—

TERESA What, I'm not allowed to call him a creep? It's like he's checking us off a list—

ELAINE He made a pass at you, too?!

TERESA No! How can you think—

ELAINE He doesn't have a list. And if he did, *I'm* the last person on it! *(beat)* Moira, I'm so, so sorry for what happened to you… but, I mean, I know I'm not Bruce's first girlfriend… I knew there were other women before me. And the fact that one of them happened to be my sister is just—it's just a fluke!

Scene Two

The porch, the following morning. ELAINE and TERESA enter through the kitchen door, carrying a large table, which they set down on the porch.

TERESA So what will you say when Bruce shows up?

ELAINE What?

TERESA After the events of last night.

ELAINE I don't see why it should change anything.

TERESA You don't—

ELAINE So don't let on that you know any of this.

TERESA Cross my heart and hope to die.

ELAINE You think you know the full story, but you don't. Give Bruce the benefit of the doubt. He is a wonderful man.

TERESA *(annoyed)* All right.

ELAINE begins straightening up the porch. TERESA starts to hang some patriotic bunting.

ELAINE You'd understand if you'd ever been in love.

TERESA I'm sure.

ELAINE Pity his brothers are already married…

TERESA What? Oh yes, you *do* like to keep it in the family.

ELAINE I'm warning you.

TERESA Why? What do you think I'm going to do? This is a weird situation, so I'm staying out of it. Why aren't you worried about what *Moira* will do? She has a lot more reason to get upset.

ELAINE But she's not. You are.

TERESA I'm just letting off steam. I'll behave when he arrives. I may not be a debutante but I know damn well how to be gracious—

ELAINE You'd better be.

TERESA *(after a pause)* You ever think about how this house is built on sand in a hurricane zone?

ELAINE My happiness is not built on sand!

MOIRA enters from the kitchen, pushing a tea cart.

MOIRA The petits fours are in the oven. Shall we set the table?

ELAINE Petits fours at a consciousness-raising?

TERESA Oh God, that's so tacky and bourgeois.

MOIRA Even a liberated woman can enjoy a good tea cake. I thought it would be fun.

TERESA Oh, it will be fun, we'll all have fun this weekend. I'll have fun with my favorite cousin and Elaine will have fun with Bruce and you'll have fun with your tea cakes. What a lark, what a goddamned lark.

The women begin to set the table.

MOIRA *(to ELAINE)* What's her problem?

ELAINE Sexual frustration?

TERESA I heard that.

ELAINE Well?

TERESA Yes, I am "sexually frustrated," if that means "frustrated by my sex, that is, frustrated by being a woman and surrounded by women"—

ELAINE You know that's not what I meant.

TERESA Well, it *should* mean that! What, you think I'm bent out of shape 'cause I don't have a boyfriend? You may be sexually frustrated, it doesn't mean everyone is.

ELAINE I am not! I'm liberated.

TERESA Ha.

ELAINE I love sex! Isn't that feminist of me?

TERESA It's not supposed to be the only thing you think about!

ELAINE But when you're in love—it happens. I'm sure Moira understands what I mean—don't you?

MOIRA Yes… I suppose.

ELAINE I can't stop thinking about him, I want him every minute—

MOIRA Thank you.

ELAINE Didn't you want him?

MOIRA I didn't want to have his baby!

ELAINE But before that—

MOIRA I guess.

ELAINE You guess.

MOIRA I didn't say no.

Beat.

TERESA Moira—did he…?

MOIRA Did he what?

TERESA I mean… If you didn't want to…

ELAINE Are you saying he assaulted her?

MOIRA What? God, no! How can you think that?

TERESA But you said you didn't want to.

MOIRA All right, I guess I'm old-fashioned. Yes, I enjoyed sleeping with him. No, I don't care to talk about it.

ELAINE You don't have to be ashamed of your desires.

MOIRA I *wasn't* ashamed. And look where that got me.

ELAINE They talk about the potency of female desire, but until I met Bruce, I never knew—

MOIRA Yes.

ELAINE It's potent.

MOIRA Yes.

ELAINE A girl doesn't just forget a man like that—

MOIRA Elaine, what do I have to say to convince you that I'm not going to interfere?

TERESA Moira's the only one of us who never minded sharing her toys.

MOIRA Teresa.

TERESA You're just going to lie down and roll over? Instead of getting upset and fighting like hell—

MOIRA Fighting for *what*?

> *ALISON suddenly appears at the kitchen door.*

ALISON Yeah—for what?

> *Beat.*

ELAINE Alison, we didn't see you—

ALISON Whatcha talking about?

MOIRA We're just getting the table ready.

ALISON You all fell silent when I came out. *(beat)* Who's fighting? And for what?

ELAINE That's a good question…

ALISON There's something you're not telling me. You think I'm too young? I'm in college—

MOIRA There's nothing—

ALISON You can't fool me. I know something's going on. *(beat)* Maybe you can talk about it at the consciousness-raising!

Scene Three

Later that day. The consciousness-raising tea party. DIANE, MOIRA, ELAINE, TERESA, ALISON, KELLY, SARAH, and MEREDITH sit around the table. The tea cart, laden with sandwiches, petits fours, and a tea service, is near MOIRA.

DIANE Men are pigs.

ELAINE Diane—

DIANE The police are pigs, that goes without saying, the president is a pig, and the White Anglo-Saxon Protestant male is the worst pig of all.

SARAH I thought they were WASPs?

DIANE No, they're not wasps, they're nothing like wasps. Wasps are beautiful, hard, shiny, like little jewels. Whereas the men we know are overfed, and jowly, and turn pink in the sun, and paw at you, and grunt at you… They're pigs. Plain and simple.

ALISON I think pigs are kinda cute.

DIANE Yeah, and then you take one in and it shits all over your floor. *(beat)* Yeah, shit, shit, shit! This is a consciousness-raising group, we have to be able to say whatever we want. Say it with me! Shit!

SISTERS Shit.

DIANE Men are *shitty* pigs! *(beat)* Oh, and you know what? Wasps are all female—like bees, and ants! *We're* the real wasps! You have a stinger, don't forget!

MOIRA Who'd like some more tea?

DIANE Now the point of a consciousness-raising group—

MOIRA Tea party—

DIANE —the point of a consciousness-raising *tea party* is that we all get together and rap about our personal experiences with the topic at hand. Which is: Men are Pigs. Who'll go first? *(silence)* OK, I'll start us off. So when I was at Holyoke, a group of us decided to get together and bathe naked under the light of the full moon. It was that year when we were all in a hippie phase. Well, we go out to the Connecticut River, and take our clothes off, and get in the water. And it's really powerful. I don't mean in a sexual way, I mean there was this sense of sisterhood. We were all there, together, under the full moon, and you know, women are tied to the moon because of our monthly cycles…

TERESA Germaine Greer says you aren't a woman unless you've tasted your menstrual blood.

MEREDITH Ew.

DIANE Try it sometime. A little tampon teabag…

MEREDITH *(setting down her teacup)* Blech!

DIANE So we're in the water, and this *man* comes by, walking along the riverbank, and stops and stares at us. The nerve of him! We were there to get away from men, and here he was, intruding on our womanly ritual—staring at us like we were working at the Playboy Club! So, you want to know what we did?

TERESA Yeah!

DIANE I came up with the plan. I remembered there was a house a little way upriver that had a fence around it with big signs: "Beware of Dog." So we convinced him to take his clothes off and get into the water with us—believe me, he didn't take much convincing—and we teased him and flirted with him and maneuvered upstream till we were right in front of that house… and then we persuaded him to scale the fence and sneak onto the property… I think we said we lived there, it was a nudist commune… and then we swam off as fast as we could. *(ominously)* We heard the dogs barking and growling, and that was the last we ever saw of him. He never came back for his clothes…

MOIRA Diane!

DIANE He deserved it.

MEREDITH You really think he *died*?

KELLY You're so morbid!

MOIRA Diane, don't you think you were provoking him—?

DIANE If a man can't look at a naked woman with respectful indifference, he's got a problem.

MOIRA Well, I just think it's more complicated than that.

ALISON But, if you don't want to be looked at when you're naked, don't go swimming naked. Right?

DIANE You are completely missing the point—

ELAINE No, we get the point, it's that you want us to be angry with men, all the time!

DIANE Why shouldn't we be?

MOIRA It's just—it's more complicated—

DIANE Moira, you're what, twenty-four years old, so you've had plenty of time to learn how the world works—how men abuse our trust, abandon us, and behave like little shits—

TERESA And if it's not one man in particular, it's society in general—which is run by men.

DIANE Surely you have *some* experience with male piggishness.

MOIRA I don't like to blame people. I don't think anyone is to blame.

TERESA You don't have to blame anyone—just tell your story.

MOIRA My story?!

TERESA *(quickly)* I didn't mean your *story*-story, I mean, just say something—

DIANE What "story-story"?

MOIRA What Teresa meant was—

ALISON I knew there was a story!

SARAH Oh really?

MEREDITH What kind of story?

TERESA Sorry. Um. Moira, you don't have to say anything if you don't want to—

DIANE The point of a consciousness-raising session is to talk about things you don't want to! For the sake of your sisters, Moira. Will you?

MOIRA *(collecting herself)* Yes. So, I told Elaine and Teresa this last night, but now the rest of you ought to hear it. *(beat)* I know you think I had some kind of romantic disappointment, and that's—that's what sent me to the mental hospital. Well, you guessed right. I was wrong not to tell you. It's not very feminist of me, but yes, we broke up and I lost my mind!

ALISON I knew it, I knew it—

MOIRA And it's embarrassing to lose your head over a man, which is why I didn't tell you, but it's true. It was more than simple heartbreak. He—he, well, he wasn't anyone we know. He was… Italian… a very poor scholarship student at Harvard—

TERESA Oh, like *Love Story* with the genders reversed?

MOIRA —very involved in the anti-war movement—

DIANE A student revolutionary! I didn't think you had it in you!

MOIRA —and we had an affair—

DIANE —or maybe you *did* "have it in you"—

MOIRA I even met his parents—lovely big Boston Italian family… And though I knew it couldn't last, I was happy. And then, well— *(suddenly vehement)* The trouble with good-looking men is that they are never content with just one woman.

DIANE Sing it, sister!

MOIRA I thought he loved me. But it was hard. Other women were always after him, and he didn't want to be tied down. *(beat)* When a woman finds a good and handsome man, she knows she'd be a fool to let him go. But when a man finds a good and beautiful woman who loves him, that's still not enough. Men like that are never satisfied! They smash things up and leave destruction in their wake—while they walk away unhurt! It is very dangerous to fall for a man like that—

> *A tennis ball bounces onstage and smashes into the tea cart. The women, startled, look in the direction of where the tennis ball came from. BRUCE enters, racquet in hand, sweating through his tennis whites like an Ivy League Stanley Kowalski.*

DIANE *(ironically)* Tennis, anyone?

ELAINE Bruce!

BRUCE Diane, charming to see you, as always— *(rumples DIANE's hair)* —and Moira— *(rumples MOIRA's hair)*

MOIRA *(setting the table to rights)* Bruce—

BRUCE What were you talking about there, Moira?

MOIRA It's nothing.

TERESA *(bitterly)* We're just being silly, we're a bunch of silly girls.

BRUCE Those tea cakes look delicious. Mind if I join?

DIANE That would be completely inappropriate—

BRUCE I won't say a word.

KELLY You're not supposed to hear what goes on at a consciousness-raising—

SARAH It's very secret. *(giggles)*

ELAINE Oh, let him stay. There's something I want you to hear—all of you. It's my turn anyway. *(beat)* I *don't* think men are pigs. I think men are wonderful and you don't know what you're missing. I think love is the most amazing thing in the world, and if you wonder how I know this, it's because *I'm* in love—with Bruce!

Silence. BRUCE grins sheepishly, laughs nervously.

BRUCE Well! Guess the cat's out of the bag—that's right, your sister and I are—you know—

ELAINE We're so happy!

BRUCE So happy.

ELAINE hugs BRUCE.

ELAINE You're all sweaty.

BRUCE I know, I should go home and freshen up—

ELAINE I don't mind. I'm so glad you're here.

BRUCE Fourth of July at the beach—wouldn't miss it!

ELAINE But this year you're here with someone *special*.

BRUCE *(tweaking ELAINE's nose)* Yes, someone very special. I should really go shower.

BRUCE starts to exit.

ELAINE Don't be a stranger! Come back for supper?

BRUCE *(calling as he exits)* Sure thing.

BRUCE exits toward his beach house.

DIANE Sweating just like a *pig*.

ELAINE I won't stand for that, Diane!

SARAH You and Bruce are together?

KELLY When did it start?

ALISON Why didn't you tell us?

ELAINE I feel like the luckiest girl in the world.

DIANE All right, enough—

ALISON I *knew* Elaine was acting weird.

SARAH Do you think he'll propose?

MEREDITH Does Daddy know?

KELLY He'll be our brother-in-law!

SARAH He'll be one foxy brother-in-law!

MEREDITH You think he's a fox? He's so old!

ELAINE All right, there's so much to tell you! Should I start at the beginning?

> *The younger sisters nod.*

Well, at Christmas Bruce asked me if he might write me a letter or two when I was away at college—

DIANE That's enough!

ELAINE Don't you want me to tell my *story*, Diane?

DIANE Not *this*!

TERESA It's *my* turn!

ALISON But this is some very big news!

ELAINE So we started corresponding, and I told him I didn't have a date for the Spring Fling Formal—

TERESA Moira's story was more interesting.

MOIRA Thank you.

KELLY He came all the way from Florida to be your date?

ELAINE Mm-hm...

SARAH How romantic!

ELAINE I felt like the luckiest girl on campus—

DIANE We know, we know. You're the luckiest girl in the universe.

MOIRA She is, isn't she? I think we should be happy for Elaine, and hope for the best.

ELAINE Thanks. It's good to hear you say that.

TERESA *(sullenly)* Congratulations. It's what you want, I guess.

ELAINE It is.

DIANE Can we get back to the consciousness-raising now?

ELAINE I think that would be all right.

DIANE Your turn, Teresa.

TERESA Um.

>   *Beat.*

DIANE You were so hot to trot a moment ago.

TERESA Men are pigs… well, you know, they run everything, and screw it up—I mean, they got us into this mess in Vietnam—

DIANE This is supposed to be about your personal experiences with the patriarchy.

TERESA Um. *(beat)* I'm drawing a blank, isn't that odd. Well, maybe I haven't been personally affected, as much as other women, but… I think that's what we have to remember, you can just wake up one day and decide to be a feminist, there doesn't have to be some event that catalyzes you, it doesn't have to be personal—

DIANE The personal is political!

TERESA Diane, I don't want you to doubt my commitment to the cause! But I haven't really suffered. I've been lucky, I guess.

KELLY But not the luckiest girl in the world!

MEREDITH *(to ELAINE)* Will we all get to be bridesmaids?

SARAH When was the first time he told you he loved you?

ALISON Will you move in with him?

DIANE *(to TERESA)* I think we're losing them.

ELAINE There's so much to tell you! Moira, is all the tea gone? Better make another pot.

Scene Four

> *Later that day, after supper. All of the WOMEN are on the porch. DIANE holds up a small drawstring bag of paisley calico.*

DIANE Look what *I* brought…

> *Everyone looks blank. DIANE holds up rolling papers.*

And *these*…

MOIRA Diane!

DIANE Oh come off it, your dad's not here.

MOIRA You… you are a bad influence.

DIANE This is the best way to end a consciousness-raising! It'll bring us closer together.

MOIRA How, by making us all junkies? Don't expose my sisters to that.

SARAH *(giggles)* She thinks we couldn't get it somewhere else.

MOIRA All right, Sarah, but you're not going to get it at *home*…

> *DIANE has started rolling a joint.*

What are you doing?

DIANE All those in favor of a little weed between cousins, say Aye.

ELAINE, TERESA, ALISON, SARAH Aye.

DIANE The Ayes have it.

MOIRA I'm starting to think it was a mistake to lower the voting age.

DIANE What?

TERESA Didn't you hear? Two days ago they got enough votes to ratify the amendment—

DIANE Right on! My God, I'm actually feeling patriotic.

> *She lights the joint and takes a hit.*

God bless America!

> *Passes it to TERESA.*

TERESA *(smoking)* God bless American *agriculture*…

> *BRUCE enters from upstage, coming down the path that leads from his beach house to the Attlees'.*

BRUCE Whoa there, what are you girls up to?

ELAINE Oh Bruce, I thought you'd never get here! You missed supper.

BRUCE I'll make it up to you tomorrow.

> *TERESA passes the joint to ALISON.*

ALISON *(smoking)* Good stuff, Diane.

> *ALISON attempts to pass it to KELLY.*

KELLY Doesn't it fry your brain?

ALISON That's just CIA propaganda.

KELLY *(looking at ALISON, TERESA, DIANE)* I'm not so sure…

DIANE You might think my brain is fried, but it's not the marijuana that did it.

ALISON Everyone smokes at college. Even at girls' schools. You can see the haze over the Quad.

BRUCE Really. It's certainly changed from when I was in school.

MEREDITH Yeah—you old dinosaur.

ELAINE He's not a dinosaur.

> *DIANE offers MOIRA the joint.*

MOIRA Don't even try.

DIANE *(offering joint to BRUCE)* Maybe some for our guest tonight, huh?

BRUCE No, thanks. I have a physical coming up.

> *The joint remains with DIANE. She takes several more hits throughout the scene.*

ELAINE Bruce has to keep himself in peak form!

BRUCE That's right—they'd never pick some fatso to be the next man on the moon, would they?

MEREDITH You're really going to walk on the moon?

BRUCE Someday. I hope.

ELAINE It's absolutely incredible, everything you have to do in order to become an astronaut.

BRUCE They do make you jump through a lot of hoops.

ELAINE I'm so proud of you. But sometimes I get discouraged thinking of how long it could be before you know if you're selected as an astronaut—and then if you are, I get frightened to think of waving goodbye to you as you go up in a rocket ship…

BRUCE Takes a strong woman to do that.

ELAINE That's what worries me.

BRUCE Well, we'll build up your strength. Look, it's started this summer. We didn't see each other for four weeks, and you handled that like a trooper. And then, like an exercise regimen, we'll see if you can go five weeks without me… six, eight…

ELAINE I don't think I could bear it!

BRUCE I think you could.

MOIRA The heart is a very resilient organ.

BRUCE Indeed. And Elaine, I can tell you've got a strong heart.

MEREDITH If she's so strong, maybe she should be the astronaut.

ALISON The first woman in space!

KELLY No—the Russians already sent one.

ALISON Really?

BRUCE Damn Russians—

SARAH You could be the first couple in space—

ELAINE and BRUCE start giggling.

What?

BRUCE We could be the first to—you know—

ELAINE Bruce!

BRUCE —in zero gravity—

Everyone is giggling.

SARAH I didn't mean it like that!

BRUCE Very kinky, Sarah!

DIANE C'mon, it sounds like fun.

TERESA I think it would make an awful mess.

Everyone laughs harder, but now they are laughing at TERESA.

What? What? It would!

MEREDITH You know what else would make an awful mess: getting your period in space—

Now everyone is laughing at MEREDITH.

SARAH Ew, ew, ew!

KELLY Then you'd really taste your menstrual blood—

MEREDITH Ew, ew!

BRUCE Maybe that's why there are no female astronauts.

DIANE That's stupid—

BRUCE Diane, it's an anatomical defect.

DIANE But Bruce, our periods connect us to the moon—so what could be more appropriate than sending a woman to the moon? Man in the moon, man on the moon, one small step for a man—why don't they ever talk about a woman on the moon? Moon, it's feminine, moon goddess, la lune, la luna, the lunar loony bin…

BRUCE Send all the women to the lunar loony bin—

DIANE To be a woman—in this society—it is only natural to go crazy. Ask Moira about it—

MOIRA Diane, please.

BRUCE That's right—the loony bin!

ELAINE That's not a very nice thing to say.

BRUCE I remember you that summer—one day you were fine, and the next, you had—poof! Up and vanished!

MOIRA Yes, that's right.

SARAH It was that Italian—

MOIRA Sarah!

BRUCE Oh really?

MOIRA I don't want to talk about it.

KELLY Oh, but Bruce is practically family!

BRUCE An Italian, huh.

MEREDITH He was her boyfriend—

>   *MOIRA, ELAINE, and TERESA shoot dirty looks at MEREDITH.*

Sorry.

BRUCE And you loved him so much you went crazy. Well, well, well.

MOIRA Yes. That's it.

BRUCE He must have been quite a guy for you to lose your head like that.

MOIRA Quite a guy.

BRUCE An Italian?!

>   *ELAINE comes up behind BRUCE, puts her arms around him and kisses his neck.*

ELAINE Brucie…

BRUCE Mm?

ELAINE You know, you've got that whole big house to yourself… and it's been so long since I've seen you… so, you know…

BRUCE Well, you certainly aren't shy…

ELAINE Bruce, I am a liberated woman!

BRUCE And I love that you're liberated… Just don't get any crazy ideas,

OK?

ELAINE What's that supposed to mean?

BRUCE Don't turn into one of those man-hating—

ELAINE Do I look like I hate men?

> *Kisses him.*

BRUCE I would say not...

ELAINE Well, come on!

> *ELAINE jumps up and runs toward the Cronin house. BRUCE chases her offstage.*

TERESA Moira.

MOIRA Mm?

TERESA You really think this could work out? With Elaine and Bruce?

MOIRA I don't know.

TERESA Do you *want* it to work out?

MOIRA I don't know.

Scene Five

> *The beach. The next day. KELLY, SARAH, and MEREDITH are sunbathing. Lying out in the sun, they are the pictures of summertime indolence. A long pause.*

SARAH I wish it were Christmas.

MEREDITH Why?

SARAH I want it to be Christmas.

KELLY Sarah, it's the Fourth of July.

SARAH At Christmas we'd be going to parties—

MEREDITH We had a party yesterday.

SARAH I'm sick of summer! *(beat)* Trip Harris isn't ever going to notice me. He likes Caroline Bates, I know he does!

KELLY Oh, Sarah. I'm sure he's noticed you.

MEREDITH Everyone notices us.

SARAH Yes, the mob of women, the seven sisters… But he's never going to notice *me*!

    DIANE enters, coming over the sand dune.

MEREDITH Hey, Diane.

DIANE Oh, hey. I thought I might find you down here.

SARAH I worship the sun.

MEREDITH She thinks if she gets a tan, Trip Harris will notice her.

DIANE And you?

KELLY We keep her company.

DIANE Hey, I didn't get to hear much from you girls at the consciousness-raising.

SARAH We had lots of questions for Elaine!

DIANE No, I mean before that… "Men are Pigs."

SARAH Oh, that.

DIANE You ever feel that way? Anything you wanted to share but didn't get the chance?

SARAH I'm with Elaine. I think men are wonderful.

MEREDITH Except she's always swearing that her life is over because some boy didn't notice her.

DIANE Sarah, that's exactly what the patriarchy wants you to do. It wants you to be dependent on them.

SARAH You're always talking about the patriarchy. I don't see why it's so important.

MEREDITH But if it weren't for the patriarchy, we wouldn't even be here.

DIANE Sunbathing?

MEREDITH No, I mean… why do you think there's seven of us? We're not Catholic. *(beat)* 'Cause they were trying for a boy.

DIANE Huh.

MEREDITH If, if Kelly had been a boy, do you think I'd even be alive? Nobody wants seven daughters, it's ridiculous.

KELLY Oh my God! I never thought of that. If I'd been a boy—

MEREDITH So I'm really glad you weren't.

DIANE Meredith, you're a smart cookie.

MEREDITH Thanks.

SARAH So Daddy only wanted me if I was a boy?

DIANE Patriarchy, Sarah. Doesn't it make you feel like shit?

SARAH I don't care! I like being alive!

MEREDITH And, you know, at least Americans don't kill girl babies like they do in Asia, right? Otherwise— *(mimes slitting her throat)*

KELLY Ew, you're so morbid!

DIANE But sometimes we help 'em out.

MEREDITH What?

DIANE You know how many Asian babies Bruce has killed? Boys and girls. You think he was in Vietnam handing out flowers and candy? He didn't even bring Elaine flowers and candy, and he's dating her.

MEREDITH That's awful!

SARAH What? That he's not giving her flowers?

MEREDITH You know what I mean.

SARAH Yeah.

MEREDITH *(beat)* I bet they would have killed me if we were in Asia.

KELLY Don't say that! Daddy loves you. I know he does.

DIANE And we love you, Meredith, you're darling.

SARAH Hey, Mer', did you know I used to be jealous of you? I wanted to be the youngest.

KELLY Because we all spoil her to death?

SARAH No, silly. Everyone knows the youngest sister is the prettiest.

MEREDITH I'm not the prettiest.

SARAH I mean like in fairy tales. There are always seven sisters and the youngest is always the prettiest and goes on adventures and marries the prince. But no one cares about the sixth sister.

KELLY Unless you like tongue twisters.

DIANE You still believe in fairy tales, Sarah Attlee?

SARAH No. I'm saying, when I was a kid.

DIANE *(laughs)* Oh, honey, you still are a kid.

SARAH Will you come for my birthday next month? Sweet sixteen!

MEREDITH And never been kissed!

SARAH You stop that!

DIANE What's the problem—that you've never been kissed, or that you have?

Scene Six

> *Meanwhile, on Fourth of July morning, MOIRA and TERESA are on the porch. ELAINE and BRUCE come out of the kitchen door and cross the porch. They are dressed for tennis and carry racquets.*

ELAINE Bruce and I will be back for lunch. *(to BRUCE)* You better not skip out on us to go shower this time—

BRUCE Moira's making lunch?

ELAINE Yes.

BRUCE What'll it be—Italian food?

MOIRA Potato salad and poached chicken.

BRUCE Oh.

ELAINE Well, I'm sure we'll work up a good appetite—

BRUCE See you in a bit.

MOIRA Have fun!

> *ELAINE and BRUCE exit.*

TERESA I don't know how you can just sit there and take it!

MOIRA I guess it's a bit strange that we've never discussed it.

TERESA Never?!

MOIRA The fewer people know, the better. So if that means I have to put up with—with all of this… I've spent two years avoiding a scandal, I'm not going to be at the center of one now.

TERESA I think a scandal is just what this place needs.

MOIRA Easy for you to say, it's not your reputation on the line.

TERESA "Reputation" is such a bourgeois concept.

MOIRA Yes—just like summering in the Hamptons.

TERESA scowls.

I happen not to mind the life we were born into, and I don't think you do either, as much as you say.

TERESA How can you not mind? The lies you told. The fact that it's more respectable to have a nervous breakdown than to have a baby, or an abortion. The way you were raised to be so goddamn passive, and then to say, "oh well, that's just how life is!" You just sit back and let it all happen—

MOIRA It's not like that. It was a very hard choice—

TERESA Yeah, I bet it's hard to be such a doormat!

MOIRA I did something big. I had to be brave. I thought you'd respect that. I'm not just your schizo sister. *(beat)* You don't know what it was like at—at the home. In a way, it was like a twisted version of being *here*. Once again, I was surrounded by women, not even women, *girls*. Once again, I was the big sister. I mean, I was only twenty-two, but most of them were fifteen or sixteen. And they weren't lively and carefree girls like you, they were so forlorn, with such sad, shameful stories. There was nothing to do but sit and think about how you'd gotten yourself into such hot water—and that's not healthy to do for months on end—and by the time I got out I probably could have used a good six months at McLean—but you see that was the one place I *couldn't* go, because you thought I had been there all along…! It's funny, isn't it? But it took all my strength.

TERESA So wouldn't it have been easier to tell the truth?

MOIRA Why are you so obsessed with getting things out in the open? You and Diane and Alison. You know, some things are better left unsaid—

A rustling beneath the porch.

Wait. What was that?

TERESA What?

MOIRA A noise—

Pause. They listen—nothing.

I must've imagined it.

TERESA You know you have nothing to be ashamed of.

MOIRA I know.

TERESA In an ideal world, there would be no such thing as shame.

MOIRA Really? I think there ought to be some shame involved when a man seduces and abandons one girl and then takes up with her sister.

TERESA Well, all right, Bruce should be ashamed of himself. And if you told your story, people would see what a creep he is—

More rustling beneath the porch. Beat.

MOIRA Didn't you hear that?

TERESA Oh God. Is Alison in her hidey-hole again?

MOIRA Oh, no.

TERESA Alison! Olly olly oxen free!

ALISON crawls out from beneath the porch. She has been crying.

Good Lord, Alison, I know you must be shocked, but there's no need to *cry* about it.

ALISON Jim Morrison died.

TERESA Oh, God.

ALISON I needed some alone time, all right? I am really torn up—

TERESA You've been sneaking around all weekend—

ALISON I wasn't trying to eavesdrop!

MOIRA You must've heard everything, didn't you?

ALISON What happened to the baby, Moira?

MOIRA I don't want to talk about it! This shouldn't become common knowledge.

ALISON How come Teresa got to know about it and I didn't?

MOIRA Because.

ALISON Don't "because" me. I'm a part of this family and I just want a little respect—

TERESA *(sings)* "Just a little bit… just a little bit…"

ALISON I mean it. What do you want me to do?

TERESA You could start by not crying over the death of some rock star. *(beat)* And how do we know you won't run down to the beach and tell the others? We have to swear you to secrecy.

ALISON It's not fair!

TERESA *(cheerfully)* No, it's not. Say it with me: "cross my heart and hope to die, stick a needle in my eye."

ALISON I'd rather stick a needle in my vein.

End of Act One.

Act Two

Scene One

Lunchtime on the Fourth of July. Everyone is on the porch, eating potato salad.

KELLY I wish Paul could be here.

DIANE Well, you know, med students start their rotations in July. He's busy. *(beat)* They say that's why you shouldn't ever have surgery the first week of July. Or a baby, if you can help it.

ALISON *(looking at MOIRA)* February might be a good time to have a baby…

DIANE What? Why?

TERESA *(simultaneously with the above)* Do we have to talk about babies?

ALISON I don't know. So he could grow up with the Spring.

SARAH Ugh, not that hippie stuff again.

ELAINE *(to DIANE)* How's Paul liking his rotation?

DIANE I don't know. I think the last time I talked to him was our birthday—two weeks ago.

MEREDITH Are you mad at him or something?

DIANE No, why?

MEREDITH I couldn't imagine going two weeks without talking to my sisters.

ALISON Well, we all went months without talking to Moira when she—

MOIRA I know what you mean, Meredith. It's hard for me too.

DIANE It's funny. Sometimes I think Paul and I are complete opposites and sometimes I think he understands me better than anyone on earth. Actually, the problem is how other people see the two of us. I'm just as smart as he is, I have just as much to contribute. And yet, I feel like I'm always in his shadow. Paul, the doctor! Paul, the golden boy! *(beat)* Being Paul's twin is what made me a feminist.

BRUCE Interesting. Then how do you account for Teresa?

TERESA What?

BRUCE You're a feminist because you resent your brother—

DIANE I do not resent—

BRUCE —but Teresa doesn't have any brothers.

TERESA Maybe when you have six sisters, you have six times more opportunity to see how much it stinks to be a woman.

DIANE It does not "stink" to be—

TERESA I mean the way society works—

ELAINE I love being a woman! Or, you know… *(sings)* "I enjoy be-ing a girl…" *(beat)* Wait, did I just agree with Diane?

TERESA *(to DIANE)* I don't get it. You have all these examples of the ways men have screwed us over, and you want us to get angry, but you also want us to say that we're proud to be women and it doesn't stink and we wouldn't be a lot happier if we were men.

BRUCE Hey, is this another consciousness-raising? No one told me…

ALISON Well then it's *my* turn—I have something to say—

MOIRA This is *not* a consciousness-raising—

DIANE Yeah, the one yesterday was kind of a bust—

ALISON Why not? This is important—

SARAH She's going to talk about Jim Morrison, isn't she?

TERESA Either it stinks to be a woman or it's fantastic, you can't have it both ways—

DIANE Well, but there are different circumstances—

TERESA And it's going to stink as long as men are in power. So then what do we do—live on female communes? And then why wouldn't the men come in and smash those up too?

BRUCE Look, I'm sorry about the tea service—

TERESA This is not about the tea service! It's about how you are never going to respect what we are trying to do, so we are at an impasse.

BRUCE You think I hate feminism?

TERESA Don't you?

BRUCE Feminism is the best thing that ever happened to the American male. Look: for the first time in history, there's a bunch of twenty-year-old girls running around, determined to sleep with as many men as possible to prove they're liberated, and determined never to get married, 'cause marriage is for squares. Why would I hate that?

TERESA I hope you don't think I'm that kind of feminist!

ELAINE *(simultaneously with the above)* I hope you're not saying I'm that kind of girl!

BRUCE *(to TERESA)* Don't be so repressed.

TERESA In fact, that is a perversion of what feminism—

ELAINE Do you really think I'm like that?

BRUCE *(to TERESA)* Aw, lighten up. Isn't it your philosophy that men and women are the same, deep down? So we have the same needs? The same primal urges?

TERESA But not all people have the same kinds of urges. Right? You have one kind of urge, I have another kind—

BRUCE Wait—you're a lesbian?

TERESA What?

BRUCE "Different kinds of urges…"

TERESA Oh God, don't be disgusting.

DIANE If she were a lesbian, you and she would have the *same* kind of urges.

BRUCE Isn't that funny? If you were a lesbian, you'd understand me! *(beat)* But you're not, right?

TERESA How can you even think—

BRUCE Teresa, you go to Vassar.

TERESA So?

BRUCE So there's some kind of Sapphic shenanigans going on after curfew, right?

TERESA I wouldn't know anything about that. You do know we just went co-ed?

BRUCE Boy, you really are a piece of work. You're the least liberated feminist I've ever met.

TERESA There are different ways of being liberated—

ELAINE Bruce, do you have to talk about this?

BRUCE I'm just having some fun.

TERESA Yeah, "fun."

ELAINE Well, it's not appropriate for you to ask my sister about her sex life—or lack thereof—

TERESA Shut up.

BRUCE Can I ask Diane if she's a lesbian?

ELAINE What is your sick fascination with lesbians?

MOIRA I wonder about lesbians sometimes. I feel sorry for them. It must be so lonely, to be an outsider like that. For your very existence to be a scandal.

MEREDITH I don't know, there might be something nice about it.

ALISON Being an outsider?

MEREDITH Just, well, they're called homosexuals, right? "Homo" means "the same." Maybe they're not lonely. Maybe they're surrounded by people who are like them. They fall in love with people who are like them. People who understand them. *(indicating her sisters)* I mean, *you* are always trying to figure men out, and Bruce, I bet you are trying to figure us out. But if you were a lesbian, you'd understand the people you fell in love with. They wouldn't be mysterious. And it might be easier to love them.

ELAINE But loving someone who's just like you—where's the fun in that?

KELLY It seems kind of narcissistic.

DIANE So what does that make your father?

SARAH What?

MEREDITH He always wanted a boy! Remember?

BRUCE Men always want to have boys.

ELAINE *(kissing BRUCE)* And maybe soon Daddy will have the son he's always wanted—or a grandson!

ALISON Well, actually—

TERESA Can someone pass the potato salad down here?

End of scene.

Scene Two

ALISON sits on the beach alone, a pad of paper in her lap, writing a letter.

ALISON Dearest, dearest Lizard King,

You're out there, somewhere, across the vast Atlantic waters, and all around the world, women are weeping and wailing and rending their garments.

It's really heavy here on earth, Jim. Everyone's got secrets. Everyone's so self-involved. My older sisters are so weird and the younger ones are so narrow-minded. I thought people were supposed to be getting more open-minded. I thought this was the Age of Aquarius.

I keep thinking, you wrote "Break on through to the other side"—is that what you did yesterday? Did you know something that we don't? Did Janis and Jimi know it too? Is it better to be dead than alive? Is that why there's so much death everywhere?

I'm going to burn this letter and then maybe some pieces of it will reach you, wherever you are.

Rest in peace, Jim.

Alison Attlee.

> *ALISON kisses the letter. She sets a candle in the sand and lights it.*

C'mon baby, light my fire.

> *KELLY, SARAH, and MEREDITH enter.*

KELLY What are you doing?

MEREDITH *(noticing the candle)* We're not Catholic.

SARAH What's that?

> *SARAH snatches the letter and begins to read it.*

"Dearest, dearest Lizard King…"

> *KELLY and MEREDITH laugh derisively.*

ALISON That's private!

SARAH "You're there, somewhere, across the vast Atlantic waters, and all around the world, women are weeping and wailing and rending their garments."

> *KELLY and MEREDITH mockingly boo-hoo-hoo.*

"It's really heavy here on earth, Jim."

KELLY Yeah, man, it's "heavy."

SARAH "Everyone's got secrets. Everyone's so self-involved. My older sisters are so weird and the younger ones are so narrow-minded—"

ALISON You weren't supposed to see that!

> *ALISON snatches the letter out of SARAH's hands.*

SARAH Tell us how you really feel.

ALISON I could tell you things…

KELLY I don't need to hear more about how narrow-minded I am, thank you.

ALISON I didn't really mean that!

SARAH And I bet you think you're so nonjudgmental, right?

KELLY *We're* narrow-minded, *they're* weird…

MEREDITH Why are they "weird"?

ALISON I could tell you something—something big—

SARAH What? Jim Morrison was murdered by the CIA?

ALISON No, about our family—

KELLY What could you possibly know that we don't?

ALISON They don't want me to tell you…

SARAH She's bluffing.

ALISON I wish I could tell you… but if I do, they get mad and if I don't, *you* get mad!

MEREDITH I'm not mad at you. I just don't believe you.

ALISON You're gonna find out soon enough and then you'll see I was right!

KELLY Yeah, and Jim Morrison's gonna answer your letter.

Scene Three

ELAINE and TERESA are on the porch.

ELAINE "And maybe soon Daddy will have a grandson!" How could I be so stupid? I nearly gave away everything there…

TERESA It's like "Don't think of an elephant." Of course we can't stop thinking about it…

ELAINE And the secrets keep piling up. I can't go on like this!

TERESA Either she should tell everyone, or she should never have told us at all. *(beat)* I keep thinking back to when we were kids here, with the Cronins staying next door. We'd all be playing on the porch, and Bruce would try to ignore us—he was embarrassed about spending the summer with a bunch of girls. How could we have known that any of this would happen? It was just ten or twelve years ago, but it was such a different time. Did going to war change Bruce, do you think, or was he always like this?

ELAINE For someone who claims not to like Bruce very much, he certainly seems to take up a lot of space in your head.

TERESA What's that supposed to mean?

ELAINE Teresa—are you jealous of me?

TERESA Don't be ridiculous.

ELAINE *(stung)* Oh!

TERESA What?

ELAINE Whenever people say "Don't be ridiculous" that always means they're hiding something.

TERESA Really. *You're* the jealous one. Why would you possibly think that I'm interested in Bruce?

ELAINE You're always arguing with him.

TERESA Well, people argue when they don't like each other!

ELAINE No! Like in the movies—the two of you, you banter. It's like *Love Story* only you're both rich!

TERESA Oh God, that's horrifying.

ELAINE He listens to you. Sometimes he hardly seems to hear what I say.

TERESA Are you worried that I like him? Or that he likes *me*? Because I *don't* like him, I can assure you. I'm trying to be nice for your sake. But

I think he's a creep.

ELAINE He's your sparring partner. And you're the kind of girl who needs a sparring partner.

TERESA That's not what I want, actually. I want someone who understands me, who I don't have to argue with.

ELAINE Someone weaker than you? You'd eat him alive.

TERESA I'm hardly that awful—

ELAINE Even if you're a feminist, there's no shame in wanting a strong man. Doesn't every woman want to be with a man who's bigger, stronger, smarter, and better than her?

TERESA How can you say that?

ELAINE Don't you want your boyfriend to be better than you are? Isn't that only human?

TERESA Well, I hardly think that Bruce is better than me. So there you have it. *(beat)* What I can't understand is why you think it's all or nothing.

ELAINE What do you mean?

TERESA You act like either you'll marry Bruce, or you'll be alone for the rest of your life.

ELAINE That's how it was for Moira.

TERESA You're not Moira.

ELAINE I don't want to imagine my life without Bruce. I love him. So of course I want to marry him and be with him forever! You say that women should have lots of options, but doesn't that get confusing? Besides, you have to make a choice eventually.

TERESA I think you see the world as black-and-white. But there are as many options as there are colors in the rainbow.

ELAINE *(ironically)* Far out, man. *(beat)* Aren't there only seven colors in the rainbow?

TERESA There's millions.

ELAINE *(beat)* OK, Teresa. We were told, growing up, that one set of things was valuable. And then we woke up one morning and the world had decided that all of those things were worthless, that we should acquire a whole new set of values. And maybe you can just swap out your values at a moment's notice, but I can't. I don't see what's so bad about wanting to be married and have a family. I mean, I'm grateful that I can vote, and I'm very grateful not to be a virgin! But I thought the point of this was freedom. Choice. I am choosing this.

TERESA And of course you happen to make the choice that society wants you to make.

ELAINE Well, why is society so bad, anyway? Maybe some things are clichés for a reason. They say love is the best thing in the world, and it *is*, Teresa, that's not a myth!

TERESA Even if the man you love knocked up your sister and—

ELAINE That's what I mean! Despite everything, I am choosing to love, rather than hate. You say men hate us—if we hate them in return, wouldn't we be stooping to their level?

TERESA It's amazing what you'll tell yourself so you can keep sleeping with that pig.

ELAINE You're just jealous that I'm sleeping with *someone*. *(beat)* You can still choose love, Teresa. You don't have to scorn it. I think you really are a loving, sensitive person, deep down, but that frightens you— so if someone hits you in your weak spot, you lash out. Bruce is like that too, you know—

TERESA Don't you *dare* compare me—

ELAINE —there you go, proving my point. Maybe that's why you and he have a spark: you're too similar.

TERESA *(beat)* Where's his weak spot, then?

ELAINE Why would I tell you?

End of scene.

Scene Four

> *Twilight. The beach. TERESA and DIANE enter from over the dune.*

DIANE *(as they enter)* No. She was just trying to get a rise out of you. You are nothing like Bruce.

TERESA You mean that?

DIANE Honey, are *you* a male chauvinist pig? God, she'd better not marry him.

TERESA She sounds pretty determined. She really wants to be married. And I wonder, too, if she's doing it to spite Moi—

DIANE What?

TERESA —um, to spite *me*, I mean, 'cause I'm against it. She's seen too many movies. She thinks the more we oppose her, the more it proves that she and Bruce are meant to be together.

DIANE Ugh, it makes me sick. Maybe we should go after Bruce instead.

TERESA What do you mean?

DIANE Convince *him* to dump her. Doesn't that sound easier? I mean, he doesn't seem all that crazy about her, he's bound to break up with her sometime—

TERESA He will?

DIANE —and you could help speed it up. Keep arguing with him. Be a nuisance.

TERESA Elaine wouldn't tell me what his weak spot is.

DIANE It's his manhood, of course!

TERESA His penis?!

DIANE I was speaking figuratively. But yes, that too.

> *BRUCE and ELAINE enter over the dunes.*

ELAINE Will the fireworks scare you?

BRUCE What? No.

ELAINE Sometimes you hear about men who come back from war and then jump at any little noise—especially gunshots or fireworks.

BRUCE Pansies.

ELAINE That didn't happen to any of your army buddies?

BRUCE They wouldn't be my buddies if they did that.

TERESA Well gee, it sure is nice to celebrate the Fourth of July in the company of a genuine American war hero!

ELAINE Teresa.

BRUCE It's OK. I've heard worse.

ELAINE He put his life on the line for our country and I won't let you insult that.

TERESA I just said, gee, it sure is nice—

ELAINE Teresa.

DIANE It's a free country.

ELAINE Thanks to men like him!

TERESA If it is, I can exercise my freedom of speech—

ELAINE It's a national holiday. Can't you show a little respect for the troops?

TERESA I do respect them, OK? I pity them, actually—the men who were drafted. But I don't respect anyone who signed up for this pointless war—

ELAINE He was very brave!

TERESA Were you deluded?

DIANE Maybe he deserves your pity too. Poor Bruce, actually believed he was doing the right thing…

BRUCE You think I believed that? *(beat)* I knew it'd be a mess. The French had a hell of a time keeping control of Indochina, why would we do any better? Don't pity me. I went in there with my eyes open.

TERESA Did you have a death wish?

BRUCE I wanted to fly planes.

DIANE Ridiculous macho bullshit—

BRUCE You know how you get to be an astronaut? You have to be a military pilot first. *(beat)* I was always fascinated by flight. Remember *Sky King*?

ELAINE "Out of the blue of the Western sky comes… Sky King!"

BRUCE King of the sky. Conqueror of the heavens. And when the space program started, I knew I'd do anything to be an astronaut. And then things fell into place: I graduated from college, they needed pilots in 'Nam…

ELAINE So you see it wasn't about war or violence or bombing at all—

DIANE That was just collateral damage?

ELAINE It was about flight!

TERESA So you—you went over there and killed people just so that eventually you might get to fly a fucking rocket ship? How is that different from murder?

BRUCE I don't have blood on my hands. I was flying the plane. Other people launched the bombs, told me where to fly. If I hadn't done it, some other guy would have.

TERESA But you *signed up* for it.

BRUCE If I got what I needed and the military got what it needed, why is that a problem?

TERESA You killed innocent people—

BRUCE They weren't innocent and they would have died anyway.

DIANE That's no reason to burn them alive with napalm!

ELAINE Napalm?

BRUCE Yes.

ELAINE I'm so naïve. I thought it was just bombs. Those poor people—I've seen pictures—

BRUCE Ah, don't be such a bleeding-heart. There was something almost beautiful about it. Like throwing thunderbolts.

MOIRA, ALISON, KELLY, SARAH, and MEREDITH enter.

MEREDITH Are the fireworks going to start soon?

TERESA Oh, they've started.

ALISON I don't hear them…

TERESA Bruce was just telling us about his days as a mass murderer.

SARAH What?

DIANE In Vietnam—

TERESA He's done all kinds of horrible things and you expect me to welcome him into our home and our family—

ELAINE Well, too bad, it's not your decision!

TERESA I'm just trying to make you see—

ELAINE It's *my* decision! In fact, I've been thinking, and—Bruce, when you go back to Florida, I want to come with you!

BRUCE What?

ELAINE Move in with you!

BRUCE That's—

ELAINE I never thought I'd live with a man without being married—God knows what Daddy will say—but I don't care even if there's a scandal! You must get awfully lonely in Florida—

BRUCE Elaine, we should talk this over—

ELAINE —and you're so busy with the astronaut training, you could use me around to do your laundry, and—

DIANE Just listen to yourself!

ELAINE What?

DIANE You're moving in with him to do his *laundry*?

ELAINE Don't tell me what to do! Teresa said I always make the safe choice, and deny myself what I really want. Well, I realized I want to move in with Bruce, and Society can go stuff itself.

TERESA That isn't what I meant—

BRUCE I don't know about this—

ELAINE Don't you want me around?

BRUCE Well…

ELAINE I know there might be a scandal, but we can survive that together—

BRUCE It's not that, it's… This is a bit sudden. *(beat)* Is there something you're not telling me? Are you—you're not pregnant—?

ALISON gasps.

TERESA Yes, Alison, they're having sex.

ALISON I knew that—

MOIRA I think the two of you should discuss this in private. Elaine, Bruce is right. It's a big decision.

ELAINE I'm not pregnant, for your information.

MOIRA I didn't think you were.

BRUCE I'm sorry, Elaine. But this is sudden, and I need to think—

ELAINE Really? I thought it was—either you know or you don't!

BRUCE You really believe that?

ELAINE It's like that for me.

SARAH I think it's very romantic for you to go off and live with Bruce—

TERESA To do his laundry? Elaine, you can't be serious—

MOIRA Please. This is between Elaine and Bruce. And I don't think anyone can influence them either way. *(beat)* I'm staying out of this.

ELAINE Thank you.

> *The fireworks begin; the group falls silent. After a pause:*

KELLY Alison—

ALISON Yeah?

KELLY Is that what you wouldn't tell us earlier? That Elaine's moving to Florida?

ALISON *(beat)* Mm-hm. That was it.

KELLY But why did she tell *you*?

SARAH I bet Alison was snooping around—

MEREDITH Shh. I want to see the show.

> *Fireworks explode, their colors reflecting off the faces of the group. Lights fade.*

Scene Five

> *The beach. Late at night. BRUCE sits on the sand, drinking a*

> *bottle of beer. There is an empty bottle next to him. Long moment. The sound of waves. TERESA enters over the sand dune. She is wearing shorts and a hoodie. She does not notice BRUCE until she nearly trips over him.*

TERESA Oh! Sorry—

BRUCE It's all right.

TERESA I'll go—

BRUCE No, come on—have a beer.

TERESA I don't think so.

BRUCE You're still mad at me?

TERESA Bruce, maybe we'll just have to have our differences, and that's that.

BRUCE What do you mean?

TERESA We're never going to see eye to eye, and maybe we should just accept that, and stop getting into arguments—

BRUCE OK then. Don't argue. Sit down.

TERESA What?

BRUCE We don't have to see eye to eye. We don't even have to talk. Don't go away. Sit down.

TERESA I guess.

> *She sits next to BRUCE. Pause.*

BRUCE So… Come here often?

TERESA Ha.

BRUCE I mean, do you have a habit of wandering down here after midnight?

TERESA Sometimes. *(beat)* Well, a lot, recently. When I need to clear my head—you know?

BRUCE Yeah.

TERESA My family.

BRUCE Yeah, your family. *(smiles)*

TERESA I guess we can be an—intimidating bunch.

BRUCE I can handle it.

TERESA Really? I don't envy any man who marries one of us.

BRUCE You're the most eligible women in the Hamptons.

TERESA Oh yes. "The seven beautiful Attlee sisters. Debutantes, like stars…" But think about it. If you marry Elaine, you'll spend every Thanksgiving with us, every Christmas, every summer at this beach house. I doubt Moira will ever get married and I don't think I will either, so it'll just be you and a bunch of girls—and you know how girls love gossip and bickering and secrets—

BRUCE I thought you were a feminist?

TERESA No, I am, I'm sorry, I love my sisters, but sometimes they're so… Well, sometimes I find it hard to handle, and I was born into this family. You marry Elaine and then what are you? A fox in a henhouse.

BRUCE Did you just call me a "fox"?

TERESA Great. I didn't mean it that way.

BRUCE I know.

TERESA And I called myself a hen, too. A "chick." Oh dear. *(beat)* You see, that's the problem, even the *words* we use, we can't escape it—

BRUCE Hey, lighten up.

TERESA You're always telling me to lighten up—

> *BRUCE catches her eye and holds the bottle of beer out to her.*

Well, all right.

TERESA takes the beer bottle.

It's kind of nice not arguing with you.

BRUCE Agreed. *(beat)* So. You feel trapped?

TERESA What?

BRUCE I'm saying, you feel trapped, don't you? In your family.

TERESA What? Well, yes, I feel trapped!

BRUCE I could tell. Me, too.

TERESA Oh, no.

BRUCE What?

TERESA You're *not* trapped.

BRUCE You all assume I'm going to marry Elaine, but have I ever said "marriage" to her? Have I promised her anything? I don't even know if I want to live with her, and you're acting like I'm already part of your family. Did I agree to any of this? I worry that I'm going to wake up one day, a husband and a father, never having walked on the moon, and not know how I got there.

TERESA But you're not trapped. You can escape.

BRUCE You don't understand.

TERESA I don't understand!? What about how I've *been* trapped, more trapped than you've ever been, and how hard I've tried to escape—I'm still trying?

BRUCE I'm just saying—you can't fight destiny.

TERESA Oh, so you think my *destiny* is to be some housewife? Just because my mother was, just because that's how I was brought up? When you look at us, and all of the expectations we were raised with, and what we had to do to physically tear them down—*that's* being trapped. And yet we still manage to free ourselves. Some of us.

BRUCE Yes, and some of you stay in the traps. And act as bait.

TERESA What—Elaine? Well, God, if that's how you think of her, you better not marry her!

BRUCE If I can be honest with you—

TERESA What, she's the Venus flytrap and you're the poor, innocent little fly? You're not a fly.

BRUCE I'm a WASP.

TERESA Yes, a wasp, with a sting… And besides, flies aren't innocent. They feed on rotten meat.

BRUCE Watch it, now.

TERESA You know what? I think we *do* intimidate you. Seven sisters, we grew up together, and you will never know Elaine as well as we do. And you feel trapped because you know that if you ever did anything to hurt her, we would never forgive you. Oh, I understand you, Bruce. But you will never understand us. And that's what scares you.

BRUCE You don't understand me at all.

TERESA Touched a nerve, I see.

BRUCE I didn't tell you I was trapped to have you throw it back in my face like that!

TERESA Only a very strong man can admit it when he's scared.

BRUCE I'm not scared!

TERESA So break up with her, then. Or better yet—talk to her about you and Moira. Get it out in the open. Clear the air. *(beat)* Oh yes, I know about that—you really think Moira would keep that from us? That's what I'm saying: you don't understand us at all. I know all about you and Moira, and it made me think you were a total creep, but, OK, now I see you're not a creep, you're just a scared little boy—

BRUCE *(seething)* Shut up.

TERESA Is that all you can say?

BRUCE You're not as smart as you think you are.

TERESA Well, neither are you.

BRUCE You're not as smart, or as strong, or as secure as you think you are—

TERESA Like I said, neither are you—

> *Suddenly, BRUCE pounces. He's lying on top of TERESA, trapping her under him. She struggles to get away.*

OW! What are you doing? Get off— You're drunk—

> *And then he's reaching for his belt buckle and unfastening his pants.*

NO! NO! Please—Bruce—this isn't funny—

> *More struggling. TERESA remains trapped. She flails her arms at him; he grabs her wrists and holds them down.*

HELP! HELP—

BRUCE Don't even try.

TERESA Don't! Please— HELP! SOMEBODY! HELP—

> *TERESA struggles. BRUCE, keeping her trapped, begins to unfasten her shorts. TERESA screams. BRUCE claps a hand over her mouth. Blackout.*

Scene Six

> *The following morning. The porch: MOIRA and DIANE are having breakfast.*

DIANE So Elaine wants to go do laundry in Florida. What about you?

MOIRA What do you mean?

DIANE You can't live at home your whole life. Why don't you move to the city? You can sleep on my sofa till you find a place.

MOIRA Maybe.

DIANE That's what you said *last* summer. Look, I know you went through a rough patch two years ago, but—

> *SARAH, KELLY, and MEREDITH enter through the kitchen door. They wear swimsuits under their clothes and carry beach towels. They cross the porch and head toward the beach during the following conversation.*

MOIRA *(to her sisters)* Morning.

MEREDITH Morning. Hey, did either of you hear something last night?

MOIRA Hear what?

MEREDITH Someone shouting. A woman, maybe? On the beach?

DIANE I didn't hear anything.

MOIRA Me neither.

KELLY Sarah and I didn't, either. Just Meredith.

MOIRA Maybe you had a bad dream.

MEREDITH Yeah.

> *TERESA slowly enters from the direction of the beach. She is in bad shape, having spent the night on the beach. Her hoodie is torn. Her hair is sandy. Her legs have several bruises and abrasions. The others stare at her.*

SARAH Boy, what happened to you?

TERESA What? Oh—

KELLY You look awful.

TERESA I was taking a walk and then the sand sort of crumbled beneath my feet and I fell—

MEREDITH Did you hear anything?

TERESA What?

MEREDITH Last night I thought I heard someone shouting for help on the beach.

TERESA I didn't hear that…

KELLY Teresa, are you sure you're all right?

TERESA I'll be all right. *(tries to smile)* You should go down to the beach… I'm just going to get cleaned up…

KELLY OK.

TERESA Watch out for sand dunes—

MEREDITH We will…

> *KELLY, SARAH, and MEREDITH exit to the beach. TERESA crosses the porch, curls up on the bench next to MOIRA, and hugs her very tight.*

TERESA Where's Elaine?

MOIRA What's the matter?

> *ALISON enters from the kitchen.*

TERESA Have you seen Elaine or—or—

ALISON *(crossing the porch)* Oh, Elaine's over at Bruce's.

TERESA She's with…?

ALISON She wants to remind him what he'll miss if he leaves her behind.

TERESA *(beat)* Go away.

ALISON You can't tell me to go—

TERESA *Please* go.

MOIRA Let her stay, Teresa.

TERESA No…

MOIRA Yes. *(beat)* Alison.

> *ALISON sits on an Adirondack chair. A long pause. TERESA remains curled up, hugging MOIRA.*

TERESA The sand. So much sand. Rubbing me raw and abrading me… getting into places where sand shouldn't go… And at first I closed my eyes and tried to forget it was happening but that just made it worse. You know when your eyes are closed you feel things more intensely, right? So I opened them and saw him, of course, big and dark and close up. And the only other thing I could see was the sky. Big and dark and far away. But full of stars. And I remembered what they say, that there are more stars in the universe than grains of sand on Earth. The stars win out. They *have* to win out. There has to be more starlight than sand… But there was so much sand! And the stars are so tiny and remote… I should have fought, I should have fought harder, oh I screamed and flailed but I should have done more—

MOIRA *(stroking TERESA's hair)* Shh… shh…

DIANE Men are such fucking bastards.

MOIRA Diane!

DIANE This sort of thing shouldn't surprise me by now, really. Whenever a man is alone with a woman late at night—especially if he's been drinking—

MOIRA Are you saying this is her fault?

TERESA I should have tried harder—I should've fought—

MOIRA I'm sure you fought as hard as you could. *(beat)* Do you know who did this to you?

> *TERESA nods.*

Will you tell me who it was?

> *A pause. Slowly, TERESA turns her head in the direction of BRUCE's beach house, then quickly looks away again.*

Oh God.

DIANE Bruce.

MOIRA You don't have to say it—

DIANE Bruce! That fucking creep! Why are we not running over there and bashing his head in?!

MOIRA That wouldn't be wise—

DIANE I never liked him! And now he and Elaine… It's disgusting!

MOIRA Teresa… Oh, my baby sister, I'm sorry. I'm so, so sorry… I should have known he'd only cause trouble… I should have stood up and said, he's done enough harm already…

TERESA It's not your fault…

MOIRA I never thought something like this would happen… not to *you*… I was so selfish not to tell…

DIANE What? Tell what?

ALISON Oh, God.

MOIRA Diane… Elaine wasn't the first of us to… with Bruce… I was.

DIANE What kind of sick, incestuous family is this?!

ALISON *He's* the sick one—

DIANE *(to MOIRA)* And why didn't *you* go to the police?!

MOIRA He didn't assault… *me*. It was my choice.

ALISON But you didn't tell us for two years!

DIANE Does everyone but me know about this?

MOIRA It's a long story. *(beat)* I didn't want a scandal. Maybe that's bourgeois of me. But I didn't want to be known as the girl who Bruce knocked up—

DIANE There was a baby?!

MOIRA Like I said, it's a long story…

DIANE Two years wasn't enough time to tell it? God, what a bastard. *(beat)* Well, he won't have it so easy this time. Teresa, clean yourself up and then we're going to the police.

TERESA No…

DIANE Or wait, *don't* clean yourself up, you'll look more pathetic that way.

TERESA I thought the police were pigs, Diane?

DIANE Come on.

> *TERESA cries and clings to MOIRA.*

TERESA *I can't—*

MOIRA I know. I know.

TERESA Moira, I'm so sorry…

MOIRA You have *nothing* to apologize for!

TERESA I mean… I'm sorry I yelled at you… You were right to keep it secret. You have to keep certain things secret, or else…

DIANE Get ahold of yourself. We're going to go to the police and make this bastard pay.

TERESA It'll be in the papers… "Rape in the Hamptons"…

MOIRA What will *she* have to pay, Diane?

DIANE Good Lord. Are you afraid? Where's your sense of justice? Where's your feminism now? Think about it. Most girls who have this happen to them are… not credible witnesses. Waitresses, or stewardesses—no money, no education, and a history of loose behavior. So they can't defend themselves in court, the prosecution tears them apart, and the rapist gets off scot-free. Most of the time they're too afraid even to press charges. *They* protect their rapists, better than any lawyer.

And so men think they can do this with impunity! But if we spoke up… Teresa, you were so outspoken yesterday, you're really going to keep your mouth shut now, when it matters? We *need* you to speak up. OK, you lost your virginity, lost your innocence—but think of what the world will gain! We can lock this creep up and send a message to all the other smug, entitled bastards in the world. But if you keep quiet, Teresa, you're letting us all down. *All* of your sisters. The ones there on the beach—and the ones everywhere else.

MOIRA This is not a good thing, what just happened. I hope you realize that.

DIANE I know it's not a good thing—

MOIRA Then stop telling her how her rape is going to save the world!

DIANE Do you want to send the message that he can get away with it?

TERESA I don't want to send any message…

MOIRA *(to DIANE)* She doesn't have the strength to be a victim.

DIANE What is that supposed to mean?

MOIRA Let's go inside and get you cleaned up.

TERESA *(to MOIRA)* Will you give me a bath?

MOIRA I will, sweetie. With bubbles.

DIANE But then how will the police—

MOIRA We're not going to the police, Diane, and that's that.

> *MOIRA helps TERESA up; they move to exit. ELAINE starts to enter from the direction of Bruce's house.*

DIANE Shit. Elaine's coming.

TERESA Oh God…

MOIRA *(looking at the others)* I'll have to tell her. Alison, you take Teresa inside and give her her bath.

ALISON OK.

TERESA OK.

> *TERESA puts her arms around ALISON. It is the first time any of the sisters have touched or hugged ALISON throughout the entire play. TERESA and ALISON exit through the kitchen door. ELAINE comes onto the porch. She is glowing and carefree.*

MOIRA Elaine.

ELAINE Good morning! Yes? What is it?

MOIRA Elaine. Do you know what happened last night?

ELAINE Last night…? Oh, I know, maybe I shouldn't have sprung that on Bruce so suddenly, but he was a perfect angel this morning…

DIANE Did you hear anything? On the beach?

ELAINE Fireworks…?

DIANE After that.

ELAINE I'm sorry…?

MOIRA *I'm* sorry. Oh God, I'm sorry. *(beat)* Bruce, you know, has… the ability to hurt people.

ELAINE Yes.

MOIRA Well, he—he hurt Teresa last night. Badly.

ELAINE I know they were arguing, but…

MOIRA No, I mean… After that. Late at night, on the beach. There was some kind of encounter between them, and… I don't know all of the details, but… but he…

DIANE He assaulted her.

ELAINE He—he—You mean—*that* kind of assault…? *(starts to cry)*

MOIRA Elaine. I'm so sorry.

ELAINE *(crying wildly)* Oh, God! Oh God, oh God! And so this morning—Oh God!

> *MOIRA moves to embrace her.*

Don't touch me—don't anyone touch me… I need a shower…

DIANE Teresa has dibs on that.

MOIRA *Diane.*

ELAINE Oh God, what do we do?!

MOIRA There won't be any—any legal repercussions. Teresa… has decided not to go to the police.

ELAINE Thank God.

DIANE "Thank God"?

MOIRA It was her choice, and… I trust that it's the right thing. *(beat)* Maybe it's foolish of me, but I tend to trust that my sisters will do the right thing.

ELAINE Oh, I know, I know… If only I'd done it two days ago, then none of this would have happened! Oh God! How is Teresa?

DIANE Well…

ELAINE That was a stupid question… I'm so stupid!

> *ELAINE, miserable, collapses to the floor of the porch. KELLY, SARAH, and MEREDITH come up from the beach, having heard the noise on the porch.*

KELLY We *know* something's going on.

MOIRA Yes.

KELLY Will you tell us?

MOIRA Yes. Have a seat. *(beat)* There's a lot of things that you ought to know.

> *BRUCE comes out of his house. He is dressed in his tennis whites and carries his racquet and a canister of balls. He walks with purpose toward the Attlee house.*

DIANE Bruce! That's right, get your filthy ass over here!

ELAINE Oh, God—

DIANE He needs to be held accountable.

SARAH I'm sorry, *what* happened?

MEREDITH Where's Teresa?

> *BRUCE comes onto the porch and approaches ELAINE. She refuses to look at him, though the rest of the women stare at him.*

BRUCE Elaine, why aren't you ready? What's going on?

DIANE You've got some nerve…

MOIRA Bruce—

BRUCE C'mon. Where's your racquet?

> *ELAINE shakes her head.*

I thought you wanted to play tennis.

ELAINE Bruce—

BRUCE What's the matter? You were in such a good mood—

ELAINE Stop pretending! Stop pretending that you didn't—

BRUCE That I didn't what? *(beat)* Look, if Teresa's said anything to you—

MOIRA *(incredulous)* What?

BRUCE I'm just saying, if Teresa said anything…

MOIRA Are you trying to say she's lying? You're despicable. *(beat)* I'm glad your son will never know you.

MEREDITH What…?

BRUCE My—my son?

MOIRA Yes. Your son. Daddy's grandson. *(beat)* There wasn't any loony bin. There wasn't any Italian. There was just you, Bruce. And the child I carried for nine months.

BRUCE Where is he?

MOIRA I don't know. They don't tell you.

BRUCE He's my son!

MOIRA Not anymore.

BRUCE *(beat)* I don't believe you. You're bluffing.

MOIRA *(bitterly)* Oh, because we girls make stuff up for the hell of it?

BRUCE Goddamn it, why didn't you tell me? For two years, not to know that I have a child… *(beat)* Unless… Last night Teresa said—

MOIRA I don't want to know what she said last night!

DIANE *Some of us heard her screaming.*

MEREDITH *(realization dawning)* Ohhh…

BRUCE —she said "Moira told us all about you and her"… *(to MOIRA)* So they all knew. They all knew that you had my baby and took him away from me—

KELLY *I* didn't—

MOIRA *(with bitter irony)* That's right, Bruce. I'm the one who goes around taking things and hurting people and smashing things up. I'm the one who should apologize to you, you bastard… *(beat)* I imagined telling you so many times—telling you and seeing the look on your face. But I never thought I would be this sad. I never thought I could hate you this much.

BRUCE Well, it's mutual. *(beat)* There's a lot of people who'd be interested to know that you had a baby instead of going to the loony bin.

I can think of a lot of people—

MOIRA *(coolly)* Well, that's wonderful, because I can think of a lot of people who'd be interested to know that you raped my sister. *(beat)* Now get off our porch.

BRUCE You wouldn't dare.

MOIRA We would.

BRUCE Has—has she gone to the police?

DIANE Wouldn't you like to know?

BRUCE You've got to keep this quiet. Do you hear me? This could—If NASA hears about this—

DIANE You should have thought of that.

BRUCE What do you want from me? You—I'll do anything if you just keep this quiet…

MOIRA Go away.

BRUCE She said—Last night—

MOIRA Don't tell me—!

BRUCE —she said you'd never forgive me if I ever—

MOIRA Then you should have listened. *(beat)* Now get off our porch. My sisters and I have a lot to talk about.

> *BRUCE exits, stunned. End of scene.*

Scene Seven

> *Early evening of Saturday, July 10. All seven sisters are on the porch, in a tableau similar to the beginning of Act One, Scene One. They are listening to a Gloria Steinem speech on the radio.*

VOICE OF GLORIA STEINEM "Our aim should be to humanize society by bringing the values of women's culture into it, not simply to put individual women in men's places. We want to reach out to every woman who is tired of the masculine mystique belief that violence is an inevitable or acceptable way of resolving conflict."

VOICE OF MALE RADIO ANNOUNCER And that was Gloria Steinem, speaking at the first meeting of the Women's National Political Caucus earlier today. Miss Steinem, the attractive author and women's liberationist—

TERESA You see how they belittle her?!

MEREDITH He thinks she's pretty.

TERESA Which means he's not taking her seriously... They'll never take us seriously...

VOICE OF MALE RADIO ANNOUNCER As the pantyhose-and-pearls brigade descended upon Washington earlier today...

TERESA Oh, God...

MOIRA Turn off the radio, Elaine.

ELAINE complies.

TERESA I don't know if I did the right thing. Would Gloria Steinem approve? Diane didn't.

MOIRA Diane doesn't know everything.

TERESA But to let a man like that go free... I wouldn't want any of you to do that...

KELLY Then why can't you—

TERESA But he *had* to go free—so I can be free...

SARAH What?

TERESA I mean... when something like this happens to you, and other people find out, they start seeing you a certain way... and you lose control of who you are... and everything you did to define yourself... because you just become that one thing, forever... Do you see what I mean?

ALISON That's deep.

MEREDITH I remember a couple of years ago, I thought people who smoked marijuana were dope fiends or freaks. Not people I knew or people I liked. Weird people, bad people. And so when you told me that you had tried it, I was shocked. And for a few weeks all I could think of when I saw your face was "marijuana, marijuana, marijuana." It's like that?

TERESA Like that.

MEREDITH That's terrible.

MOIRA Don't be upset, Meredith. I think the world will be better for you.

TERESA Mer', we're counting on you.

SARAH You know what story always makes me think of us? Especially when we're at the beach? "The Little Mermaid." There's seven sisters in that one, too. And it's the youngest one who comes up out of the sea and joins the world of men.

MEREDITH She had to lose her voice to do it.

> *The Judy Collins album is still on the record player. ALISON turns it on. "Both Sides Now" begins to play.*

TERESA No, don't—it's scratched, it's ruined…

> *ALISON takes the needle off. A beat.*

KELLY Well, we still have to have music.

ALISON What about the other side?

TERESA What?

ELAINE "Both Sides Now"…

ALISON It's not scratched on the other side.

MOIRA Well, flip it over.

ALISON turns the record over and begins to play the song "Sisters of Mercy." Tableau. After the first verse, music fades. Lights fade.

End of play.

Boreas, or Hard Pack

by Lise Miller

BOREAS, OR HARD PACK

The first public reading of *Boreas, or Hard Pack* was on October 21, 2011 at EXIT Theatre, as part of San Francisco Olympians Festival II: Heavenly Bodies. It was directed by Lise Miller and featured the following cast:

Tony Cirimele	HAP
Jan Gilbert	GINA
Leota Tisdel Rhodes	MOLLY
Keshuv Prasad	STAGE DIRECTIONS

Characters

HAP, a 42-year-old snowplow dealer.

GINA, Hap's 42-year-old wife.

MOLLY, Hap and Gina's teenage daughter.

Curtain up on a present-day New England farmhouse kitchen—just before dawn. This old-fashioned kitchen is furnished with a new leather couch and a big, glass-top dining table. On the table are some tacky Christmas gifts in crumpled wrappings.

Through windows upstage center and stage right we see a whiteout of snow falling on massive snow drifts. Our middle-aged hero, HAP, darts on stage left wearing a bathrobe and a pinched, determined expression. He roots among the gifts.

HAP God! Where could I have put that fucking folder?

He halts, hands on hips. His wife, GINA, wafts on stage left. She leans against the window casing and gazes at the snow.

GINA Gorgeous. Look, Hap!

He glances at her.

I bet we've already got five feet. *(to herself)* I'm so glad we moved.

HAP Have you seen a blue folder?

GINA Before I went to bed?

HAP Before the party.

GINA I don't think so. Where?

HAP I brought it home from the dealership before we went back for the party. Did you see where I put it?

GINA I didn't see you with a folder.

HAP A blue folder!

GINA I heard you. You didn't have one when you came home.

HAP You were busy putting on makeup.

GINA For *your* party! *(beat)* Why don't you tell me what's in this folder, and I'll help you look for it.

> *She crosses to the table and lifts up the gifts to look around.*

Why do you need it at five o'clock in the morning on a Sunday?

> *He snatches the gifts from her hands and nudges her aside.*

HAP Nothing! Forget it!

> *GINA moves back to the couch and sits on her folded legs to keep warm. She watches as HAP continues frantically to scrounge.*
>
> *Their daughter, MOLLY, a teenager, enters stage left. She wears a vintage shift dress. She makes a beeline for the gifts and lifts them admiringly. A glass Chinese cat. A set of bath gels and lotions.*

MOLLY Raging office party, Dad.

GINA We're looking for a folder.

HAP *I'm* looking. Do you mind?

GINA It's blue.

> *HAP throws up his hands.*

MOLLY What's in it?

GINA Have you seen it?

MOLLY No. What's in it?

HAP None of your business. Both of you. Go back to bed. I'm going to the dealership. I must've left it there.

GINA How're you going to leave? Look at the driveway.

MOLLY Our car looks like a fairy mound.

HAP Somebody's got to come out here and plow.

> *GINA stands up.*

GINA I'll call someone.

> *While HAP extends his search to the rest of the room, GINA rifles through the handbag she left open on the table. She turns to MOLLY.*

Did you borrow my phone?

MOLLY Why would I do that?

GINA Then can I borrow yours?

> *MOLLY looks through her own purse, also on the table.*

MOLLY Did somebody take my phone?

GINA You can't find yours either? I'll look around. Help Daddy find his folder.

HAP No, don't.

MOLLY What happened? It's not here!

GINA You can use Daddy's.

MOLLY I don't want to use Daddy's. Where's mine?

GINA Hap, could you find us your phone, please?

HAP storms off stage left.

MOLLY You know how bad this is? If it's lost?

GINA We'll find it.

MOLLY Yours, too. Doesn't it bother you?

GINA I'm just enjoying the snow. Look! It's enchanting.

MOLLY Oh please.

MOLLY takes a closer look at her mom.

Is this about the party last night?

GINA I had a good time.

MOLLY A good time doing what? *(beat)* You were outside with Bo.

GINA Bo. I can see why your dad partnered with him. He's so… good.

MOLLY looks even more closely at her mom. HAP enters stage left, empty-handed.

MOLLY You *bitch*! What have I ever done to *you*?

MOLLY bursts into tears, dives onto the couch, and sobs.

HAP What's going on?

GINA I told her about something that happened last night. Well, didn't *happen*. Bo made a… miniature pass at me.

MOLLY He only did it to hurt *me*, because he knew my friends wanted me to break it off and I couldn't convince him I don't give a shit what they say—or you guys say!

GINA Are you saying you've been having an illicit affair with Daddy's partner?

MOLLY Bo, Mom! Bo! Don't pretend he's just Daddy's partner. You just *said* you almost slept with him!

GINA I certainly almost did *not*!

Her words hang in the air.

HAP This is why I'm getting *out*. That man is tearing this family to pieces.

GINA No! We have to hold onto the business; we just moved here.

HAP I don't even like snowplows. I don't even like living up here, with your damn, smug, proto-Mennonite clan.

MOLLY That doesn't mean you can just cut out Bo! You two have a *contract*!

Beat.

HAP Did you hear that from Bo?

MOLLY It's *obvious*. It's a *partnership*.

HAP He's been talking to you about the business.

MOLLY No! He hasn't!

GINA Hap, don't be paranoid.

HAP He has! He's talked about us. Did he tell you he makes me take all the new sales and then closes them himself? Did he say how he and I used to hang out, but now I can't bring myself to even share a *beer* with him because he made fun of me when I brought in a Bellini? *(in imitation, sneering)* "What's with the pink booze, Li'l Happy? Is that what they drink on Long Island?" He did, right? Talk all about me? How I suggested we sell snow-blowers? He *laughed*.

MOLLY He never talks about you, Dad. That's boring! He talks about… arbitrage.

HAP Arbitrage!?

MOLLY And what metals melt at what temperatures.

HAP What metals…? What?

MOLLY And Canadian snowplows. Bo wants to deal in those. In Canada, he says, plows are huge. They have tank treads.

HAP Bo thinks we can sell snowplows the size of tanks?

GINA I bet those can really… get it done.

MOLLY Bo could!

HAP Bo! Bo! *I* know Bo. You don't. You think he's this… dark, charismatic force. This… Greek god manning a fleet of… snow chariots with 500 horsepower. "Hap, let Bo do it. Isn't Bo handsome? I bet he wants to open three more dealerships; you should really let him." You know what Bo is? A selfish, vain asshole. Screw all of you!

GINA Hap, what was in that folder?

HAP Nothing. A deal. My *own* deal!

GINA Selling what?

HAP Snow blowers! A dozen Toro Snow Blowers.

GINA Off the books?

HAP *On* the books! My own, *private* books! And after I get another bunch of deals, I'm buying him out. I'm sick of him treating me like I'm his goddamn driver's ed student. I sold German cars—in New York! I don't need his vacant chassis test-driving my daughter and pulling my wife into the backseat for a disgusting nuzzle.

GINA It was a modest fondle.

MOLLY What the fuck? You *slut*!

HAP Shut *up*! Bitches, both of you. I need to get that folder before Bo finds it.

MOLLY He's probably already found it.

> *A snowplow roars offstage. They all look stage right. GINA rushes to the window.*

GINA Hap, it's got *tank treads.*

HAP Oh God.

> *The roar grows deafening. GINA screams and cowers. We hear a creak and a boom as a wall of snow descends on the house. Stage right goes dark. The family scurries under the dining table.*
>
> *Red light flashes through the window upstage center. We hear a snowplow offstage back up: BEEP BEEP BEEP BEEP.*

What the fuck is he thinking?

MOLLY See? He's not "just an asshole."

GINA Somebody call 911.

HAP He took our phones.

GINA At the party.

MOLLY I can talk to him. Bo! Bo!

> *MOLLY runs to the window upstage center, but the window goes dark. With a muffled thud, a wall of snow hits that side of the house, too.*

Oh my God, Bo, stop it! I love you!

> *BO, using his snowplow, only roars and beeps in reply.*

GINA Why did you sell something right under his nose?

HAP Listen to yourself.

GINA He wouldn't have done this if I'd encouraged his advances.

MOLLY *AdvanCES?* You skank!

HAP Molly…

MOLLY Whatever, Mom! You were only cheating on Dad. Dad was cheating on *Bo.*

> *End of play.*

CHRONUS

BY BENNETT FISHER

CHRONUS
A PLAY FOR VOICES

The first public reading of *Chronus* was on October 14, 2011 at EXIT Theatre, as part of San Francisco Olympians Festival II: Heavenly Bodies. It was directed by Jessica Holt and featured the following cast:

Colin Johnson	CHRONUS
Chris Quintos	MARIA
Myron Freedman	ARTHUR
Leigh Shaw	PIPER

Characters

John CHRONUS

MARIA Chronus

ARTHUR Petersen

PIPER Clyde

There is a percussive STOMP that happens throughout—like the tolling of a clock or the 'clack' of wooden blocks in Noh theater. Whatever choice the director makes, it should remain consistent throughout the play.

Part One: The Stone

PIPER appears.

PIPER Every once in a while, a moment comes along like a razor and divides time in two. Everything before. Everything after. You don't get to move back.

STOMP

PIPER recedes. CHRONUS appears, flanked by MARIA and ARTHUR.

CHRONUS Good evening…

A few minutes ago, I called Congressman Hastings to formally concede and congratulate him on his victory. I am grateful for the hard work and support of my staff, lead by my dear friend, Arthur Petersen, our dedicated volunteers, and my lovely wife, Maria, and our two boys, Cassidy and Michael.

It was a close race, and we fought well. We fought for important issues, for the right to freedom and prosperity that is every American's privilege, for small and sensible government, and for integrity and accountability in our leaders.

The people of Tucson have chosen to keep Congressman Hastings as their representative for another term, but I urge the congressman to consider the extremely narrow margin of the outcome as a mandate for him to always consider, truly consider the other side, and do what's best for *all* of his constituents.

Ladies and gentlemen, I'm going to speak candidly, the way I've always spoken…

I am frustrated and I am concerned. And not so much because we lost, that's not what this is about.

No, I am concerned for the future of this country, and the future of my children.

I am concerned that we live in an America that will let itself be beguiled by lofty rhetoric.

I am concerned that we live in an America that values eloquence over experience.

I am concerned that we live in an America that spends more time dreaming about the future than taking a sober look at the present.

I am concerned that we live in an America that is incapable of acknowledging that there are limits to what a government can do and what a government should do.

I am concerned that we live in an America that spends too much time hoping and wishing and not looking at the tangible things, the concrete things, the legacy left for my children and for your children.

And I refuse, I *refuse* to be victimized, besieged, entrapped by that

America—the America that prefers the glittering lie and not the hard truth, the liberal fantasy and not the grounded, conservative reckoning.

I refuse to accept that America, and I refuse to subject my children to that America!

I would rather eat my children…

>   *STOMP*

…than have them live in that America.

>   *STOMP*

ARTHUR If he said anything after those words, I didn't hear it. Time slowed to the stutter of a crawl. We were somewhere in that miserable silence between the unchangeable words and their inevitable consequence.

>   *STOMP*

>   *MARIA and CHRONUS recede. PIPER appears.*

PIPER Arthur Petersen?

ARTHUR Fuck off.

PIPER Are you Arthur Petersen?

ARTHUR Fuck off, I'm drinking.

PIPER I came all the way from Phoenix—

ARTHUR Good for you.

PIPER From McCain headquarters…

ARTHUR McCain?

PIPER Yes. We met at an RNC function in the spring.

ARTHUR Oh?

PIPER I'm not sure if you recall.

ARTHUR No… Yeah, yeah… umm…

PIPER Piper.

ARTHUR Right…

PIPER I'm wearing a name tag.

ARTHUR I'm sorry, I'm a little drunk.

PIPER My name tag reads Piper Clyde.

ARTHUR Great… Why aren't you at the McCain headquarters?

PIPER We got our ass kicked.

ARTHUR But there's a party or…

PIPER We. Got. Our. Ass. Kicked.

ARTHUR Yeah… Well, I'd rather be in Phoenix tonight.

PIPER Phoenix is the past. I'm not interested in the past. I'm interested in the future.

ARTHUR What's the future?

PIPER John Chronus.

ARTHUR What?

PIPER I'm serious.

ARTHUR Who *are* you?

PIPER I'm Piper Clyde.

ARTHUR You do realize why I'm drinking right now?

PIPER Two years is a long time—

ARTHUR You think people are going to forget?

PIPER Young, astoundingly successful businessman, true conservative, not a career politician, not part of the Washington machine, wife helps with the Hispanic vote...

ARTHUR Would-be child-eater...

PIPER You believed he'd win a congressional seat in a district that's been solid blue since—

ARTHUR He said he would eat his kids—

PIPER And you almost did it—

ARTHUR *Eat. His. Kids.* On national television.

PIPER Local television.

ARTHUR Your guy just lost. Mine buried.

PIPER My mom used to say, when God closes a door, he opens a window.

ARTHUR Great—

PIPER But I say, who the fuck wants to go out a window? I think you need to say fuck the window and open that door the fuck back open.

ARTHUR I'd really just like to drink now—

PIPER John Chronus has the potential to speak to a new demographic. One that matters.

ARTHUR And what demographic is that?

PIPER It doesn't have a name.

ARTHUR Great.

PIPER The Palin demographic, maybe. The people that she—

ARTHUR Palin lost, McCain lost, Chronus lost—

PIPER Palin didn't lose. McCain lost.

ARTHUR If it makes you feel better to—

PIPER And I'm not talking about feelings, I'm talking about facts.

ARTHUR Look—

PIPER Fact. John Chronus took a district that's been solid blue since the '90s and was a razor's edge away from making it red.

Fact. John Chronus polled better among moderates and independents than any previous Republican candidate in the last six years.

Fact. John Chronus polled better among Hispanic voters than any Republican candidate in the state, for any office.

ARTHUR Not enough to win—

PIPER Not in 2008. Midterms are all about discontent. Democrats got a mandate now, but I blame 90% on the fact that Bush was Bush and McCain was McCain. They're not in the picture in two years. Palin, Cantor… People like them, that's the future.

ARTHUR The hell they are.

PIPER Yes. People like them and people like Chronus.

ARTHUR Chronus is nothing like Palin—

PIPER I'm talking about a new wave. We need people to reenergize the base. And in Arizona we need to reenergize the base without alienating moderates and Hispanics.

ARTHUR Listen, I get it. God slammed the door in your face tonight. Me too. It's disheartening. Let's just accept that we lost and move on—

PIPER This is moving on.

ARTHUR No, it isn't.

PIPER You know John Chronus remains a viable candidate.

ARTHUR He was until he said something idiotic.

PIPER No rational person would actually believe that he meant it.

ARTHUR What's rational got to do with it? People get worked up about the phrasing, not the sense.

PIPER No—

ARTHUR Same as it ever was. Message, message, message. But the message now is "I'm a punch line."

PIPER "Extremism in the defense of liberty is no vice."

ARTHUR Goldwater? Really?

PIPER I guarantee you there's a way to spin it.

ARTHUR You are projecting a ridiculous fantasy onto a pile of shit. Turning around and jumping back into it right after you lost doesn't make you any less of a loser—

PIPER No, it makes you a winner next time around.

ARTHUR If you think you can sell me on this tonight, you're mistaken.

PIPER I don't need to sell you tonight.

ARTHUR No?

PIPER No. I'm here to give you this.

ARTHUR What is…

PIPER An internal report. I figured the rest of the staff is too distracted tonight to miss it…

ARTHUR When did you compile this?

PIPER Doesn't matter. Too late for it to make a difference…

ARTHUR Hmm.

PIPER You know that saying that your army is always ready to fight the last war? We had some people on staff who insisted it was going to be 2000, but it wasn't. Some people insisted it was going to be 2004, but it wasn't… So, of course, when this gets circulated… Well, there's some reluctance to apply any of the…

ARTHUR What is it?

PIPER This is the future, Arthur. The most mathematical, unbiased breakdown we're capable of… All the data indicates that we are poised to ride the tide of true, populist conservativism. We just need the right candidate.

ARTHUR John's not going to recover from that comment—

PIPER You don't get it. Look at the data. John Chronus is not going to win *in spite* of what he said tonight, but *because* of what he said tonight.

ARTHUR Hah.

PIPER Just read, OK?

People look at the restrained, measured grandfather and they don't see statesman anymore. They see politician. They see insider. Establishment. Weakling.

ARTHUR Really?

PIPER Look at McCain.

ARTHUR Hmm.

PIPER And then Obama gets in there, two years trying to push education or health care or environmental regulation, raise taxes or increase spending… Government's a dirty word again.

ARTHUR Hmm. *(beat)* Not wasting any time, are you?

PIPER I don't want to camp out at the RNC for three years, especially not with Steele at the helm. I'm getting back into it.

ARTHUR You'd really jump to a congressional campaign after working on a presidential…

PIPER He won't be running for Congress. He'll be running for Senate.

ARTHUR Senate?

PIPER Now's the time. Pendulum's swung all the way to one side. We're going to catch it swinging back. Read the material. Call John.

ARTHUR Yeah… *(beat)* I'd really like to. But I can't.

PIPER Why not?

ARTHUR He's gone.

PIPER Gone?

ARTHUR Just walked out of the hotel. Got in his car, drove off. Gone.

PIPER Where?

ARTHUR Nobody knows.

> *STOMP*
>
> *PIPER and ARTHUR recede. CHRONUS appears.*

CHRONUS I believe that the speed at which time seems to pass depends on your greatness.

There was a homeless man in an alley off the parking lot, shrouded in blankets, and I thought for him, each minute of night spent trying to find shelter from the desert wind, each minute of day spent trying to find shelter from the desert sun, each of those minutes must stretch to a ceaseless, unbearable eternity.

And then I thought how insignificant that momentary, insect life is compared to the life of a city, of a country, of a continent, a planet, a star, the universe, where eons pass without significance on the cosmic conscience.

And I thought how quickly the year had passed since I resolved to run, and how endless that moment had seemed when I opened my mouth without thinking in front of all those microphones. And I wondered, how fast does time pass for me now? Now that it's over?

> *STOMP*
>
> *MARIA appears.*

MARIA There was a homeless man in an alley off the parking lot. Whenever I see a homeless person, I always wonder who they were before. I don't care who you are, nobody's born in a dumpster. Not in this country.

STOMP

MARIA and CHRONUS.

MARIA What the fuck!?

CHRONUS I'm sorry…

MARIA The whole night, John, the whole night…

CHRONUS I'm sorry…

MARIA I don't even remember falling asleep—Were you just going to let me sleep?

CHRONUS I—

MARIA Were you just going to let me sleep here on the couch, waiting for you to show up?

CHRONUS Maria, I'm really sorry…

MARIA You should call Arthur. Have you called Arthur?

CHRONUS I sent him a text.

MARIA You sent him a text? When?

CHRONUS About an hour ago.

MARIA What? Where was my text?

CHRONUS I'm sorry—

MARIA Jesus Christ, John… If I didn't know better, I'd think it was another woman.

CHRONUS It wasn't another woman—

MARIA I *said* I know it wasn't. You just decided to drive off and then stay out all night and not call.

CHRONUS I said I was sorry.

MARIA Asshole.

CHRONUS I just… I needed some time. I needed to think. It's not going to happen again.

MARIA You look like hell.

CHRONUS Yeah…

MARIA We talked about this, you know.

CHRONUS Talked about what?

MARIA Talked about you not taking it so hard if you lost.

CHRONUS I told you, I just needed to clear my head—

MARIA Don't take that tone with me, John—

CHRONUS Listen, sometimes—

MARIA No! You don't get to cut me out like that.

> *Beat.*

CHRONUS I know… *(pause)* I'd like to go lie down for a while if that's…

MARIA Talk to me, John.

CHRONUS What's there to talk about? We lost.

> *Pause.*

MARIA Don't get upset.

CHRONUS I am upset.

> *Pause.*

MARIA John…

CHRONUS What?

MARIA I don't know if...

CHRONUS What?

MARIA Arthur was talking to someone from McCain headquarters last night... She wants you to consider a Senate run.

CHRONUS Senate?

MARIA Arthur says she had some data that indicated—

CHRONUS Senate?

MARIA Yes, John. The Senate.

CHRONUS The Senate is a whole other—

MARIA Exactly. No more liberal stranglehold from Tucson, no more bump from Obama—

CHRONUS Look, Maria, I really need to lie down now...

MARIA When we decided to run, we committed.

CHRONUS I'm not running—

MARIA You don't get to shut me out! *(short pause, more collected)* Baby, let's at least just meet with this woman...

CHRONUS Maria... No. I'm sorry. No.

Pause.

MARIA Do you remember the night Michael was born?

CHRONUS Of course I do...

MARIA What do you remember...

CHRONUS Maria, I really need to go lie down.

MARIA I remember when the doctors first allowed my husband to hold his son, my husband started crying—

CHRONUS Maria—

MARIA And you know, and he wasn't just a little emotional. He cried in a way that I have never seen a man cry, and it was fierce, and primal, and so full of love, so full of the most immense, overpowering love and joy and…

But, of course, the doctors were terrified. They thought he was going to drop the baby, they thought that he was too overcome.

But I remember there was no mistaking it for anything other than a beautiful thing.

Don't be afraid of that passion, John.

CHRONUS I don't stand a chance.

MARIA This woman thinks you do.

    STOMP

    PIPER appears.

PIPER The planets need to be aligned. OK? I've done my homework.

You started a good network here in Tucson. Strong street team, smart staff, some good donors, nothing extravagant yet, but the seedlings of something that can grow to handle a Senate race. You have an impeccable business record and made tremendous inroads in an otherwise liberal district.

And, more importantly, you have time on your side, for the next two years. In two years, funders will be looking for conservative candidates who are not the familiar faces that blew it the last election. And, as for the public, well, Democrats have two of the three branches, and two years to fuck it up, which I assure you they will because they always do.

CHRONUS You think we can win?

PIPER I think we have a real shot.

CHRONUS That's not good enough.

PIPER It has to be good enough. Look, it's not just a hunch. You think I want to waste a whole hell of a lot of time if it's not statistically significant? There's a window for you in these next two years.

CHRONUS And after those two years?

PIPER I'm a strategist, not a prophet. Can't see that far ahead…

>   *STOMP*

>   *MARIA and PIPER recede.*

CHRONUS Maria's asleep. Michael and Cassidy are asleep… I assume Michael and Cassidy are asleep.

It's 3:33. Michael likes to make wishes when all the numbers are aligned.

I never grew up with a digital clock in the house. A minute wasn't an event, it was something that just slithered along with the hands of the clock.

Last time I was up like this…

People use that expression "came over me." "I don't know what came over me." And I *don't* know what came over me when I spoke those words in front of the cameras, the press, the volunteers, my staff, my family, but it wasn't something that possessed me from the inside.

My words came over me, were thrown over me like a net and I was an animal ensnared, inarticulate and desperate. And when I broke free of that covering, I broke free of words, broke free of that endless campaign, finally broke free of the place itself.

I walked right out into the parking lot, got in my car, and drove. Drove away from the lights of Tucson to the interstate, and then off the interstate into the shapeless desert. I drove to the place that was like a blank page at the end of the book, where you could look out and just see indiscriminate flatness hurtling off in all directions.

It was a place where time has no hold. A patch of desert with no memory. Flat and empty since and until. A year would pass through it like water through a sieve. But I held it in time. My presence cleaved it to the now, stained it with November 4, 2008. I came to that patch of ground like a god, gave it the here and the now.

And then I said "Fuck it."

There was champagne I had forgotten to take out of the car. Some good stuff. Something not for the night of victory, but for a day or so after, when I could savor its importance…

Best laid plans…

Champagne's a bad choice if you want to get solemnly, determinedly drunk all by yourself. The whole bottle went down and then came right back up. The carbonation, I think. I don't have much of a tolerance for a man of my build.

I thought I just about finished when I felt something else, and, in my last heave, there was a little stone. A little pebble fell out among the rest, coarse and uneven and… utterly mundane. Mundane in a way that's uncomfortable to look at.

I'm sure there's a scientific explanation for why it was there, but I thought to myself at the time…

"I've hardened this thing inside of me, like coal into a diamond. This is my pit…"

Then I got back in my car and slept it off until I could see the sun, and find my way home.

Michael says his kindergarten teacher talks to them about what's inside all of us. I wonder how far to look in. I've seen what happens when you discover something you don't want to see.

Somewhere, out in the desert, there's a part of me that should have stayed on the inside.

Somewhere inside me, there may be another stone.

>   *STOMP*

>   *PIPER appears.*

PIPER Hello?

CHRONUS Are you awake?

PIPER I am now.

CHRONUS I can't sleep… I… I'd ask for your advice, but I suppose you'd just tell me to run. So…

Pause.

PIPER Look, John…

CHRONUS What?

PIPER You didn't call me at three-thirty in the morning because you were on the fence.

CHRONUS I am.

PIPER You're not. Own it.

CHRONUS I'm calling you at three-thirty in the morning because I don't know what to do—

PIPER Bullshit. Own your decision—

CHRONUS I haven't made a decision.

PIPER OK. You're worried you won't be able to hack it? Fine. Party doesn't need you, then.

CHRONUS This is how you're making your pitch?

PIPER I'm going to use both barrels on anything that steps in our way. I need to know you'll do the same. Senate is a lot bloodier than Congress. More money, bigger operation, harder schedule, more scrutiny. *(short pause)* Why do you want this, John?

CHRONUS I want a better future for my children.

PIPER I'm not Barbara Walters.

Short pause.

CHRONUS I… I really don't know, Piper.

PIPER If a candidate *can* tell why, they don't want it. It has to be like breathing. You want it because there's no other way. It's not about right and left. It's not even about right and wrong. It's about weak and strong. Accept that you're one of the strong.

> *Short pause.*

CHRONUS All right.

PIPER All right yes?

CHRONUS All right yes. Both barrels.

Part Two: The Sickle

> *STOMP*

> *CHRONUS, alone.*

CHRONUS On election night two years ago, I embarrassed myself and my family, but I believe it would be even more embarrassing to stand aside and renege on my promise to my country and to the people of Arizona.

I embarrassed myself with a phrase, but our leaders in Washington have embarrassed themselves with their actions.

They have embarrassed this country by encroaching on the freedoms that make us great.

And, ladies and gentlemen, they do more than embarrass, they lead us away from the path of progress and down the path to ruin!

Economic ruin!

Political ruin!

Social ruin!

And moral ruin!

It staggers me how far we have let ourselves sink, and it angers me to think of how much further we might yet sink if we choose to ignore our responsibility.

And if our government continues to ignore its responsibility, how can the American people trust it to make the right decisions? To stop overspending, to eliminate the deficit, to pay down our staggering debt?

President Obama has refused time and again to take responsibility, to come up with a plan that acknowledges that we have hard choices. And Congress is equally ineffective: unable or unwilling to stand up to his tax-and-spend liberal agenda. Both groups use the same line we've heard before: have faith, and I promise you it will get better. Well, tonight, I think that the people of Arizona, the people of Arizona and the American people are tired of empty promises.

This is not about Democrats or Republicans. This is about the future of America. The politicians in Washington have lost all credibility. Their political careers are more important than their service to their country and those they represent.

But I'm a businessman. I get it. In business, if you spend more than you make, your company goes under. In business, if you don't get the job done, you're out the door. And when I see how Washington is somehow able to exist in a world where you don't have to do your job, where you don't have to be responsible, ladies and gentlemen, when I see that and I see what it does to America, to ordinary Americans like the people of Arizona, when I see that, I get angry!

I'm not ashamed of my anger.

I am not going to be cowed by the media, the pundits, the pollsters.

I am not going to be duped by Washington, by the liars and hypocrites of both parties.

I am not going to leave the problems for someone else to fix while I still have blood in my veins and air in my lungs.

I'm not going to do that because that's not what being an American is about!

My father came to this country with two hundred and fifty dollars in his pocket. He worked a night shift as a garbage man and taught himself to read English during the day.

He rose up the ladder in the sanitation company because he was committed, because he didn't shy away from a challenge or ask for a lighter load. He saved up to marry, saved up to buy a house, saved up to send us to school. He taught us never to ask for a handout, but to find the power in ourselves, to believe in what we can accomplish and believe in what this country will let us accomplish so long as we try hard enough.

I believe in what my father taught me.

I believe because it's got me this far.

I believe because it's brought me a successful business, a loving wife, a wonderful family.

I believe because as I meet and talk with people across this great state, I see similar stories of struggle and perseverance.

And, ladies and gentlemen, though I hate to ask for anything, tonight I am asking for your voice and your vote!

I am asking for your strength and your support!

I am asking you to rise up with me and make this country great again! Thank you!

    STOMP

    PIPER, ARTHUR, MARIA appear.

PIPER The speech has to change.

MARIA Our numbers go up every time we make that speech.

PIPER If we want to win this primary, we can't win it inch by inch.

ARTHUR I think we're polling pretty strong for February.

PIPER We're a distant second—

MARIA Not distant—

PIPER And that's assuming the current field is set. We need endorsements. We need to get the attention of the funders, the attention of the media, attention of the public before the big boys enter the race and drown us out.

ARTHUR Who's going to enter?

PIPER Attorney general, for one—

MARIA Please.

CHRONUS What do you suggest, Piper?

PIPER Cut the embarrassment shit.

ARTHUR I agree. We cannot keep apologizing for election night.

MARIA We're not apologizing. We concede the flaw to turn it into a strength.

PIPER It's shackling us to the past. We're letting it define us.

ARTHUR Yes.

MARIA I don't think so.

CHRONUS What are your other suggestions?

PIPER More on the attack.

ARTHUR More against the Republicans, not Obama. Let's get specific.

PIPER Yes, good. And... *(hesitates)*

CHRONUS And what?

PIPER Not the story about your father.

CHRONUS You don't want my father in the speech?

PIPER No... It's a lovely story, just... You're still not polling well on immigration with—

MARIA I don't understand. The circumstances are entirely different.

PIPER It's not... It's not proving to be a helpful association. I don't think.

CHRONUS You don't think?

PIPER We need to bring your favorability numbers on immigration up.

Short pause.

CHRONUS OK. Take it out.

PIPER We can always put something back in at some other—

CHRONUS It's fine. Take it out. When can I look at something new?

PIPER I think we can get something by tomorrow morning.

CHRONUS Right…

CHRONUS and MARIA recede.

PIPER Hmm.

ARTHUR starts to laugh.

What?

ARTHUR You didn't know John's dad, did you?

PIPER No.

ARTHUR Of course not. That's a stupid question… I met John through his father.

PIPER Oh?

ARTHUR Sanitation. Used to joke that we crawled up from the sewer.

PIPER Complicated relationship?

ARTHUR Most people wouldn't say it that politely.

PIPER I see.

ARTHUR But that is a very polite way to say it. Very polite. Campaign terminology.

PIPER My job.

ARTHUR He's great in campaign terms: strong personality, hard worker, self-made man…

PIPER I'll bet.

ARTHUR Even I listen to the speech and I… well, he's absolutely reshaped by the language.

PIPER Well, there you go.

>   *Short pause.*

ARTHUR Been a lot of reshaping.

PIPER The landscape's reshaping.

ARTHUR Interesting idea. The adaptable candidate…

PIPER Are you just going to continue to make observations?

ARTHUR You sold him on the fact that he's the future of the party. Who he is *now* is the future.

PIPER There seems to be some code that you're expecting me to parse, and I really don't—

ARTHUR I know what your next step is.

PIPER You do?

ARTHUR Yeah. Maria knows too. Want my advice?

PIPER No.

ARTHUR Be careful.

PIPER OK—

ARTHUR I'm serious. You don't think I thought about the same issue in the last campaign? You don't think I wasn't tempted? But I bit my tongue. I said, this is the man I'm running, not the man I wish I was running.

PIPER If it's not a dynamic thing—

ARTHUR You don't understand. Some things don't change. With them… it's a partnership. Truly.

All I'm saying is think about every other card you can play before you play that card. Because they won't look at you the same when you do.

PIPER Yeah.

ARTHUR Yeah. You're welcome.

> *STOMP*
>
> *ARTHUR and PIPER recede. CHRONUS appears.*

CHRONUS Our campaign takes up seven hotel rooms. I lie down to sleep, and the apparatus of the campaign is just a few inches from my head, stretching out along the side of the building, a chain of rooms worrying on into the night.

> *STOMP*
>
> *MARIA appears.*

MARIA Each day moves you closer to the date. Even at rest, you're keeping pace.

> *STOMP*

She wants me out.

CHRONUS What?

MARIA Out of the public eye, off the campaign trail, I don't know.

CHRONUS Why would she want you out?

MARIA Immigration.

CHRONUS What?

MARIA The stuff with your dad's story is only the prelude.

CHRONUS You're saving us with the Hispanic voters.

MARIA How many Hispanics in this state are registered Republican?

CHRONUS You're converting more with every event.

MARIA What Piper says. I guarantee—

CHRONUS No, no—

MARIA People see me next to you and they think—

CHRONUS Oh, come on—

MARIA Explain why the numbers are so low then? What other possible explanation could there be for—

CHRONUS If it's upsetting you, I don't know, start campaigning in Tagalog.

MARIA Don't joke.

CHRONUS I'm not joking. Look. They put you in a box if you let them. Just don't let them. OK? Let them know the real you. Like Piper says, you got to frame the debate. So, maybe, I don't know, you come out with a hard-hitting speech against illegal aliens or—

MARIA When have I given a speech? A real speech?

CHRONUS I don't know—

MARIA I shake hands and smile at people and talk about our kids. You want me to talk policy now?

CHRONUS Well, do you want to?

MARIA John, it's not about what I want. It's about—

CHRONUS Look, I'm just throwing out ideas here—

MARIA It's about an image for the campaign that—

CHRONUS That's why I'm saying we shape the image—

MARIA No, John, it's not… I don't know. I feel like I'm an albatross.

CHRONUS What?

MARIA Albatross. Like I'm—Did you never have to read that? Like in high school?

CHRONUS What the hell are you talking about?

MARIA Forget it.

CHRONUS OK… Hey—

MARIA What?

CHRONUS *(A joke)* Say something in Tagalog at the next meeting. I want to see the look on Piper's face.

MARIA You think I'm enjoying this? Do you think I like butting heads with her at every—

CHRONUS What? No. Look… I come home, I just want to… I just want to be home. No campaign stuff for a few hours. That's all.

MARIA *(Oozing sarcasm)* Terrific.

CHRONUS What?

MARIA During the day it's, you know, Arthur and Piper, Arthur and Piper—

CHRONUS What are you—

MARIA And then we get back here and you're too tired to talk to me—

CHRONUS I am talking to you—

MARIA If this is a partnership, then it's a partnership, OK? I'm not—

CHRONUS Maria, I want you involved, it's just—I come home and my face is sore from smiling and—

MARIA I'm not asking you to smile—

CHRONUS I can only take so much and—

MARIA Learn how to take more! *(short pause)* This is the life, John, this is the reality, and if I only get to talk to you at night, and you're too tired to listen, then it's not going to work.

CHRONUS OK... So what's going to work?

MARIA Don't talk to me like I'm a child—

CHRONUS I'm not—

MARIA And don't act like a child.

CHRONUS How am I—

MARIA Playing it off. Running away. All of it. All of this avoidance. The child world is for liberals, John. It's weak. I'm telling you what's happening, what it is. I'm telling you what Piper's going to push for in the next strategy session. I'm telling you so you can make a choice, so you can lead. I don't care how many hands you shake or how much smiling you do, you don't switch that off when you come home.

> *STOMP*
>
> *ARTHUR appears.*

ARTHUR You don't win by winning, you win by not losing. It's about who takes more punishment and comes out the other side standing up.

> *STOMP*
>
> *PIPER appears.*

PIPER Campaign manager is of the few jobs left that's entirely adversarial. Businesses can merge. Lawyers can settle. Not so here. My father played chess competitively. When a player realizes he's lost a match, game ends. You know you're beaten and you leave. Here, you think you're beaten, change the game. Play rougher.

> *STOMP*

John, I hate to say this, but… We've entered crisis mode.

MARIA That's a little dramatic.

PIPER We need to be doing better than we're doing.

MARIA We can always be doing better.

PIPER That's not a very productive position to take.

MARIA You need to let the new speech do its work. You need to let the voters get acquainted.

PIPER Just because the storm hasn't hit doesn't mean it's not on the horizon.

ARTHUR What storm is that?

PIPER The attorney general.

MARIA Piper, he's not in the race.

PIPER He just hasn't announced. The second he enters, he'll be far enough in the lead we'll all come after him at once. It's in his interest to wait. I've seen the numbers.

MARIA I seem to recall another set of numbers.

PIPER You think I'm the only person with access to that data? Wake up. This is how the party operates. John's one of the new breed but there's a whole litter. Frankly, John, you need to dial it up.

ARTHUR Piper's right.

PIPER Thank you.

ARTHUR Even if we can't be sure, it's too much of a risk to ignore. We need to take aim.

MARIA Aim at a candidate who is not running?

PIPER If the election is held tomorrow, he wins. Tough on crime, tough on unions. Lots of experience.

MARIA John has experience.

ARTHUR Not public office.

PIPER Attorney general's weak spot is immigration. We have to be on the right side of that issue before he gets in so we can nail him when we announces.

MARIA You drag us too far to the right on immigration in the primary, we're going to eat it in the generals.

PIPER We're not going to make it to the generals if we don't move right.

ARTHUR Listen, the attorney general worries me too, but I think we keep the focus on Washington.

MARIA We're getting traction with the new speech.

PIPER No. Too Obama. Too lofty, too many platitudes.

ARTHUR Then we take some out. We get into the specifics of tax-and-spend liberalism, specifics of health care reform, specifics of bailouts and over-regulation. There's plenty.

MARIA There is plenty. We don't need immigration to do this.

ARTHUR We've branded him as an outsider. That's the card we play.

PIPER We tried the outsider card with McCain.

MARIA You all switched decks so many times with McCain, you forgot to—

PIPER The attorney general chews up our outsider image in a second. And do you know why? Because he has a record.

CHRONUS The ATF thing?

PIPER Absolutely the ATF thing. He's a bona fide pain in their collective balls.

CHRONUS Hmm.

PIPER The speech is great, John. But it's not enough. We need a Teflon issue and we don't have one... I think that issue is immigration.

MARIA You're a businessman. Let's keep talking about small businesses...

PIPER We can fold immigration into small business. Illegal workers—

MARIA I think it muddies it—

PIPER If we make the race about immigration, when the attorney general—

MARIA The race is about the economy. The economy and Washington insiders—

PIPER The race is about what we make it about. Listen, I didn't want to bring this up earlier, but I think we need to take a serious look at the image we're presenting on the campaign trail—

CHRONUS What do you mean?

PIPER What I mean is—

ARTHUR *(decidedly changing the subject)* Look, Piper, John. Let's back up a minute. Simplify. Issue aside, we need a bump. We need to solidify our position in case the field changes.

CHRONUS Where are we with endorsements?

ARTHUR No one's committed.

PIPER Attorney general gets in, that's endorsements from the governor on down. Maybe even from McCain. Which, again, is why I feel that immigration—

ARTHUR Look, John. I think we need to move.

CHRONUS Move how?

ARTHUR Move further off the road.

CHRONUS You've lost me.

ARTHUR Tea Party.

MARIA No.

ARTHUR Why not? We get an endorsement from, I don't know, some of the key guys. Cunningham and Williamson and—

PIPER We start flirting with them, my friends at the RNC are not going to like it.

ARTHUR If it gets us through the primary, they'll like it fine. They're still registered Republican.

PIPER True.

MARIA When a Republican candidate loses the primary, they're out. Tea Party candidate loses, they run as an independent. It will send a red flag up among the donors.

ARTHUR What, the donors that have already given us money—

MARIA Don't be idiotic, Arthur. Potential donors—

CHRONUS The campaign's going to need money, Arthur.

ARTHUR This is your Palin demographic, Piper. All they did was give themselves a name.

MARIA It's going to be a problem.

PIPER No. Arthur's right. The problem is John's the right candidate, but we're still running the old campaign.

ARTHUR Yes.

PIPER All we did was plug a new variable into the same equation.

CHRONUS You think the Tea Party's the solution?

ARTHUR I think if we need to attack, then let's attack. Let's commit. You want to hit the attorney general, then let's really hit. You want to be the outsider, then let's really get outside. Piper's tired of moving forward by inches, so I think we have to get creative. We don't grab that group, someone else will.

CHRONUS OK… Make it happen.

STOMP

ARTHUR and MARIA recede.

PIPER The economy.

CHRONUS Government doesn't know how to run business. Business knows how to run business.

PIPER Don't forget your company is a leading employer for Arizonans.

CHRONUS I will not forget that.

PIPER Good. Military.

CHRONUS They are protecting us, we need to protect them. Strong military is essential.

PIPER Guns.

CHRONUS We have a right to defend ourselves.

PIPER Government spending.

CHRONUS Government can't hold your hand. We have to downsize. That's what you do in a tough economy.

PIPER Budget.

CHRONUS I balanced my company's budget, the government should too.

PIPER Deficit.

CHRONUS We can't spend more than we make.

PIPER Bailouts.

CHRONUS Bailouts are rewards for failure. Don't chain the free market.

PIPER Use the word illegal.

CHRONUS For what?

PIPER Bailouts.

CHRONUS Are they illegal?

PIPER They should be.

CHRONUS Bailouts should be illegal.

PIPER Taxes.

CHRONUS Your money, not the government's. Raising the personal income tax is hard on families. Raising taxes on business is bad for the economy.

PIPER Family values.

CHRONUS Parents know what's best for their children.

PIPER Immigration.

CHRONUS Worked for my dad.

PIPER Don't be clever. Illegal immigration.

CHRONUS Is illegal.

PIPER Come on, John. Spell it out.

CHRONUS I-L-L-E-G-A-L.

PIPER John—

CHRONUS What?

PIPER It needs to matter for you in the speech.

CHRONUS It does.

PIPER Convince me. Here. Now.

CHRONUS I will. I will, trust me. I'm just tired…

PIPER That's no excuse.

ARTHUR appears.

CHRONUS Hey Arthur.

ARTHUR Ready?

CHRONUS Yes. Let's go.

STOMP

ARTHUR, PIPER, and CHRONUS recede.

MARIA Piper takes us to this meeting hall in a suburb outside of Prescott. The building's, I don't know, like an Elks Lodge, maybe, or, you know, for Scouting. I felt like I took Michael places like it when he was a Cub Scout, for their little troop meetings.

And the people there are kind of like overgrown Cub Scouts. Some actual military uniforms but mostly this regalia of jeans and plaid and pins and the flag, the flag is everywhere, and of course, around all of it, that unmistakable yellow. The yellow ribbons and the yellow banners with snakes. We come out onto the stage and it's just a hive of yellow and buzzing. Only about thirty-five people, but enough pomp, enough anticipation for a battalion.

John gives the speech. The new speech.

There's always some modifications—John can do that, he can feel the audience and draw or compress an idea, spin one phrase into five. Arthur worries it's too spontaneous but Piper and I recognize that there's a precision to the fluidity, attuned to the receptiveness of the crowd.

He begins, and I notice the modifications as he starts to warm up, as he registers the ebbs and flows of the buzzing, but then, at a certain point, the change is too variable. I lose the speech, somehow, and I am unable to tell whether John has changed the language, or whether those same semi-fixed phrases have flared into something altogether different with this kindling.

I try to listen and scrutinize each word, but my mind seems to be reverting to an infant state, which recognizes but cannot comprehend, cannot order, cannot connect sound to meaning.

And then the language vanishes altogether, and John is no longer making words, but making sounds. He is buzzing with the crowd, and their noise is not an excited hum but a roaring torrent of rage and hope. The sound could boil water, cut the skin like a sandstorm.

Piper says this is a trial run. There are larger groups in the Phoenix area that we're due to speak to the next night. While Arthur looks over the schedule and makes revisions, she's on the phone with one of the organizers. I'm next to John in the back of the van.

We can't talk while she's on the phone, but John has this smile. Not a candidate's smile. Something quieter and deeper. The lips thin and stretched, the eyes gleaming but intent.

Part Three: The Harvest

STOMP

ARTHUR appears.

ARTHUR It lasts a week. For a week, no one is worried. For a week, we take pride in the fact that we've found the vehicle that will take us towards victory. They are eating it up—on the deficit, on taxes, on personal liberties, the economy. Boom, boom, boom, boom, boom, boom, boom, boom, boom. All down the line. And then, like that, we go from hot shit to shit. We had a three-point lead the day before he announced, and I jinxed it. I exhaled. It's like the campaign's gone from the spring of youth rapidly into old age. Each day we're weaker, each day there's less time.

STOMP

PIPER appears.

PIPER I thought I was watching them, but they're watching us much closer. We had numbers *to* watch. I've been staring at a curtain waiting for it to open. No real idea what's behind it. Now we're scrambling to get data. Real data. And I'm stranded in this kind of… All I have is hope and faith. Hope. God, how embarrassing. How insipid.

STOMP

MARIA appears.

MARIA In one of the more obvious ploys to chip away at us, the attorney general makes his announcement at the courthouse in Tucson. In his speech, he mentions working for the people is not like running a business. I joke that there's absolutely no reason for him to be at the courthouse in Tucson, unless he's getting his driver's license renewed. No one is amused.

STOMP

CHRONUS appears.

CHRONUS The voters are on our side. In a week, when this settles, we'll discover that we're in control.

MARIA Honey, we can't just wait it out.

CHRONUS He wants to bring it on, let's bring it on.

ARTHUR I fucked up.

CHRONUS Come on, Arthur.

ARTHUR We should have played the Tea Party card later. He's going to make his way around to all the same stops we did and—

CHRONUS Let's do a speech at the courthouse in Phoenix. Tit for tat.

MARIA John. Serious up.

CHRONUS What? We climb one ledge, there's another one rising up after it. If we make it past the primaries, we have a whole other race.

MARIA If the attorney general's going right, let's go left. Appeal to moderates. We're more electable.

ARTHUR With no political record? Won't work.

MARIA You backed us into a corner so far to the right—

PIPER That corner gives us volunteers, canvassers, people on the ground. It gives us the mechanism to—

ARTHUR We need to reenergize the base in Tucson.

PIPER No, no, no, no, no. Too liberal. We need—

MARIA If we start slipping in our district, there's blood in the water—

PIPER We're already slipping, we've slipped.

MARIA Moderate voters—

PIPER Blood is everywhere!

MARIA Moderate voters can get behind John's—

PIPER You have no idea what you're talking about—

CHRONUS Enough!

> *Everyone is quiet.*

OK, let's simplify this. The Tea Party gave us a bump. We need another bump. Where's the next bump?

ARTHUR There is no next bump.

MARIA There has to be.

PIPER Immigration.

MARIA We did immigration.

PIPER When? Two lines in a few speeches? We need to do more. Go further.

MARIA What, visit the Minutemen? Invade Mexico?

PIPER I'm talking about changing the focus of the race. If we stick to the economy, the attorney general—

MARIA As a business leader, the economy is where John has the most expertise—

PIPER Let's look at the facts. For one minute, let's just look at the facts, all right? Can we look at the facts? Can we look at the—

CHRONUS Piper—

PIPER The attorney general's a friend to business. No-go there. The attorney general fought the health care initiative. No-go there. The attorney general took on the teachers' unions. No-go there. The attorney general took on the ATF and the federal government. Immigration is the only area where he's weak. He hasn't prosecuted aggressively enough. He's talked with those path-to-citizenship guys. If we go after him there, and if we go after him relentlessly—

MARIA It will kill us in the generals. The Hispanic bloc—

PIPER If you have a solution, instead of just criticism, I'd really like to hear it. Otherwise, I think it would be more productive if you—

ARTHUR We're going to need support from the Hispanic community.

PIPER Our objective is not some sort of glacial paradigm shift so that, one day, the great-grandsons of current Hispanic voters will register Republican. Our objective is to win the primary.

ARTHUR You talked about a new tide of populist—

PIPER The world doesn't change overnight. If we want to turn this around today, now, immigration is the only way.

ARTHUR No.

PIPER Yes. *(beat)* What do you think, Maria?

MARIA What? As the representative for all Hispanic people in Arizona? I'm half Filipina, you bitch.

CHRONUS Maria.

MARIA What I think is that this emphasis on the short term has bit us in the ass. I think we are continuing to hedge our bets to try and please everyone and shortly we will please no one. I think we need to actually take a committed stand with a group, on a principle we care about, and I think we have to stop cowering and hit back. Hit back on everything, not just immigration.

    Short pause.

PIPER You know, you're right…

MARIA Thank you.

PIPER I don't need your advice.

CHRONUS Hey.

MARIA Fuck you!

PIPER If we try to hit back on every single issue we look desperate. It gives him an immediate advantage. Each time we take a swing and don't connect, people see, and it sets us back. You take Goliath down with one, precision shot.

CHRONUS It has to be immigration?

PIPER Immigration connects with voters.

MARIA Connects with the Tea Party.

PIPER They are our only friends now. And I can't be sure how long they'll stay on our side. You're not the only person capable of giving a rousing speech, John. We need to let them know that you're steadfast in their court…

CHRONUS OK… How do we do that?

ARTHUR We do what we have done. We drill those talking points. We drill them and drill them and drill them and drill them—

PIPER Not going to be enough. I think, I think we should consider, we should *consider* a pledge.

ARTHUR Pledge?

PIPER You know, with… *(snaps her fingers, trying to remember)* You know who I'm talking about.

ARTHUR I really don't.

PIPER Cunningham.

ARTHUR Oh God—

PIPER Zero tolerance on immigration. No path to citizenship, no amnesty, no—

MARIA Absolutely not.

PIPER We take the pledge, we take the higher ground.

ARTHUR And we become immediately compromised. I don't care if it's Norquist on taxes or Cunningham on immigration. Taking a pledge will hamstring us.

MARIA You're looking for the silver bullet, it doesn't exist. We can close the gap, but we have to rely on—

PIPER Immigration is a weapon—

MARIA Cunningham is an idiot with a talk show. He's not—

PIPER Cunningham has a huge base of supporters—

MARIA If you have him take the pledge, you turn him into something he's not.

PIPER Do you support amnesty, John?

CHRONUS No, no I don't think so.

PIPER You don't think so?

CHRONUS I—

ARTHUR John, I think this is a bad idea. If we force you to take a position—

PIPER Politics is all about taking positions. Would you want a senator without convictions, without opinions, without—

ARTHUR I'd want a senator who thinks. I want the senator who isn't shackled to some—

CHRONUS Please—

ARTHUR That's what the Tea Party is all about. Independence, the people, grass roots. That's why John speaks to them. That's why John—

PIPER We're doing this for the Tea Party. The Tea Party is one of the most vocal groups out there against illegal immigration.

MARIA Wait a minute, wait a minute, when did we start doing things for the Tea Party?

ARTHUR That's not a unifying issue—

PIPER You can't selectively hear what you want to hear.

MARIA Excuse me? I thought we were running for Senate because we believe what John believes, because we share a certain set of convictions—

CHRONUS I agree with Arthur. I don't like the idea of limiting our options.

PIPER Your options are limited, like it or not.

ARTHUR Piper, listen, this is not about immigration, this is about the philosophical principle of not committing yourself to—

PIPER Philosophical principle? You think you can come out of this without owing anyone anything, you're mistaken.

MARIA We've made it this far.

PIPER Excuse me?

MARIA I said we've made it this far.

PIPER Yes, all right, we've made it this far. But the problem is, we have further to go.

MARIA We'll get there.

PIPER Why am I the only person in this room who appreciate that there's a difference between the politics you want to practice and the politics you have to practice? We're conservatives because we understand that people don't live in a dream world. If everyone else in this room wants to continue with the fantasy that we can only do what we're 100% comfortable with and somehow pull it off, then I don't know what I'm doing on the campaign. You promised me both barrels, John.

CHRONUS I know.

MARIA John has convictions.

PIPER How does not making a promise line up with those convictions, Maria?

MARIA You're out of line—

PIPER I want your husband to win—

MARIA You've been out of line this whole meeting—

PIPER I want your husband to win and I am giving him the tools to win—

MARIA You don't get to decide everything that happens on the campaign—

PIPER Regrettably, no—

MARIA What did you say?

PIPER Maria, when are you going to realize that whatever skill you have smiling and holding children does not translate into concrete, policy—

MARIA You cannot talk to me like that—

PIPER With the speech, with the Tea Party, now with immigration. Arthur and I are trying to make this work and you continue to just—

MARIA Because I don't have my head completely up my ass—

CHRONUS Stop!

> *STOMP*
>
> *PIPER and ARTHUR recede.*

If you're going to be at the meetings, you cannot go after my staff like that—

MARIA John, I'm—

CHRONUS I allow you to attend the meetings because I value your perspective—

MARIA Allow me to attend? Value my perspective?

CHRONUS But when you start to undermine—

MARIA Who the fuck do you think you are?

CHRONUS When you start to undermine my campaign manager and—

MARIA You said this was a partnership—

CHRONUS That doesn't entitle you to—

MARIA Is this a partnership? Is it?

CHRONUS Maria—

MARIA Yes or no—

CHRONUS Yes. But—

MARIA No. No "Yes, but." You promised me we—

CHRONUS I don't fight with Arthur on every issue. I don't fight with Piper on every issue. I listen to them and I—

MARIA Piper doesn't know what she's doing—

CHRONUS She does. She has the experience, she has the perspective—

MARIA Perspective?

CHRONUS Yes—

MARIA Perspective from what? From the McCain campaign? A losing campaign?

CHRONUS She is a professional campaign manager—

MARIA Oh, I'm sorry, since when does working on a losing campaign qualify you for—

CHRONUS Don't diminish her qualifications just because you don't agree—

MARIA You're right. I don't agree. She is pushing you too far to the right.

CHRONUS Because it's the primary. Because she knows we need the base—

MARIA It's not the base anymore. It's a bunch of lunatics—

CHRONUS They are real Americans—

MARIA Oh, please. Building a fence on the border? Requiring everyone to carry proof of citizenship? Those ridiculous accusations about Obama's birth certificate?

CHRONUS This is the conservative base—

MARIA The conservative base is people like you and me. Small government, low taxes, pro-business. These people are fanatics.

CHRONUS These people are my supporters.

MARIA John, that is exactly the problem.

Short pause.

CHRONUS We're not going to win if you continue to involve yourself the way that you are.

MARIA What?

CHRONUS You know exactly what I'm talking about.

MARIA No, John. I don't.

CHRONUS OK… You feel guilty about your heritage. You feel guilty because you know it's hurting the campaign—

MARIA John—

CHRONUS Let me finish. You feel guilty, and rather than acknowledging your guilt, limiting your role, distancing yourself, whatever, you want to shift the campaign back to the center. You want to make it a non-issue when it is the issue, it is the issue.

Short pause.

MARIA What is your policy on immigration, John?

CHRONUS Maria—

MARIA What's your policy?

CHRONUS You know my policy—

MARIA No. I don't. No one on the campaign does.

CHRONUS I've been—

MARIA That's the problem. Not me. You.

John, you don't need to be in lockstep on every issue. You can be for amnesty, for a path to citizenship…

CHRONUS Maria—

MARIA Arthur's right. You want a candidate that thinks. If you believe something, believe it, and convince your constituents that it is the right thing to believe. That is what the people expect—

CHRONUS I've already laid out what I think about immigration—

MARIA Vague and non-committal. You're not fooling us, John. And you're not fooling the voters.

CHRONUS I'm not trying to fool anyone.

MARIA I know, baby. *(beat)* I just hope…

Short pause. MARIA doesn't finish her idea.

CHRONUS What?

MARIA You're not doing this for me, are you?

CHRONUS No—

MARIA I was born here. And I'm not required to feel one way or another because I'm half Hispanic. Opposing the issue is not opposing me.

CHRONUS I know—

MARIA And it's not opposing your dad. Or my dad. Or anyone who comes—

CHRONUS I know—

MARIA Do you?

CHRONUS Please stop berating me.

MARIA OK…

Short pause.

CHRONUS It's so close.

MARIA I know.

CHRONUS So close, just… I'm not sure how we get closer.

Short pause.

MARIA Do you not want to take the pledge because you don't want to, or because you're afraid to—

CHRONUS I don't know… Cunningham has over a million listeners. Piper thinks it's a good idea.

MARIA Yeah, well…

Pause.

CHRONUS I just… If I'm elected, I can do something. If I'm not, I can't.

MARIA I know.

CHRONUS We just need to get there. Somehow.

STOMP

MARIA recedes. ARTHUR appears.

ARTHUR I know I shouldn't, but I'm starting to imagine my working relationship as chief of staff. Being in Washington. Whether or not we can afford to be this adversarial in Congress. Do I go to drink with the other senators and their aides, or punch them in the nose in the hallway?

STOMP

CHRONUS I feel like a werewolf in reverse. Turn back into human form at the end of the day, back into a monster in the morning.

ARTHUR Nature of the business, John.

CHRONUS Didn't feel like this last time.

ARTHUR You've dialed it up on this campaign. That's a good thing.

CHRONUS Hah.

ARTHUR It'll get you elected.

CHRONUS You really think so?

Short pause.

ARTHUR Senate is a long shot. Zero to Senate. We didn't go in steps. City Council. State Senate. Congress. Senate. Might have been easier, if nothing else, we'd have more experience campaigning… But we're very close, John.

CHRONUS Fucking immigration…

ARTHUR Yeah…

CHRONUS Never been to Greece, do you know that? Maria and I went to the Philippines what, once?

ARTHUR The tech conference in Manila.

CHRONUS Exactly. How many generations do you need to be here to be an American? Really? When do you stop being something else?

People here act like they just congealed out of the sand and rocks and I'm just this thing, this imposter. Hypocrites.

ARTHUR You're right.

CHRONUS Or do you think it's the name?

ARTHUR What?

CHRONUS The name. Chronus. Too foreign.

ARTHUR I don't know. Bobby Jindal's a governor. His name is Jindal. Obama's *president*—

CHRONUS You know what I'm talking about—

ARTHUR You want to make excuses, fine. Go cry about it into your latte.

CHRONUS Jesus, Arthur—

ARTHUR Do you want coddling or do you want to lead?

CHRONUS What do you think?

ARTHUR Then act like it. *(beat)* You're afraid of the person you are out there. But that person is powerful. *That* person is a leader. *That* person is not beholden to anyone or anything. *That* person commands respect.

    Short pause.

CHRONUS You're right… *(beat)* I won't take the pledge.

ARTHUR What?

CHRONUS Don't need it. Fuck that and fuck the attorney general. He won't look so pretty after a week of me going right for his throat—

ARTHUR You're kidding, right?

CHRONUS Hell no. I'm going to rip out that fucker's larynx in my next speech. See if I don't.

ARTHUR No, John. About the pledge.

CHRONUS No. What are you talking about?

ARTHUR Because I got a call from Cunningham. They're expecting you to make an announcement at the rally. We're booked for tomorrow.

CHRONUS Arthur, I'm not taking the pledge.

ARTHUR John, you have. I just talked to him.

CHRONUS What?

ARTHUR You've already taken it. They've been told you have.

CHRONUS How is that possible?

ARTHUR I don't know.

> *STOMP*

> *ARTHUR recedes. PIPER appears.*

PIPER A good campaign manager allows the candidate to have the illusion of control. If that sounds deceitful to you, then you ignore all the actions that the campaign manager does to get his or her candidate elected. That's the greater test of loyalty. You take power to give them power.

> *STOMP*

CHRONUS What are you doing talking to Cunningham?

PIPER When did I talk to Cunningham?

CHRONUS They think I'm taking the pledge.

PIPER Well, you should.

CHRONUS I didn't call Cunningham.

PIPER I'm lost…

CHRONUS You're forcing my hand in something I don't want to do?

PIPER Hah. Don't *want* to do? Don't *want* to do? Listen, John—

CHRONUS No, you listen. John Chronus is not going to take a pledge for any—

PIPER Don't refer to yourself in the third person.

CHRONUS Don't interrupt me—

PIPER John, separate what you want to do from what you need to do.

CHRONUS What I need is to trust my staff. To be free to make my own decisions—

PIPER Do you give your CEOs, your board the same amount of grief?

CHRONUS My CEOs and my board don't cut me off at the knees—

PIPER Why do I have to defend every single choice I make for this campaign? We have enough opposition from the opposition, all right? Let me do my job and—

CHRONUS Go behind my back and—

PIPER Let me do my job and *win you this election! (beat)* Christ, John, that's what it's about. This is the *Senate*.

CHRONUS I don't care—

PIPER You should. You should. Do you have any idea how far we're leaping here? And if we get in then we are *in*. You get the entire party apparatus behind you. The funders, the endorsements, the big names. And in Arizona? Shit. Once every six years? Cake.

CHRONUS I need people I can trust.

PIPER You can trust me to win this.

CHRONUS That's not enough.

PIPER John, you don't pay me to be your friend. I'm not a friendly person—

CHRONUS It's not about that—

PIPER You'll have Arthur as your chief of staff. I'll move on to another campaign. Come November, I'm gone—

CHRONUS You think that gives you license to—

PIPER Both barrels, John. I need you to free my hands—

CHRONUS Free your hands like with Cunningham?

PIPER Free my hands so that I can do some damage. So that I can go after the people that are standing between you and the office. So that I can make the calls that get us—

CHRONUS Piper, frankly, I don't feel like you've always made the right call—

PIPER Oh, please.

CHRONUS And I think the data speaks for itself—

PIPER You don't know how to read the data, John. Just because Maria thinks—

CHRONUS Don't bring her into this—

PIPER Why not? You brought her into this. Everything I suggest, she comes right back against it—

CHRONUS Maria is a partner in my—

PIPER Some partner...

CHRONUS Excuse me?

Short pause.

PIPER OK... John, I'm going to be blunt. You're a great candidate, but you're new to this... There comes a time where you have to accept that you cannot reinvent the way the process works. It's an ugly thing and it stays ugly. I know your wife—

CHRONUS Leave my wife out of it—

PIPER Your wife is deluded. She's pushing us the wrong way in the meetings, and, as much as I hate to say it, she's hurting us on the campaign trail. When she stands next to you, she creates a visual association with—

CHRONUS Don't—

PIPER It's the truth, John. It's shameful that some voters feel that way, but it's the truth. Accept it. Move on. Let me get back to work.

CHRONUS No. *(beat)* I'm sorry. You're out.

> *STOMP*
>
> *PIPER recedes. MARIA appears.*

MARIA I believe in fate, I suppose. But I cannot tell whether it makes us stronger. Are we empowered by the knowledge of powerlessness, or is it a way to cosmically shift the blame? To reorder the cruelty of randomness into purpose.

If I had been standing a few more yards away from Cunningham at the speech… John's walking with him out of the pavilion, and he gets close enough to reach out and grab my shoulder.

The chance of a few yards, but the words felt like they steamed up from the earth, from something primal, inevitable, and inescapable.

"John, honestly, until your wife called, I wasn't sure that you were completely on our side with this. I'm happy you are. I value that loyalty and commitment. You're keeping a promise, and we'll keep ours to support you."

And I realized in that moment that when I decided to call, I knew nothing good would come of it.

The partnership's broken. Of course he'll find out. Of course he'll feel betrayed.

But maybe if he wins…

I think that's what love is.

After it's over, John and I walk back to the car. We drive back to the hotel. Bit by bit we shed the supporters, and the volunteers, and the staff, and the handlers until we are alone together. But there's no challenge, no reprimand, no argument about what the partnership should be. We go home and we do not talk about the campaign.

He just says he needs to call Piper, opens the sliding glass door, and steps out into the desert night with the cordless phone.

> STOMP
>
> MARIA *recedes.* PIPER *appears.*

CHRONUS We never made an official announcement. You can return and everyone saves face.

> PIPER *does not respond.*

Piper, are you there?

PIPER I'm still here.

CHRONUS Look, I made a mistake... You're right. I can't read the data.

PIPER Don't joke with me, John.

CHRONUS Listen, Piper...

PIPER Never, never in my career—

CHRONUS I know, I know... I made an assumption... *(beat)* I need you back on the campaign.

PIPER I cannot be looking over my shoulder, John.

CHRONUS I promise you it won't—

PIPER I need something more concrete than a promise.

CHRONUS Piper... I can't fire my wife...

PIPER I'm going to say this once. I'm not coming back unless you shut her out of the campaign. She doesn't advise on policy. She doesn't come to the meetings. She appears at the events that I specify in the manner I specify.

If I get the feeling that you two are conferencing at home, at night, when

Arthur and I are away, I'm done.

And I need you to lock it up. With the speeches, with the message, with what we're pushing and how we're pushing it and who we're pushing it to. I need you to harden up and own the role.

And if you're able to do all of that, I'll deliver you. Come November, you'll be looking at houses in Arlington and scheduling visits with private schools.

If you're not… Well, in another two years, there's a whole new crop of John Chronuses. Congressional, senatorial, gubernatorial. And I know they'll be willing.

Have I made myself clear?

CHRONUS Just come back, Piper.

STOMP

CHRONUS recedes. ARTHUR, and MARIA appear.

ARTHUR How many endless candidates have there been that promise they'll change something? Evidently someone believes, or we wouldn't have the cheering hordes.

STOMP

ARTHUR recedes.

MARIA There's the man and the politician. The two are not the same. That should be obvious but—understanding and accepting are not the same.

STOMP

MARIA recedes.

PIPER There are the politics you want, the politics you practice. That's the way it goes. It's the part of the system that cannot be changed.

STOMP

PIPER recedes. CHRONUS appears.

CHRONUS We cannot make excuses. The solutions to America's problems rest in the hands of everyday Americans. That is the conservative ideal: we acknowledge that we are responsible, not the government. We cannot define ourselves by our misfortune, we cannot demand help we are not entitled to. When calamity strikes, we must resolve to pick up the pieces and move on.

Americans are tired by politics as usual. Americans are demanding a new voice, a voice that carries the strength of our great heritage, of our founding fathers and founding documents.

I believe the responsibility of our beloved nation is embedded within the hearts of patriots from all walks of life, every race, religion, and national origin, all sharing a common belief in the ideals that keep our nation great. When we have the courage to stand by those ideals, we become worthy of them.

Our government has failed us, but we have failed by entrusting power to the incompetent, and by accepting their rule without objection.

It is ours by right. And we have to take it back.

We have to take it back.

> *Long pause. CHRONUS almost starts to say something, but does not. He retches, spits something up into his palm. He looks at the object—a pebble—then drops it to the ground. CHRONUS recedes.*
>
> *End of play.*

Europa

by Claire Rice

Europa

The first public reading of *Europa* was on October 28, 2011 at EXIT Theatre in San Francisco, California as part of the San Francisco Olympians Festival II: Heavenly Bodies. It was directed by Neil Higgins and featured the following cast:.

>   Xanadu Bruggers   EUROPA
>   Kai Morrison   ZEUS

Characters

> EUROPA, *a beautiful woman in love.*
>
> ZEUS, *the man EUROPA is in love with. He plays a guitar.*

Setting

> A hotel room on the island of Crete. A romanticized present or a point in the past wrapped in nostalgia.
>
> ZEUS sits on the edge of a bed in a hotel room. He plays at a guitar. EUROPA enters from the bathroom in her underthings, barefoot. She waves her red dress like a red cape of a matador.

EUROPA Toro! Toro!

> ZEUS puts down the guitar and acts the part of the bull in a bullfight. He growls and stomps and charges at the cape, which she pulls away just in time. He rounds the room and comes at her again, stomping and charging and rolling his head. She shakes the dress and calls to him again.

Toro! Toro!

> And he charges again. But this time he catches her up in his arms. Breathless, they hang there in that moment, looking into each other's eyes. She feels his body with her hands. He buries his face in her neck, her hair, her breasts. She pulls back his head and looks him in the eye. She caresses him.

ZEUS Come with me, lady.

> He takes her to the bed and lays her down. They make love. Sweet,

gentle, and soundless. They revel in each other's bodies beneath the sheets. The audience is not a voyeur to this act. It belongs to the lovers alone. The time shifts and changes around them, even as they fall asleep. They began in the afternoon. Without the lovers taking note, it becomes evening, late night, early morning, then almost afternoon. ZEUS gets out of bed, stretches, goes to the bathroom, puts on some clothes and takes up his guitar. Sitting, looking out the window, he plays. EUROPA wakes.

EUROPA That's pretty. What is it?

ZEUS Just something that's in my head.

EUROPA Should we order in breakfast?

ZEUS I'm not hungry. Are you?

EUROPA I guess not. If you aren't going to eat, I don't want to. What should we do today?

ZEUS Anything you want.

EUROPA You were the one who wanted to come to Crete.

ZEUS I wanted to come to Crete with you. And I have. I've gotten everything I wanted. Now I want you to have anything you want.

EUROPA I like the sound of that. Anything I want.

> *EUROPA gets up and goes to the bathroom. She continues the conversation.*

What about the museum?

ZEUS OK.

EUROPA The cafes?

ZEUS OK.

EUROPA A walk on the beach?

ZEUS OK.

EUROPA Dancing?

ZEUS OK.

> *EUROPA emerges from the bathroom. She throws on her red dress and puts up her hair.*

EUROPA You know what I want? Let's order fruit and chocolate for breakfast. Oh, but you said you weren't hungry.

ZEUS I'm not, but you can eat if you are.

EUROPA I don't want to eat alone.

ZEUS I don't want you to be hungry. Please. Get something to eat.

EUROPA What about champagne? Would you share some champagne with me?

ZEUS Sure. Anything you want.

EUROPA Anything I want. It's like I'm a queen.

ZEUS You are. Queen of Crete.

EUROPA Ha!

> *He plays on. EUROPA picks up the phone.*

Yes. This is the Queen of Crete in room 505. I would like a fruit and cheese plate sent up with chocolates, your best juice and a bottle of champagne. Well, that sounds just fine. Yes. Oh, lovely. Thank you.

> *She hangs up the phone. He plays on.*

Good news. It comes with cheese and bread. What a decadent breakfast!

ZEUS Sounds delightful.

> *She kisses him. He plays on.*

EUROPA Should I have ordered coffee? Did you want coffee?

ZEUS Whatever you want. I'm fine.

EUROPA Whatever I want. I think after breakfast we should go shopping. I feel like I need a new bag and maybe new sandals. Oh, and I didn't bring shampoo. We'll have to go get some.

ZEUS Whatever you want.

EUROPA For the Queen of Crete.

ZEUS For the Queen of Crete.

She giggles and starts putting on her makeup. He plays on.

EUROPA You know what your song reminds me of?

ZEUS What's that?

EUROPA The moon. Spending its time going around and around this planet. When you think about it, they are so close, but they never touch.

ZEUS They can't touch. They would destroy each other.

EUROPA I know. That's what the song reminds me of.

She puts on her makeup. He plays on.

EUROPA Have you heard from your wife?

ZEUS No. She usually doesn't try to call me while I'm gone.

EUROPA Why?

ZEUS She knows I'll be back.

He stops playing. There's a knock at the door. ZEUS opens it. A cart is brought in. He pays for it and shows the bellhop out.

EUROPA When?

ZEUS When what?

EUROPA When will you have to go back?

ZEUS I don't have to go back.

EUROPA When will you go back?

ZEUS I don't want to talk about this.

EUROPA I do. And I get whatever I want. I am the Queen of Crete, and you are on my island.

ZEUS I'm going back tonight.

EUROPA Tonight?

ZEUS Maybe sooner.

EUROPA It's already almost noon.

ZEUS I know.

EUROPA That's so soon.

ZEUS You should stay. Have a good time.

EUROPA I didn't think I would be here alone. I wasn't planning on it.

ZEUS Don't worry. I left some cash for you in the safe. You can stay as long as you like.

EUROPA From queen to whore in a matter of moments.

ZEUS That's not what I mean. If you don't want it, leave it in there.

EUROPA What's my going rate?

ZEUS Stop it. You didn't mind when I paid for the flight, the hotel and the breakfast. I assume you thought I was going to pay for everything for as long as we stayed here.

EUROPA In trade for services rendered.

ZEUS You don't have to take the money.

EUROPA But you will leave me alone on this island. Or maybe not. Am I the only Queen of Crete?

ZEUS Yes.

EUROPA But there are so many islands out here, aren't there?

ZEUS This one is yours.

EUROPA Well, I just hope you feel like you got your money's worth after only one night.

ZEUS What were you expecting?

EUROPA You made me believe I was something more to you.

ZEUS I wanted to touch you. Even for just a moment. I wanted to pretend you were the woman who would make me stay.

EUROPA You just wanted to know what it would be like if I loved you, but you knew you wouldn't love me.

ZEUS Your love is worth having, even if only for a moment. I've never wanted anyone else in the whole world to be happy the way I want you to be happy. I want to give you more happiness then I'll ever ask for myself. Ask me anything, and I'll give it to you.

EUROPA If I asked for your love, would you give it to me?

ZEUS I said I would give you anything you wanted. Just ask.

EUROPA What if I said the only thing that will make me happy is you?

ZEUS Do you want me to stay?

EUROPA Are you offering?

ZEUS In this moment, I'll give you anything you want, my queen. Anything at all.

EUROPA If you go, will you come back?

ZEUS Maybe. But I don't think so.

EUROPA I'll wait for you if you ask me to.

ZEUS I want more for you than that.

EUROPA *(thinks)* No. I don't think I want your love after all. You'll never stay. You might be here with me for another hour or another day, or even a year, but you'll never stay.

ZEUS *(waits)* What are you going to do today?

EUROPA I think I'll get a better place to stay, something more fitting for a queen. I think then I'll find a nice café where I can read the newspaper, watch the old ladies go to and from church, and write bad poetry. Maybe I'll start looking for a job, like teaching English classes and giving tours to American tourists. I guess after that I could do just about anything. I've always wanted to learn to sail a yacht or open a restaurant or write a book. Maybe I'll get married and have five children. Maybe not. I don't know. I guess I could do anything I want. It's a frightening prospect. Anything I want. What a great burden an open and unknown future is.

ZEUS What can I do for you?

EUROPA Say hello to your wife for me.

>   *End of play.*

Too Near the Sun

by Jeremy Cole

Too Near the Sun

The first public reading of *Too Near the Sun* was on October 21, 2011 at EXIT Theatre, as part of San Francisco Olympians Festival II: Heavenly Bodies. It was directed by Jeremy Cole and featured the following cast:

Tony Cirimele	OTTO
Robert Cooper	DAEDALUS
Maro Guevera	GUSTAV
Charles Lewis III	KING MINOS
Keshuv Prasad	ICARUS
Stacy Sanders Young	AGNES

Characters:

In Crete:	**In Germany:**
DAEDALUS, *an architect*	OTTO LILIENTHAL, *an inventor*
ICARUS, *his son*	GUSTAV LILIENTHAL, *his brother*
KING MINOS, *a king*	AGNES FISCHER LILIENTHAL, *his wife*

At rise: DAEDALUS and ICARUS on one side of the stage—they are in mythical ancient Crete. OTTO and GUSTAV LILIENTHAL on the other—they are in actual 19th-century Germany. We soon hear KING MINOS and AGNES yelling offstage, both sides:

KING MINOS *(calling from offstage: angry)* Daedalus!

ICARUS Did you hear that, Father?

AGNES *(calling from offstage: angry)* Otto!

GUSTAV Did you hear that, brother?

KING MINOS *(louder, accenting the last syllable)* Daeda-LUS!

DAEDALUS Oh my gods… Is that the *King* shouting?

AGNES *(louder, accenting the last syllable)* Ot-TO!

OTTO Uh-oh. I don't like the tone of voice she's using.

KING MINOS *(much louder)* DAE...DA...LUS!

AGNES *(much louder)* KARL WILHELM OTTO LILIENTHAL!

ICARUS Papa!

GUSTAV Otto!

ICARUS He said your name in *syllables*:

GUSTAV She used your *full name*:

ICARUS & GUSTAV *(simultaneously)* ...that's not a good sign.

KING MINOS *(entering)* Architect!

AGNES *(entering)* Husband!

KING MINOS Traitor!

AGNES Fool!

KING MINOS Do you hear me, Daedalus?

DAEDALUS Forgive me, Sire, were you calling for me?

KING MINOS Yes! You assisted that infidel Theseus!

DAEDALUS No!

KING MINOS Yes! You saved him from the Minotaur!

DAEDALUS No!

KING MINOS Yes! You provided him with the means to escape the Labyrinth.

DAEDALUS Your Highness, please...

AGNES Do I have your attention, Otto?

OTTO I'm sorry, my love, were you calling me?

AGNES Yes! You stole my best sheets!

OTTO No!

AGNES Yes! You stripped them right off the bed!

OTTO No!

AGNES Yes! You didn't even take the time to replace them!

OTTO Agnes, please…

KING MINOS I could have you executed.

AGNES I could just kill you.

DAEDALUS Please, Sire, I beseech you, hear me…

OTTO Now, Agnes, if you would just calm down and listen…

KING MINOS No one knows how to escape the Labyrinth, Daedalus, except the man who built it: YOU.

AGNES The sheets are gone, Otto. Only one other person sleeps in that bed: YOU.

KING MINOS & AGNES *(simultaneously)* What could you possibly have to say in your defense?

KING MINOS Is this how you repay my kindness? When you were accused of killing your own nephew, who took your side? When you were set to be executed in your own country, who gave you asylum? And then you give Theseus not only the means to escape, but you go so far as to create a diversion for him—keeping me busy with your latest designs for an aqueduct… The effrontery! The gall! I have many ways of punishing treason, Daedalus, and most of them are bloody. And painful. And slow.

 Silence.

But… You are valuable to me, so I will be kind and spare you the tortures I would assign a less talented subject. Therefore, due to your own selfish actions, you and your son have now become permanent residents of Crete. And I have work for you. For *both* of you. Oh, yes, young… young…

ICARUS Icarus, Sire.

KING MINOS Ick—what? No, never mind, it doesn't matter. *Neither* of you will be spared. Get plenty of rest tonight, men, for tomorrow your great trial begins. The two of you—pathetic father and unfortunate son—will build me a marvel. Something to make people forget the Labyrinth. A tower. With turrets. The tallest in the world.

    KING MINOS exits.

ICARUS He hates me.

DAEDALUS No… You simply do not matter to him. Which is not such a bad thing… As long as you are invisible, you are safe.

AGNES What on earth could you want with my sheets?

ICARUS I'm sorry, Papa.

AGNES I'm waiting, Otto…

ICARUS I know how much you wanted your freedom…

DAEDALUS Oh, my dear boy… He never meant to free us. I was right to help Theseus. This tirade of the king's simply proves it. But now it seems I must learn to help myself: by turning my energies toward devising an escape…

ICARUS But we tried that before. The land is too rugged—the sea too rough. Besides, his army patrols the one and his navy the other. We could never hope to get past them.

DAEDALUS You lack imagination. King Minos does not yet control the sky, my son. The *heavens* are not his…

AGNES Some time before the century turns would be nice.

OTTO Yes, well, you see, we—

AGNES "We"?

OTTO That is to say, Gustav and I… we were working on an ornithopter…

AGNES *Gesundheit.*

GUSTAV *(jumping in excitedly)* We were almost finished: we had already built the frame, and...

> *AGNES stares—she is in no mood to hear GUSTAV's comments.*

Begging your pardon.

DAEDALUS Listen to me, Icarus.

ICARUS Yes?

DAEDALUS We must begin collecting feathers.

ICARUS Feathers? What kind?

DAEDALUS Any kind! All kinds! This project will require hundreds of them. Thousands, possibly.

ICARUS I can start gathering stray feathers, but those are not many... in fact, very few... it would take forever... Wait! I know! I can ask the cook to save all the feathers from the fowl he serves the King.

DAEDALUS Brilliant boy! That will give us chicken, duck, goose...

ICARUS Pheasant, quail and grouse!

AGNES *(to OTTO)* Continue, Otto. I'm all ears. So you were making this... horny-bopper.

OTTO *Ornithopter*... it's basically a man-made bird... and once we had the frame completed... we were so excited to finish the project that we simply couldn't wait to make the long trip all the way into town to buy the fabric we needed, so...

AGNES ...you stole my sheets.

GUSTAV *(simultaneously with the above)* ...we stole your sheets.

> *AGNES glares daggers at GUSTAV.*

Begging your pardon.

AGNES Very well. I asked for an explanation and I got one. A disturbing and rather childish one, mind you, but... Are you quite finished with them, now, Otto? May I please have them back?

GUSTAV The sheets? Have the sheets *back*?

OTTO Well, you see...

GUSTAV They're not coming back.

OTTO Gustav...

GUSTAV Those sheets are *gone*.

AGNES Otto. In about one minute, I am going to disembowel your little brother. It will be a mercy killing.

GUSTAV We can't return them.

OTTO We can't return them, *dearest*, because we had to attach them to the frame we built—

AGNES You had to attach them? To a frame? What, like a canvas? For *painting*?

OTTO *(jumping in before GUSTAV can)* Ja! Exactly!

GUSTAV *(who can't take a hint, apparently)* But not for painting.

  AGNES glares.

Begging your pardon.

ICARUS I'm curious, Father...

AGNES I'm confused, Otto...

ICARUS Why are we collecting feathers? What will you do with them?

AGNES This talk of frames and thing-a-ma-bobbers... it makes no sense to me. What exactly *did* you use my sheets for, Otto? In plain, simple German, please...

OTTO & DAEDALUS You would not believe me.

ICARUS Yes, I would.

AGNES Humor me.

DAEDALUS With your help,

OTTO With Gustav's help,

DAEDALUS I am going to create...

OTTO I had set about building...

OTTO & DAEDALUS ...wings.

> *AGNES looks skeptical and shakes her head, but ICARUS is thrilled and moves downstage center in wonder.*
>
> *Dream sequence—ICARUS in imaginary flight.*

GUSTAV Icarus dreams he's flying
Dancing high among the clouds
Slicing through the phantom air
Performing for the crowds

KING MINOS Now an aerial diver
Falling upward toward the sun
Now swimming through the evening sky
Accountable to none

AGNES The gentle winds buoy him along
Like currents in a stream
Eddies swirling round him
As he navigates a dream

ICARUS Shepherds and milkmaids stop their chores
To gaze up at the sky
And watch with awe and wonder
At this comet streaking by

OTTO Now, he sees a cheering crowd
Below him in the town
Now, he's landing softly
Like a feather floating down

DAEDALUS Icarus dreams of glory
Not a trace of fear or dread
While Daedalus dreams of leather straps
And feathers, wax and thread

Split scene, as before—Crete and Germany.

OTTO Gustav, I need your help.

GUSTAV Of course, brother, what do you need?

DAEDALUS Icarus, I have a task for you…

ICARUS Yes, Father, what is it?

OTTO We need to do a little research… well, all right, a LOT of research…

DAEDALUS I need your help to plan our escape.

GUSTAV Research? *Ach*! Sounds boring.

ICARUS Of course, Father! Anything! I'll do anything you ask!

DAEDALUS That's my darling boy.

ICARUS & GUSTAV What do you want me to do?

OTTO If we are going to expand our knowledge of flight,

DAEDALUS then we need to study with the experts.

GUSTAV Who would that be? Hot air balloonists?

OTTO That's not flight, that's levitation. No,

DAEDALUS & OTTO I want you to watch the birds.

GUSTAV *(deadpan)* The birds.

ICARUS *(deadpan)* Watch. Birds.

DAEDALUS Yes!

OTTO Not merely gaze at them…

DAEDALUS but study them…

OTTO There are a lot of bird-watchers out there, but they're only interested in identifying them, collecting them, not in determining what makes them tick…

OTTO & DAEDALUS If we're going to be successful,

DAEDALUS We need to observe how they stretch their wings,

OTTO How they arch them,

GUSTAV …and how high…

DAEDALUS How they flap them,

ICARUS …and how rapidly…

OTTO How they hold them still to glide,

GUSTAV How they turn,

DAEDALUS How they adjust to the wind,

ICARUS Like the way the wind blows our floating fire lanterns?

DAEDALUS That is not flight, that's levitation… But, yes, something like that.

OTTO How they control their speed,

GUSTAV …and how they dive…

DAEDALUS …and especially… how they land.

ICARUS I'll start studying them immediately, father.

GUSTAV You can count on me, big brother. *(beat)* "Our home town gave us ample opportunities for observation. Since numerous families of storks had taken up residence on the roofs of the barns, the greater part of our immature nature study was spent watching our friend the stork. Often we could get very close to him, even with the wind behind us, since his powers of smell are small. However, when he finally did notice us, instead of running *away*, as one would expect... he hopped *in our direction* until lifted by the force of his wings. It became obvious to us that rising *against* the wind must be easier than *with* the wind, because without some compelling cause, that shy bird would never have advanced *toward* us as he did..."

AGNES Gustav Lilienthal, 1911. In his introduction to Otto's book: *Bird Flight as a Basis for Aviation. (beat)* What is this, Otto?

OTTO A manuscript.

AGNES Your depth of perception never fails to astonish me, husband. OF COURSE it's a manuscript, *dummkopf!* I mean, what IS this? *"Bird Flight as the Basis of... Fliegekunst."* What does that mean? What on earth is *Fliegekunst*?

OTTO *Fliege* means "flight" and *Kunst*—

AGNES *(overlapping on "Kunst")* Kunst means "art"—yes, Otto, thank you, but I happen to understand German... being a native speaker and all... It's just that I've just never seen those two particular words smashed together like that before.

OTTO Together they mean the study of aircraft.

AGNES Air-Craft? Like what? Hot air balloons?

OTTO That's not flight, that's levitation.

AGNES There's another kind?

OTTO Well, no...not yet. But there will be. I'm working on a sort of human kite at the moment that—

AGNES A human *kite*?

OTTO Yes, well... of a sort. I haven't named it yet, but...

AGNES How about *Mensch-Drachen*? It means "Human Kite"...

AGNES & OTTO *(simultaneously)* ...in German.

OTTO That's clever, Agnes—very witty...

AGNES You haven't named it, yet, but you expect me to believe that there's a study devoted to it. So "Fliege-Kunst" is the study of something that hasn't been named yet? That hasn't even been INVENTED?

OTTO I know that seems a bit prophetic—

AGNES Not *prophetic*, Otto, *stupid*. Did we have the word "mathematics" before we had numbers? Did someone coin the term "grammar" before we had words?

OTTO Technically, that would not even have been *possible*…

AGNES I have exactly one nerve left, Otto…

OTTO Very well, Agnes, to answer your question: There have been many flying machines *built*, but—

AGNES …none of them have actually flown.

OTTO This is true.

AGNES Yet you continue to call them flying machines. When they should be called… what? *Falling* machines? *Stationary* machines? *Sculpture*?

OTTO I didn't know you were so interested in the nomenclature—

AGNES I am NOT interested! It's foolishness! Semantics! Whether you call your contraption a kite, a cloud or Kaiser Wilhelm doesn't interest me in the least!

OTTO Why are you so upset? It's a *hobby*…

AGNES It is not a hobby, Otto! It is an obsession! And why shouldn't I be upset? Upset at being abandoned; upset at feeling like a widow even though my husband is still very much alive; upset that you spend more time with your brother and this *Fliege*… *SCHEISSE* than you do with your own wife and children…

OTTO I'm sorry, Agnes, I don't mean to slight you. It's just that—

AGNES That what? That we're not important to you? Perhaps we should cover ourselves with feathers and flap our arms. Perhaps then you might notice that you have a family. One that loves you… that needs you and wants to spend time with you…

OTTO Now, Agnes, you must know how I feel about you—

AGNES HOW must I know that, Otto? How would the *children* know? I can't even remember the last time we shared a meal together. All I know is that this obsession of yours has occupied every waking moment of your life; that it has kept your brother close to you, while it has pushed everyone else away. If your parents were still alive, I feel certain that they, too—lacking wings and beaks and tailfeathers—would be as invisible as the rest of us who don't happen to be a part of your great adventures in flying—sorry—FALLING through the air!

OTTO I know I've neglected you… but please believe me when I say it was never intentional… This is my life's work, Agnes. Yes, it's only theoretical at this stage, I know that, but it won't always be. To invent an aircraft is nothing. To build one is *some*thing… But to fly one… Now, that… THAT is *everything*. I'm aiming for that. I'm aiming for "everything." It has been my great goal since childhood, Agnes. It haunts my dreams. Please, please don't ask me to give it up.

AGNES How dare you, Otto! How *dare* you!

Silence.

Give…it…up? Why in the world would I ask such a thing? How very little you must think of me, indeed. I am asking you to find room in your schedule for your family, Otto. That is all. A little time while the children are still young. Perhaps you could include us in your experiments? Or at the very least allow us in as spectators…? Do you think you are the only person who is fascinated by flight? Do you think Gustav is the only person on the planet who can possibly help? I saw the mess you two made of my sheets… Your brother may be devoted, but his sewing skills are the stuff of nightmares. You'll be wanting seams that don't rip apart, if you ever do get one of your inventions airborne.

Silence.

What's wrong, Otto? What's the matter?

OTTO Agnes Fischer Lilienthal, I think I'm falling in love.

AGNES Well, you certainly took your time.

> *ICARUS, DAEDALUS, GUSTAV and AGNES study birds, speaking very softly as OTTO confides to the audience:*

ICARUS ...all birds' wings are curved and terminate in points...

GUSTAV ...birds with long necks have short tails, and vice versa...

DAEDALUS ...as soon as a bird flies forward, its wings no longer make perpendicular movements, but describe slanting paths in the air, meeting the latter obliquely...

AGNES ...pigeons show this peculiarity very clearly, and the wings execute such powerful rotations, that it appears as if the upstroke would contribute to the lifting effect...

ICARUS ...birds that can remain stationary in calm air assume an inclined position, so that the wing-beats are not directed up and down, but partly forward and backward...

GUSTAV ...many birds lift their wings more rapidly than they beat them downwards...

DAEDALUS ...this is especially so in large birds with slowly beating wings, such as crows...

AGNES ...in order to keep the bird aloft, its body must execute a swinging motion, both when moving upwards and downwards...

OTTO *(simultaneously with the above)* People are forever asking me "Why?" "Why do you do it, Otto?" "What would possess you to do such a crazy thing?" "What makes you think you can FLY?" The answer is simple. I tell them I already have. It's true. It happened when I was no more than... what? Five years old? I was a tiny child—a shrimp. My mother always said "*Ach*, Otto, you eat like a bird! Always picking at your food. Take a bite, why don't you? A nice mouthful?" So it shouldn't have been a surprise that I was able to fly. But it was. It was a surprise to everyone.

We went to a nearby park to fly kites. I always begged to join in, but I was too small, they would say. Sometimes, though, Papa would let me hold the string once the kite was in the air. I couldn't control it, though, my motor skills were not developed enough yet, and the kite would fall and crash. Until that one day... Papa was flying a box kite—I always loved those—and when he handed me the cord, I grabbed it with both hands. The kite stayed up! It didn't crash like all the kites before! And then the wind picked up, and before I knew what was happening, I was in the air and floating across the park! My mother was screaming, but I wasn't afraid—I was thrilled! I was flying! I could FLY!

ICARUS ...all birds facilitate their flight by running against the wind...

GUSTAV ...many birds try to attain the forward velocity needed for rising by hopping in great jumps...

DAEDALUS ...since the bird, while in flight, is not in contact with any other body than the surrounding air,

OTTO I suppose everything I have done since then has been an attempt to recapture that first life-altering experience. That rush of air, that sense of weightlessness, that incomparable freedom. I'm not a religious person, but ever since that day in the park, I fully understood why the angels have wings. Heaven, I'm convinced, isn't heaven if you're earthbound. Only when the restraints of gravity have been released can one ascend to heaven. Only through flight can one achieve...grace.

AGNES ...the lifting force must have its origin in the air...

ICARUS ...a bird circling or sailing with still wings expends very little muscular energy...

GUSTAV ...when the stork distributes two wing-beats per second over a distance of ten meters, he advances five meters...

DAEDALUS ...the wing of a bird, moving up and down, possesses different velocities at every point; near the body its velocity is nearly zero, and it increases toward the tips of the wings...

KING MINOS Good afternoon.

DAEDALUS Your Highness! I'm sorry, I didn't hear you.

KING MINOS That was intentional, I fear: I was feeling mischievous. You've hurt yourself!

DAEDALUS Oh, that—merely a wax burn. I was—careless—with a candle...

KING MINOS It must have been a really large candle...

DAEDALUS Yes.

KING MINOS I thought you would be busy designing that tower for me.

DAEDALUS I am, Your Highness. Late into the night. Hence, the candle…

KING MINOS Then why do you have young, uh… you know…

DAEDALUS Icarus?

KING MINOS Yes. Why do you have him studying *birds*?

> *Silence.*

My men find the boy watching them, marking down their movements, mimicking them as though he, himself, were trying to fly.

> *KING MINOS laughs, and DAEDALUS laughs with him—a bit too heartily.*

DAEDALUS Icarus! Trying to fly! What a thought!

> *They laugh a bit longer, then KING MINOS stops abruptly. DAEDALUS follows suit.*

Your Excellency, I admit it. I am guilty. My son is indeed, watching the birds at my request. But his activities—though they may seem rather odd—are actually integral to my work on your—forward-thinking—tower project. This structure you want us to build will be taller than any that has ever been built before, and its upper stories will be high up in the sky, which is the province of the birds. I have Icarus watching them closely—studying them, if you will—so that we may determine where best to build this tower. We don't want it to be in an area that is too windy, for that location would not only be difficult—even deadly—for the workers to build in, but it may also prove too drafty once it has been built. Likewise, we would not want to build in a place that the birds themselves avoid—for they may sense problems that we cannot know. Since we cannot see the wind and the air currents, we must watch the birds, instead. I know whereof I speak, Your Highness: I did this very same type of study with bulls before I built the Minotaur's Labyrinth, and that project turned out quite well, if I say so myself…

KING MINOS It served quite well, indeed. That is, until Theseus killed the Minotaur, escaped the Labyrinth, stole my daughter and fled the country.

DAEDALUS Yes. That was… unfortunate.

KING MINOS And you still haven't paid for your part in the affair.

DAEDALUS I was led to believe that this tower project was my payment.

KING MINOS Is that what you believe? Huh. Well. Have you made any actual progress on your drawings for the tower, or have you gone completely to the birds?

DAEDALUS *(gesturing offstage)* I have made a great many drawings, Sire, if you would care to see them…?

> *They exit.*
>
> *The actors speak the following lines over DAEDALUS' litany of architectural terms.*

OTTO Daedalus works so diligently, his work invades his dreams

KING MINOS Diagrams spring to life before his eyes, or so it seems

AGNES He awakens in the morning, as out the pictures pour

DAEDALUS *(softly, dreaming)*
anteroom, atrium, colonnade, eave…
architrave, mullion, pediment, sill…
balcony, vestibule, portico, frieze…
balustrade, facade, entablature, ledge…
casement, entryway, transom, joist…
cornice, finial, parapet, ramp…
cupola, mansard, pilaster, stoop…
foundation, handrail, keystone, stair…

ICARUS Then, methodically, he copies what he dreamt the night before

GUSTAV Yet, if you watch him closely, you might notice little things

KING MINOS In the margins of the paper, there's a scrawl that looks like… wings?

AGNES A line that curves up quickly, then slowly takes a downward drift

ICARUS With numbers marked "resistance" and "velocity" and "lift"

GUSTAV While his hand is softly tracing out schematics for the tower

OTTO His mind is working to unlock the wind's amazing power

KING MINOS Working on two levels

AGNES In the shallows, and the deep

ICARUS Working in his waking

GUSTAV Working in his sleep

ICARUS My father is relentless. Where another person would be happy to invent one amazing thing, he has already done that and is now working on two more—*at the very same time.* His mind is filled with measurements—for the tower, for the wings… He cannot seem to reconcile the two—veering back and forth between them as if they were opposing armies. Personally, I am much more excited about the wings, but the tower is going to be amazing, too. Like the Labyrinth. I remember how much I loved playing in the Labyrinth while it was being built… But once the Minotaur was housed there, I was forbidden to enter. All I ever heard from my father was "no." "Don't go near the Minotaur, Icarus." "Stay away from the Labyrinth, Icarus." Now, finally, he has a project I can participate in. Wings! Flight! I know he can do it—my father is a genius. Who else would have thought to use wax to mold the wings? As a type of mortar it is both malleable and strong, and if he needs to alter it, he merely has to melt the wax and start over! It is true that I am not as much help to my father as I would like to be, but I certainly share his dreams. He may be my father, and I his son, but in our fascination with flight we are twins. *(beat)* Wake up, Father, the sun is already up.

DAEDALUS I can't do it anymore, son. I'm exhausted. And it is futile.

ICARUS Why do you say that? You have never failed at anything.

DAEDALUS This cannot be done, I'm afraid.

ICARUS But why?

DAEDALUS Well, for example: birds run into the wind to get enough lift to fly.

ICARUS Then so will we.

DAEDALUS It is not that simple. You and I weigh so much more than birds, there is not a wind strong enough, nor could we ever run quickly enough, to become airborne.

ICARUS You must still be half-asleep, Father. The answer is obvious.

DAEDALUS Obvious, is it? Enlighten me.

ICARUS Birds also jump from trees and gain their speed from falling…

DAEDALUS With weights like ours, we would need an awfully tall tree.

ICARUS Or a really tall…

ICARUS & DAEDALUS Tower!

DAEDALUS You are a brilliant man, my son. It is time for us to get to work!

ICARUS On the tower?

DAEDALUS On those wings!

> *OTTO appears wearing wings.*

GUSTAV Ready for takeoff?

OTTO Ready.

AGNES Be careful, *liebchen*!

OTTO Always, my love…

GUSTAV On your mark…

OTTO Hold on, Gustav. Not so fast. Patience is a virtue.

> *He kisses AGNES, then gets into position.*

OK. I'm ready.

GUSTAV On your mark… get set… GO!

> *OTTO runs offstage. Sound of a crash.*

Ouch.

AGNES & GUSTAV That had to hurt.

> *They run off after OTTO, as ICARUS enters wearing wings. DAEDALUS follows.*

DAEDALUS Are you ready, my son?

ICARUS No.

DAEDALUS I thought you were excited to begin flying.

ICARUS Flying, yes. Falling, no.

DAEDALUS That is why you're jumping off a *cliff*. The water below is much softer than the ground below the tower will be.

ICARUS It's still a long way down.

DAEDALUS Not so very far. I see boys diving off this cliff every summer.

ICARUS Ask one of *them* to do this.

DAEDALUS Now, now…

ICARUS Why don't YOU jump off the cliff?

DAEDALUS According to my calculations, this cliff is high enough to get you airborne, but not me…

ICARUS That's encouraging.

DAEDALUS Don't worry, Icarus. If the wings don't work, I will dive in after you.

ICARUS You might as well go first, then.

DAEDALUS Are you ready?

ICARUS No.

DAEDALUS Icarus.

ICARUS I'm ready! I'm ready…

DAEDALUS All right, now: Arms out. Legs braced. And… GO!

> *ICARUS runs offstage and we hear his scream die away.*

Damn.

> *DAEDALUS runs after, as OTTO, GUSTAV and AGNES return.*

GUSTAV With the adjustments you made and this stronger wind, we cannot fail!

OTTO "Pride goeth before a fall," Gustav… But I have to admit that I *am* feeling more confident today.

AGNES I don't know whether to pray to St. Christopher or St. Jude.

OTTO Thank you for the vote of encouragement, my darling.

GUSTAV Are you ready?

OTTO Don't be so anxious. I'm the one doing the jumping. All right. I'm ready.

GUSTAV On your mark… get set… GO!

> *OTTO runs offstage. Sound of a crash.*

AGNES *Scheisse.*

GUSTAV He'll be fine.

> *Pause.*

Eventually…

They run off after OTTO, as ICARUS enters wearing wings. DAEDALUS follows.

ICARUS These wings feel heavier than the last pair.

DAEDALUS They are heavier than the last pair.

ICARUS I'm going to sink like a rock.

DAEDALUS Don't worry about the weight, these wings have a larger mass, so they will catch more air, and keep you aloft longer.

ICARUS How much longer?

DAEDALUS That is what this test flight will tell us.

ICARUS Wonderful.

DAEDALUS Are you ready?

ICARUS No.

DAEDALUS Icarus.

ICARUS I'm ready! I'm ready…

DAEDALUS All right, now: Arms out. Legs braced. And… GO!

ICARUS runs offstage and we hear his scream die away.

Damn.

DAEDALUS runs after, as OTTO, GUSTAV and AGNES return.

GUSTAV Shouldn't you wait until your fracture heals?

OTTO And waste this weather?

GUSTAV *(to AGNES)* Talk to him, sister. I tried…

AGNES Otto, you don't want to risk breaking the other clavicle, do you?

OTTO It's not a bone I use that often, anyway.

AGNES I wouldn't be so certain… That's not the point, anyway. Don't you think you owe it to science to give this experiment your very best? You are not at your best while you are still healing.

OTTO I appreciate your concern, my love, but I'm testing this model TODAY. Gustav!

GUSTAV Are you ready?

OTTO As I'll ever be.

GUSTAV On your mark…

AGNES I can't look.

GUSTAV Get set…

AGNES Hail Mary, full of grace…

GUSTAV GO!

> *OTTO runs offstage. There is a pause, as AGNES and GUSTAV watch thunderstruck.*

AGNES Oh my God…

GUSTAV He did it.

AGNES He really did it.

AGNES & GUSTAV He's flying!

> *They run off after OTTO, as ICARUS enters wearing wings. DAEDALUS follows.*

ICARUS Please don't make me do this.

DAEDALUS Courage, son. Rome wasn't built in a day.

ICARUS We are Greek, father. Why should we care what the Italians do?

DAEDALUS I was making an analogy.

ICARUS And I was pleading for my life…

DAEDALUS You weren't hurt in the previous attempts. You just got wet.

ICARUS I nearly drowned!

DAEDALUS But you didn't, now did you?

ICARUS That is my greatest fear—drowning.

DAEDALUS You will not drown. I won't let you. Now remember: "If at first you fail your deed…"

ICARUS "Try again till you succeed."

DAEDALUS Exactly. Are you ready?

ICARUS No.

DAEDALUS Icarus.

ICARUS I'm ready! I'm ready…

DAEDALUS All right, now: Arms out. Legs braced. And… GO!

> *ICARUS runs off-stage. A pause while DAEDALUS watches thunderstruck.*

Gods be praised. He did it! He's flying!

> *KING MINOS enters.*

KING MINOS Daedalus, I thought I could find you here.

DAEDALUS *(leaping out of his skin)* Sire…?

KING MINOS I hear you have been coming down here quite a lot, lately.

DAEDALUS Yes, the walk helps me to clear my mind, and of course, I am able to study the seagulls…

KING MINOS Ah, yes. The birds that are going to help you build your tower.

DAEDALUS Yes.

KING MINOS Rubbish, Daedalus. How can the birds possibly help you build a TOWER?

DAEDALUS But they already have, Sire.

KING MINOS Enlighten me.

DAEDALUS Have you ever seen a gull descend in a spiral?

KING MINOS Of course...

DAEDALUS He does it without flapping his wings. Something about that motion made me realize that it isn't simply beautiful, but it is economical—they don't exert as much energy when they spiral down.

KING MINOS Yes, and SO...?

DAEDALUS So... I have designed for the tower a spiral staircase.

KING MINOS A what?

DAEDALUS We do the same thing that birds do—when we see a steep incline, rather than charge straight down, which places a strain on our muscles, we walk down in a roundabout way, or by zigzagging to make the descent less jarring and painful. I have developed a circular staircase that allows one to walk up and down the tower around its perimeter, rather than placing a series of straight staircases within it. The birds taught me that.

KING MINOS A circular staircase! I was wrong to question your motives, Daedalus. I apologize. You have reminded me once more of your genius—your ability to see beyond what the rest of us see. We have all seen birds circle, but only a mind like yours could develop a concrete use for that concept in the earthbound world of men. I am proud you are my architect.

DAEDALUS Thank you, Sire.

KING MINOS I have taken up enough of your time.

KING MINOS starts to leave.

But before I go…

DAEDALUS Yes, my lord?

KING MINOS Does your son… uh…

DAEDALUS Icarus.

KING MINOS Yes. Him. Does HE show any signs of inheriting your genius?

DAEDALUS He is not… *unintelligent*, my lord. Why do you ask?

KING MINOS I might have a use for him someday. When you are no longer with us. Good day.

KING MINOS exits. DAEDALUS watches him for a moment, then runs off after ICARUS, as OTTO, AGNES and GUSTAV enter.

GUSTAV It works! Your glider works!

OTTO I suppose…

AGNES You flew, Otto! It's what you've dreamed of. Aren't you excited?

OTTO I didn't go very high.

GUSTAV Your feet were off the ground.

AGNES Why do you need to go any higher than that?

OTTO Agnes, really…

AGNES That's not a stupid question. The higher you go, the more it will hurt if you fall.

OTTO But the higher I go, the *further* I'll go. I lost height gradually the whole time I was in the air just now. Listen to me: "the whole time"—it was only seconds! I didn't go very far, at all. That was barely more than a jump.

GUSTAV You couldn't see yourself, but I *could*, and let me tell you—it was a lot more than just a jump.

AGNES It was much more than a jump, Otto. You *floated*.

OTTO I'll have to take your word for it.

AGNES You just need a stronger wind.

GUSTAV Or a higher hill.

OTTO One without trees? And a steady wind? It could take us years to find such a place. And what if—when we did finally find it—it was in France?

GUSTAV & AGNES Eccch.

OTTO Indeed.

GUSTAV Then you'll just have to build one.

OTTO Build a hill? Are you crazy?

AGNES This is Gustav you're talking to. The answer is "yes."

GUSTAV What's so crazy? It's just dirt.

AGNES Gustav! That's insane.

OTTO It is, yes. But that's *such* an insane idea… that it just might work.

AGNES *Mein Gott*… You are actually going to build a hill, aren't you, Otto? Of course you are. And you'll name it *Fliege Berg*, no doubt.

OTTO "Flight Mountain!"

AGNES How very curious: I can actually *feel* my gray hair growing in.

GUSTAV How high are you thinking, Otto?

OTTO Oh, somewhere between ten and twenty meters should work.

AGNES Ten METERS? That's over two stories tall! Forget about your brother, Otto, YOU are the crazy one. You'll kill yourself!

OTTO Perhaps. But I'll be flying!

AGNES Otto!

GUSTAV My brother is relentless. Where another person would be happy to make one or two successful glides, he is now nearing two *thousand*. He measures everything: wind speed, wind direction, temperature, humidity, the height he achieves, the duration of the glide, the distance he travels, the drag on the wings… but it's destroying him that he can only glide passively, relying on so many other conditions. Without a hill and a steady wind, he is grounded. He dreams of powered flight. Holding onto stationary wings can only get one so far. If man is to travel under his own power, then our man-made wings must flap, must beat against the air in order to free us from the wind. There is no other way. Although I'm not as gifted at mathematics and science, I share my big brother's dream—his vision of people in the sky. There may be years between our births, but in our fascination with flight we are twins.

DAEDALUS Listen to me carefully, Icarus. We have a long way to go, so we'll have to alternate between active periods and gliding periods in order to conserve our strength. Don't try to go too fast.

ICARUS Yes, Father: "Don't go too fast."

DAEDALUS That is correct. A nice constant speed will allow you to go further using less energy. Fly in a straight line: the shortest route will give us the best chance of survival.

ICARUS Yes, Father: "Fly in a straight line."

DAEDALUS Also, we'll be flying over the water, which can be dangerous. Don't fly too low, or else your wings may absorb moisture from the sea and become too heavy for flight. Are you listening?

ICARUS Yes, Father. "Don't fly too near the sea."

DAEDALUS There are no clouds today, and the sun will be particularly hot, which is dangerous, as well. Don't fly too high, or else the wax of your wings may melt.

ICARUS Yes, Father. "Don't fly too near the sun."

DAEDALUS Go over these thoughts in your mind: Conserve energy, keep in a straight line, don't fly too—

ICARUS *(seeing that his father is worried)* Why don't I follow behind you, Father, and watch what you do.

DAEDALUS I make things too complicated, don't I? Thank you, son, that's a wonderful solution: just do as I do. That makes me feel much safer.

GUSTAV Otto, do you want me to attach the *prellbugel*—er—shock absorber to the glider?

OTTO No, it will take too long, and I want to get several glides in before dark.

GUSTAV The wind is awfully choppy, Otto, I'd feel better if we added the rebound rods—they've saved you in the past.

OTTO I was a pile of broken bones!

GUSTAV But you were a *living* pile of broken bones. Those bent willow-rods absorbed the bulk of the impact from your fall and spared you to fly another day.

OTTO Yes, of course, you're right. Just let me get a couple glides in first, I don't want to miss this wind.

GUSTAV Then we'll attach the *prellbugel*?

OTTO Then we'll attach the *prellbugel*.

GUSTAV Thank you for the compromise, Otto. That makes me feel much safer.

> *OTTO, DAEDALUS and ICARUS prepare for flight. DAEDALUS on a stool, perhaps, OTTO and ICARUS on something taller—ladders, perhaps? They begin to fly.*

AGNES I had seen him fly so many times by this point that it was no longer news. I don't know what made me look up…

KING MINOS I was impatient and curious to see what progress was being made on my tower, otherwise I would never have looked up…

KING MINOS & AGNES …but I did.

AGNES Other women's husbands hang hammocks behind their houses.

KING MINOS Other kings' architects build towers to be fortresses.

AGNES Mine built an artificial hill.

KING MINOS Mine built his to be a launching pad.

AGNES Completed, it stood fifteen meters above the plain.

KING MINOS Not yet completed, it was already taller than anything I had ever seen.

AGNES Other women's husbands build model trains…

KING MINOS Other kings' architects build monuments…

AGNES & KING MINOS …mine builds wings.

AGNES I must confess, the sight of him flying was always exciting to me…

KING MINOS I have to admit, the sight of him soaring through the air was thrilling…

AGNES …naturally, I was worried, as well…

KING MINOS …of course, I was also very angry…

AGNES & KING MINOS …but…he's…FLYING!

AGNES I was always terrified of him getting hurt… but despite my worries, I was so proud of him:

KING MINOS I had planned to kill him for the loss of my daughter and the Minotaur, yet in spite of myself, my heart swelled with pride:

AGNES He was the first person on earth who had ever flown on man-made wings…

KING MINOS *My* architect had unlocked the secret of the skies, and he alone could fly…

AGNES …well…

KING MINOS ...that is...

AGNES & KING MINOS ...except for Icarus...

AGNES ...but that's just a myth.

KING MINOS ...but he was just a boy. I had forgotten about him... yet there he was... lagging behind his father. The contrast between the two was startling. Daedalus was so focused... flying at a steady speed in a straight line north, but Icarus... he seemed to be *playing*—now zigging and zagging, now climbing and diving, now describing lazy circles in the air... falling farther and farther behind his father's diminishing figure.

AGNES A man in flight...

KING MINOS Two men in flight...

AGNES & KING MINOS I couldn't take my eyes off it.

GUSTAV Otto was gliding along smoothly, when all of a sudden, the wind gusted and lifted him way up in the air—

AGNES Over five stories high... I never knew something could be so beautiful and so horrible—

GUSTAV & AGNES at the very same time.

KING MINOS Icarus, seemingly drunk on his newfound abilities, began climbing higher and higher—as if he were trying to reach the sun... Then something happened, something awful... feathers slowly floated down and Icarus started thrashing about, as if trying to tread the air. Daedalus turned and saw his son just as the poor boy lost the battle...

> *ICARUS freezes in his struggle, DAEDALUS freezes in a turn toward him.*

DAEDALUS, AGNES, GUSTAV, KING MINOS (*in a stage whisper*) NO!

> *OTTO and ICARUS fall slowly to the ground.*

GUSTAV Without a wind,

DAEDALUS Without his wings,

GUSTAV My brother…

DAEDALUS My Icarus…

GUSTAV & DAEDALUS …fell.

GUSTAV Without the willow rods attached to break his fall, Otto crashed into the ground—the glider shattering on top of him.

AGNES Yet he was still alive!

GUSTAV Those who were watching ran to his side and rushed him to the nearest hospital.

AGNES He was in great pain and kept repeating to those who were carrying him—

OTTO *(delirious)* My name is Otto Lilienthal, my name is Otto Lilienthal…

AGNES A fact they already knew.

DAEDALUS How far he fell! How terrified he must have been! I tried to fly back to him—to catch him—but I was too far away. He fought fiercely, but his wings were a horrible impediment to him—he thrashed, he flailed, but the more he struggled, the more he spun out of control. He could not right himself in time… the impact was great, his young bones were shattered, and yet, the same tattered wings that could not keep him aloft, kept him afloat. As I neared him, my dear sweet boy looked up at me, and said:

ICARUS I failed you, Father, forgive me. You must be so disappointed in me…

DAEDALUS I was overcome with emotion, seeing my child so broken, so vulnerable. My voice would not come out—I could not speak. I could not tell him there was nothing to forgive—he was just a boy who thought flying was fun—and what boy wouldn't? My poor child was raised in captivity—always helping me with my work—never given a childhood, never allowed to play. *Of course* he would have found it irresistible to fly higher and higher—and I should have known that. I should have flown *beside* him, not in front. It was my fault. I couldn't save my own son, and now, as I circled him in the water, the sea slowly began to swallow him whole—before I could comfort him, before I could ask for HIS forgiveness, my only, my Icarus, hampered by his own fractured limbs and those curséd wings, sank into the sea and drowned.

AGNES His back broken and bleeding internally, Otto lingered until the next morning. All of us were there—Gustav, myself, the children—all of us praying for him to pull through.

KING MINOS Daedalus was the genius who designed the Labyrinth. The Minotaur? Merely another hungry beast. Surely of the two it is Daedalus who will be remembered. And Theseus? A thief who could have done nothing without the architect's assistance. Of the two, we will remember Daedalus. Ariadne was simply another daughter who eloped, Icarus just another boy who didn't follow his father's instructions – barely worth a footnote, either of them, but Daedalus, now HE will be remembered. Not Ariadne, Theseus, the Minotaur, nor Icarus, but Daedalus will be the household name. But let us not forget that he would have been nothing without me. If there is any justice, time will not forget my contributions…

GUSTAV My brother will be remembered. He invented the efficient steam engine that allowed him to open his own company and finance his work on flight. He pioneered a profit-sharing program for his factory workers long before it was the fashion. He accumulated twenty-three patents in his lifetime and invented the popular Anchor Stone building blocks for children, but most of all, he was the Glider King! The first man to make repeated, sustained flights using heavier-than-air craft. He designed eighteen different gliders and flew great distances—up to 350 meters! Surely, in the years to come, no one will be able to discuss air flight without thinking of my brother. His will be a household name.

AGNES Otto drifted in and out of his wits and was lucid for only a very short time.

GUSTAV Regaining consciousness just before he passed away, he looked up at Agnes, caught her eyes and said then,

KING MINOS Daedalus tried to cheat me, now the piper must be paid…

OTTO *Opfer müssen gebracht werden.*

AGNES "Sacrifices must be made."

End of play.

Nyx

by David J. Duman

NYX

The first public reading of *Nyx* was on October 15, 2011 at EXIT Theatre, as part of San Francisco Olympians Festival II: Heavenly Bodies. It was directed by Stuart Bousel and featured the following cast:

Juliana Egley	NYX
Kelley B. Greer	WOMAN
Eric Hannan	MAN

A black stage.

NYX, a Goth-fabulous hottie, saunters onstage full of sexy swagger. She is ageless. Timeless.

When NYX is giving her monologues, the stage is dark save for a spot illuminating NYX's face and torso, gradually darkening down her body until her knees are shrouded and her feet completely swallowed in darkness.

NYX I am Goddess of the Night. Primordial ancestress. Daughter of Chaos. Mother of Dreams; Retribution and Deception; Doom and Blame. Zeus, King Himself, fears me. I gave birth to Hemera, Day springing from Night—the eternal mystery of my darkness providing the illusory illumination of temporal truths. I rule the ether and I rule reality. Every man and woman comes back to me and leaves me only with my permission.

Lights up.

NYX is behind a checkout counter at a Wal-Mart store.

A CUSTOMER walks up with his groceries.

NYX checks them through.

Twelve forty-seven is your total.

The CUSTOMER hands NYX a twenty-dollar bill. NYX hands the CUSTOMER change.

Five fifty-three is your change. Thank you and have a nice day.

The CUSTOMER walks away. Pauses. He turns to protest.

Lights dim.

I am born from the fabric of time. My forthcoming is the harbinger of old age. I rule the Fates from the corner of my temple with Chronus chained to the walls and him drunk on Lemnian wine, murmuring prophecies. I interpret his fragments into truths and dispense my judgments via the Moirae, those loyal Apportioners, throughout the world. My Hesperides guard the immortal apples, secreting them against the knowing of mortals.

Lights up.

NYX is in an office in a high-school administration building. She sits behind a desk.

A STUDENT comes in and sits down across from her.

The STUDENT hands her a portfolio. She looks it over.

I'm going to be honest, based on your strength of schedule and standardized test scores, I think you're setting your college sights too high.

She hands back the portfolio to the STUDENT.

The STUDENT bursts into tears.

Lights down.

And I bring you Sleep through my fair son Hypnos! My only joy! He surveys the world of men, bringing temporary end to their troubles or enhancing their troubles through the deprivation of his gifts. That baiting place of wit! That balm of woe! You indifferent judge between high and low!

Lights up.

A bedroom.

A MAN is in bed, tossing and turning, unable to sleep. He sits up and picks up a bedside telephone. He dials.

> *Lights down on the MAN, lights up on NYX, dressed as a nurse, answering the telephone.*

Ambien? You're out? I'll have the doctor call in a refill. Take a bunch and call me in the morning.

> *The MAN hangs up.*

Well, he sounded nice. Kinda cute, actually. But no! Philotes! My daughter, beautiful and loving, tasked simultaneously with administering the pleasure of sex and the affection of friendship. She's a true goddess for the twenty-first century and it's fitting that the manifestation of those dueling, confounding intimacies emerged from the womb of darkest Night.

> *Lights up.*
>
> *A bedroom.*
>
> *NYX is now in bed with the MAN.*
>
> *She kisses him on the cheek.*

See? You didn't need that Ambien after all. You just needed someone to tire you out. You can call me to tire you out any time.

> *She gets out of bed and begins to dress.*
>
> *The MAN gets out of bed and puts his arms around her.*
>
> *NYX pats his arms and squirms out of his embrace.*

Hey! Tut-tut. None of that mushy stuff, please. You know that.

> *She finishes dressing.*
>
> *She starts scrolling through her iPhone.*
>
> *The MAN sits back down.*

We still on for the Giants game next week? Awesome. Oooh! Lincecum's pitching. I'll wear something slutty. Ta!

> *She exits with a flirty sashay.*

Lights down.

I am the mother of Death! Thanatos, the more emboldened brother of Hypbos, who enacts the Fates' demands, pulling men from their world and into the world of the gods. Will they make it to Elysium? Or will they find themselves locked away in eternal night?

Lights up.

NYX is sitting next to the MAN. They're watching a Giants baseball game.

NYX is cheering wildly. The MAN tosses peanuts into his mouth.

Woot! Go Timmy! Go go go! Yeah! Yes—what? Boo. That was a strike. That was a strike. Wasn't that a strike? That was a strike. Oh! Strike three! Yer out! Sit your ass down, Furcal. You can't handle the heat! You *can't* handle it.

The MAN starts to choke on a peanut.

Lincecum's got to be the best pitcher in the majors, right, babe?

She turns and looks at him.

Babe? You OK, babe? Are you choking?

The MAN nods.

NYX looks at him contemplatively.

Hrm.

The MAN keeps choking.

That's sometimes the way it goes.

She turns away from him and starts cheering again for the Giants.

He keeps choking. He's turning blue.

Timmy! Another K! Yeah!

She looks over her shoulder at him.

Fine. Not this time. There's still some use to you yet. Get up.

> *He stands and she starts slapping his back. She then administers a few abdominal thrusts, sending the offending peanut flying.*

> *He sits back down, coughing profusely.*

There you go. You're welcome.

> *She returns her attention to the game.*

Go Timmy! Strikeout! Number three! Hell of an inning, Timmy! Timmy! Timmy!

> *She pats the MAN on the back. He's still coughing.*

Still coughing? No no, that's good. Rest up. You'll need your strength later. Or at least I will.

> *Lights down.*

I was the first and I will be the last. I'll be in every corner of your life from the trivial to the profound, touching every facet of your day. And night. Because before there was Earth, there was Night. And I haven't left since.

> *End of play.*

Hyperion to a Satyr

by Stuart Eugene Bousel

Hyperion to a Satyr

The first public reading of *Hyperion to a Satyr* was on October 15, 2011 at EXIT Theatre as part of San Francisco Olympians Festival II: Heavenly Bodies. It was directed by Stuart Bousel and featured the following cast:

Timothy Beagley	HAL
Tonyanna Borkovi	CHLOE
Kevin Copps	HYPERION
Juliana Egley	SERENA
Eric Hannan	PAN
Dashiell Hillman	ALLEN
Kelley B. Greer	STAGE DIRECTIONS
Jennifer Lucas	CLARA
Brian Martin	PETER

Characters

HAL, 39, a third-generation Greek-American businessman and former golden boy

HYPERION, 70, his father, a second-generation Greek-American business tycoon

PETER, 14, Hal's son, an intelligent but belligerent American teenager

CHLOE, 29, a statistics analyst working for Hyperion, plucky and sexy

PAN, 25, a hipster musician and annual Burner

SERENA, 36, Hal's sister, a doctor, brilliant, elegant, kind, distant

ALLEN, 23, Hal's cousin, Clara's lover, precocious, handsome, extremely California

CLARA, 39, Hal's ex-wife, Peter's mother, a polite, restrained NorCal society matron

Setting

In and around contemporary San Francisco
Various unspecified locations in Nevada

Act One: Solar Eclipse

Prologue: Before

> *HYPERION stands at a podium, addressing an audience. He wears a white suit.*

HYPERION Who is my son? This is the question my father asked on his deathbed. This was the last thing I ever heard him say. I don't think he knew I was in the room at the time. Or at least, I'd rather think that than the alternative. Which is a weakness in me, but not a weakness that concerns me. We didn't have a good relationship, my father and I. We didn't have a bad one either. It was probably fairly typical of the time. Men of my generation. My father was poor, an immigrant. He was a doctor in his own country, a minor diplomat in his own community, a nobody here, a man running a men's shoe store in Concord. The lower middle class made lower by a large family and a bad neighborhood. My brothers and I wanted none of it. Six of us, total, and we all knew that there had to be something better and that we could have it here—not in the old country, not in some other time, but now, in America, just across the Bay. And one by one, each of us found our own version of the dream while my father stayed in Concord, tied to the store, chained in place. My father could never really let go of the past, just like he could never really learn English, but because he never wanted to do the former the latter was, naturally, impossible, and that, my friends, is how you screw yourself over at the roots: trying too hard to protect them, forgetting you need to change. Something we all do, at some point. It's just a matter of seeing how. Sadly, that is the blind spot. The son spot, as I like to say, because it's usually your sons who will finally make you aware of it. Our children are a promise we make ourselves that we cannot collect upon. My father knew that and that's why he called for his son that day—calling out in his delirium to a room full of sons.

Scene One: Reveille

> *CLARA's kitchen. HAL, CLARA and PETER, arguing over breakfast.*

HAL I said no.

PETER Why?

HAL You know why. You're fourteen years old.

PETER I'm fifteen.

HAL You are fifteen in two months, one week, one day, give or take several hours.

PETER I'm almost fifteen.

HAL Until you are eighteen—which will be in three years, two months, one week, one day and—*(checks his watch)*—sixteen hours, you will still be under my legal control and thus unable to overrule me on this front. You are not going and that is final.

PETER Pan said you wouldn't let me.

HAL Pan was correct.

PETER Pan will be with me the whole time. Pan has done this like… a million times already. Pan will make sure nothing happens to me.

HAL Pan is sorely overestimating his ability to be a responsible adult.

PETER You never let me do anything fun.

HAL That's not true. I've let you do lots of things that were fun. I just won't let you do anything fun that involves copious drugs, worshiping of false idols, and not showering for nine straight days. Which means, specifically, I am not letting you go to Burning Man. Please feel free to ask about doing anything else. There is a fifty percent chance I'll be happy to grant my permission.

PETER I fucking hate you, Dad.

HAL Well, I love you, Peter.

PETER FUCK YOU!

> *He storms out. HAL goes back to his breakfast.*

CLARA Worshiping of false idols?

HAL You know how I feel about bad art installations by trustafarians.

CLARA You're being overdramatic.

HAL I thought I was being funny.

CLARA Not to a fourteen-year-old.

HAL He's almost fifteen.

CLARA I'm aware, though not to the actual minute. *(beat)* You could stand to be around more.

HAL Honey, you know if I could be, I would be. For both of you.

CLARA I'm not the one who needs you, Hal.

HAL Yes, I'm aware of *that*.

CLARA I'm a grown woman—he's a child.

HAL He's a teenager.

CLARA That's worse.

HAL Your boyfriend—

CLARA Leave Allen out of this.

HAL I figured if we were going to talk about one teenager we might as well bring up the other—

CLARA Allen is twenty-three.

HAL Yeah, but not when you started sleeping together.

CLARA He was not a teenager.

HAL He was nineteen and seven days, Clara, and don't argue with me, he's my cousin.

> *A beat. CLARA wipes her mouth with her napkin, stands, starts collecting dishes.*

CLARA Well, this was a disaster. I hope the rest of your day is enjoyable.

HAL I wasn't the person who invited me over for breakfast.

CLARA If you're going to just deflect this onto me and our issues rather than talk about your son, I'd rather you just go.

> *A moment. HAL wipes his mouth and stands.*

HAL The part where I told him no? That was me being a father.

CLARA No, that was you being your father. The man I married would have been grateful his son wanted to go to Burning Man and not Disneyland.

HAL Yes, well, the problem with that guy, Clara, is that he can't afford this house and our son's school and pretty much everything else that makes up your life—

CLARA I am aware of what you have sacrificed and I am grateful but that's not how a teenage boy adds up the world. And he is a teenage boy, Hal. He's five seconds away from manhood and if you want to be anything more than a visitor in his life I'm telling you now—you're running out of time. And I'll forgive you, Hal, but I don't know that he will.

Scene Two: Morning

> *HAL's office. He moves to sit at his desk. CHLOE enters.*

CHLOE Ten AM, meeting with the Thrinacia Cattle Company. Ten-thirty AM, meeting with the people from Odyssey to discuss the acquisition of the cattle company. Eleven-fifteen AM, meeting with Thrinacia Cattle Company to discuss meeting with Odyssey and possible counter-offers. Noon. Brainstorm with the Republic.

HAL Cancel that. I have a lunch meeting.

CHLOE With who?

HAL My kid's music teacher.

CHLOE Do you need me to—?

HAL No, I already called him on the way in. This is personal stuff.

CHLOE Oh.

HAL Don't worry about it.

CHLOE Should we move the Republic meeting to tomorrow?

HAL Not sure. What's on the docket for the afternoon?

CHLOE Two PM, press conference with Hercules.

HAL About what?

CHLOE He's publicly apologizing for that business over Libya.

HAL You mean when he tried to shoot me?

CHLOE He mistook you for someone else.

HAL And that makes it acceptable? I'm not going to that.

CHLOE You have to. I've already said you would and it's good for the company.

HAL I have no desire to make nice with a moneyed Republican vigilante.

CHLOE He votes Green Party, actually.

HAL Really?

CHLOE No, I made that up. You still need to do it. He's a shareholder.

HAL So are a lot of people.

CHLOE I think he's genuinely sorry and trying to be a nice guy about it.

HAL Then why can't he send a fruit basket like a normal person?

CHLOE He's worth half a billion and that's not how it's done on this level, is it?

HAL Fine. Push the Republic meeting to Monday. Apologize profusely. I actually like those guys. How long does the charade with Hercules go on?

CHLOE You'll be able to make your dinner with your sister.

HAL Perfect.

CHLOE Her gift is wrapped and waiting for you at the front desk.

HAL We got her something good, right?

CHLOE You got her something she'll like.

> *HYPERION enters.*

HYPERION Hal.

HAL Dad.

HYPERION Excuse me, honey-pie. I need to have a word with my son.

CHLOE Of course, Mr. Hyperion.

HAL I have clients coming in twenty minutes from now—

HYPERION Is it the Thrinacians?

HAL Naturally.

HYPERION Fuck 'em. They can wait if they have to.

HAL Figure out a way to stall them, Chloe.

CHLOE Don't worry about it, Hal.

HYPERION Do it nicely, sweetheart.

CHLOE I always do it nicely, Mr. Hyperion.

HYPERION I'm sure you do, pussycat.

> *She exits.*

HAL Dad, you can't talk to her like that.

HYPERION Sure I can. She likes it.

HAL She likes it until she sues us.

HYPERION She isn't going to sue us. She likes you too much to sue us.

HAL Is there a reason for this conversation? Because I have had a rough morning and believe it or not, I do have things to do.

HYPERION Calm down, son, I'll get out of your hair, I just thought there's something you'd like to hear from me before you read about it in the papers.

HAL What? Are you getting a divorce?

HYPERION I would never divorce your mother. She's a peach. Guess again.

HAL You're bailing out Wall Street? We're funding a shuttle launch?

HYPERION Just whose kid are you?

HAL OK, Dad, out with it. I need this like I need a hole in the head.

HYPERION You're no fun. Where do you get that from? *(beat)* I'm stepping down.

A long pause.

HAL I don't believe it.

HYPERION Well, you should. It'll be in all the papers next week.

HAL But… does that mean—?

HYPERION I'm not giving it up. I'll still own it. I just won't be running it.

HAL Who will?

HYPERION It pains me tremendously you don't immediately assume that it's you.

HAL Right, well, it's not me, is it?

HYPERION No.

HAL Of course not. Thanks, Dad. Great talk. I need to get to my meeting—

HYPERION Aren't you curious who it's going to be?

HAL Not particularly, no. *(beat)* Unless I'm being fired. Am I being fired?

HYPERION You're not being fired. *(beat)* I'm passing over command to Allen.

> *A long moment.*

See, I knew you'd want to hear that from me rather than reading it in the *Chronicle*. *(beat)* Anything to say?

HAL He doesn't even have a degree.

HYPERION Neither did I.

HAL He's twenty-three.

HYPERION I was twenty when I got my first promotion—

HAL Not to Executive Director of a billion-dollar—

HYPERION The details don't matter. I think he's qualified and therefore he is. *(beat)* Of course, he'll need your support and guidance. You know the ropes—

HAL Oh forget that.

HYPERION Don't be jealous. You never wanted the title—you've told me that many times—

HAL Look, if he's not qualified one hundred percent, right now, then I don't see why he gets to just take over, above me—

HYPERION Because the boy's a better fit, son. He's got an eye to the future you don't have, and a charisma you also lack—

HAL The man is screwing my wife.

HYPERION You divorced her.

HAL Because she was screwing him! *(beat)* Surely you see why this decision would… affect… me, don't you?

HYPERION I do. Doesn't change the decision. *(beat)* You're never going to make that meeting, son.

HAL *(grabbing his briefcase)* Well, whose fault is that?

HYPERION Are you seeing your sister tonight?

HAL *(stuffing some papers in)* Yes.

HYPERION Tell her I send my regards—happy birthday and all my love.

HAL I think you're about the last person she wants to hear from and I can tell you why—

HYPERION Don't go there, son. You can't hurt me, so don't bother.

HAL Why? Why can't I hurt you?

HYPERION Just can't. I'm too far above it. *(beat)* Have a good meeting.

Scene Three: Zenith

A park. HAL sits on a bench, his hands over his eyes. PAN enters.

PAN Hey Hal! What's happening, man?

HAL looks up.

HAL Hey. Thanks for coming.

PAN No problem. So what's up, man?

HAL I wanted to talk to you about Peter.

PAN Yeah? Little dude's totally kicking ass at the guitar.

HAL I'm… glad to hear that.

PAN I hope there's not some kind of problem, because he's one of my best students and—

HAL Well, no, there's not really any kind of problem, it's just that… Do you want lunch or anything? I'm buying.

PAN It's cool, man, I'm on a cleanse. But we can go somewhere if you want.

HAL No, I'm fine. I'm trying to stick to these protein-shake things anyway—

PAN Oh cool. I get that. It helps when you're trying to build muscle mass.

HAL Well… I'm not really trying to do that.

PAN No? You look like you been working out.

HAL It's just this suit. It fits me well.

PAN It's a nice suit.

HAL Thanks. Anyway, about Peter—

PAN He brought up the whole Burning Man thing with you, didn't he?

HAL This morning. I was over there for breakfast and we had an argument about it—

PAN That dumb kid. No offense. I told him you'd never let him do it.

HAL Did you suggest to him he shouldn't tell me?

PAN No, of course not. I was telling him about Burning Man, he said he wanted to go, I said he'd need your permission and that I doubted you'd be cool with it.

HAL Ah.

PAN Oh, shit, I'm sorry. I realize that makes it sound like I think you're a douchebag.

HAL That… wasn't… my take on what you—

PAN I mean, I know you're not a douchebag, man. I mean, you're very cool for like…

HAL Like what?

PAN Like… a guy with that suit, you know?

HAL Right. *(beat)* Look, Pan, I really do have a lot of respect for your talents and your dad is one of my best friends—

PAN It's cool, man, I, I know where this is going—

HAL I also know Peter really looks up to you, and everything, and he should—

PAN Hey, thanks.

HAL I just… would prefer you not, you know… set my own kid against me.

PAN Well… it's not like I did that.

HAL Well, that's kind of how it seemed this morning.

PAN Well, that might be how it seemed but that isn't… my fault… or anything. I mean if you and Peter have some kind of problem or whatever—

HAL We don't necessarily have any problems—

PAN I just told the kid about how I'm going to Burning Man again and then practiced some scales with him. Anything beyond that is… you know. Whatever.

A long moment.

HAL I'm sorry.

PAN For what, man?

HAL I shouldn't have… you know… dragged you out of your day for this.

PAN Oh, whatever. I had the time. I don't leave till tonight, and I'm all good to go so—

HAL I'm having a hard time connecting with him lately.

PAN Yeah… I can see that. I mean, I get the impression you're not around much.

HAL Has he said that? I mean… does he say anything about me… to you?

PAN Not really, no. I know he really admires you but…

HAL But?

PAN I mean, you don't come up in conversation much. Which is kind of weird.

HAL Why?

PAN 'Cause he's a teenager. I mean, think about it, dude. When you were fourteen didn't you complain about your parents all the time?

HAL So he doesn't complain about me?

PAN Nope.

HAL Well, that's… good, I guess.

PAN I don't know. Complaining about someone can often be another way of saying you care about someone, you know? He complains about his mom.

HAL Yeah, so do I.

PAN See what I mean? *(beat)* I think he gets the impression you… don't really… you know… give a shit about him.

HAL He's hardly the first son to feel that. *(beat)* Does he ever talk about Allen?

PAN Oh, man, you don't want to go there—

HAL So the answer is yes, then?

PAN Well, Allen's around a lot more.

HAL Well, that's good, right?

PAN Yeah, sure, I mean, yeah, but... doesn't mean you couldn't be around more too, you know? I mean, you used to be. Way back in the day.

HAL Yes, well, things have changed.

PAN Things generally do. *(beat)* How is your sister, by the way?

HAL Good. It's her birthday.

PAN I remember.

> *HAL's phone beeps. He checks it.*

HAL I have to go.

PAN It's cool.

HAL Thanks for meeting me.

PAN Hope it helped. Sorry if I—

HAL You didn't do anything wrong.

PAN Listen, if you ever want to hang out during the lessons, you're more than welcome to. Like I said, he's a pretty fucking awesome player, for a kid—

HAL Yeah, thanks. Maybe I will.

PAN You should, dude. I think he'd really like that. *(beat)* Tell Serena I said hi, OK?

Scene Four: PM

> *HAL's office. He walks in to find ALLEN sitting at his desk, smiling broadly.*

ALLEN What's the story, Morning Glory?

HAL You're about the last person I want to see right now.

ALLEN I just watched the broadcast of you and Hercules. Priceless, Morning Glory. Fucking priceless.

HAL Yes, well, you're not the only one of us who knows how to lie with a smile.

ALLEN Oh, cut him some slack. He's a big dumb teddy bear but he means well.

HAL He tried to shoot me.

ALLEN He thought you were a terrorist.

HAL Why does that make it better?

ALLEN I don't know. What happens in Libya stays in Libya.

HAL Yes, well, apparently not. And to what do I owe this pleasure?

ALLEN Clara told me about this morning.

HAL Ah. So now you've come to lecture me.

ALLEN Maybe a little.

HAL I guess it's better than having you gloat.

ALLEN Well, I was planning to do that too.

HAL I would expect no less.

ALLEN You know, Sunshine, there is no reason why you and I can't be friends. I think I've always been a decent guy to you.

HAL When you're not using my face as a foothold to boost your upward ascent.

ALLEN It's a competitive world. A man has to do what a man has to do. You take it all way too personally and you shouldn't.

HAL It's my company, my wife, my kid—

ALLEN Oh, come on, you don't care about Sun Enterprises—

HAL I definitely care about my wife.

ALLEN She cares about you too, Glitter Boots, which is why what you said to her this morning was hurtful—

HAL Stop being a nice guy. It makes me feel like I can't trust you.

ALLEN Well, you can't—

HAL Thank you for conceding that.

ALLEN But it doesn't mean we can't be friends.

HAL Put that on a T-shirt for me, please.

ALLEN Aw come on, Morning Glory, why are you always such a downer?

HAL Being immune to your charm does not make me a downer.

ALLEN It does if you're me. It's also going to make it much harder on us both when I'm your boss.

HAL You're not my boss, Allen. Let's get that real clear right now.

ALLEN Well, hold on a moment—

HAL Hold this, fucker: you may be nominally in charge when Dad steps down, but when he dies I will own half of this company and my sister, Erin, who thinks you are a lump of crap and will do whatever I tell her, will own the other. I'll follow your lead because I'm expected to—but you will be asking, not telling me, where you want to go if you want to avoid a shitstorm to end all shitstorms. Get me?

ALLEN Nice, Sunshine. Keep that up and we'll get along much better.

HAL When did you stop being a nice little kid and start being such a dick?

ALLEN What?

HAL The person you are now is not the person you were.

ALLEN Who was I? Somebody you actually respected or somebody you just didn't have to deal with? Because I suspect you really mean that since you barely know me aside from the assumptions you make about me and you definitely didn't know me before I became a giant pain in your ass. My whole childhood, I was waitlisted while you had every door opened for you and it wasn't until I was sixteen that I realized it wasn't because of who you are but because of who your fucking father is. Your father, from whose ass all the sunshine in the world emanates. You know what my earliest memory of him is? When I was five and my mother went to him after her divorce and asked him to borrow some money to go back to college and your father said to her, point blank and in front of everybody, "I don't see your future as a worthwhile investment." Well, at least I'm proving *myself* a worthwhile investment. So tiptoe around me, Glitter Boots, because I am packing a huge fucking stick and I'm not afraid to use it.

CHLOE enters.

CHLOE There's a call waiting for you on line one, Hal.

ALLEN Why hello, Sunflower.

CHLOE Allen.

ALLEN Did you hear the news?

CHLOE No.

ALLEN Really? That's surprising. Everyone in the building has been talking—

CHLOE I don't listen to gossip. *(to HAL)* It's your son.

ALLEN Speaking of gloating.

HAL Get the hell out of my office, OK? *(to CHLOE)* Thank you.

CHLOE Do you need me to call security on this one?

ALLEN What are they going to do? Shine my shoes and fix me a drink?

CHLOE Excuse me. I think I hear my name being called on the other side of the building.

ALLEN Bye-bye, Blossom.

CHLOE exits.

She is so cute.

HAL She hates you.

ALLEN I know. I love it. She likes you though.

HAL We get along.

ALLEN No, she really likes you. You should think about that. You could definitely stand to get laid, Bright Eyes.

HAL She's my co-worker.

ALLEN Boundaries are for small people.

HAL Are we done here? I need to take a call.

ALLEN Oh, yeah, right. Your kid needs his chance to take a piss on you. Enjoy that.

HAL Go to hell.

ALLEN And a jolly good day to you, Morning Glory. One last arrow, if I may.

HAL Shoot.

ALLEN Peter. Burning Man. You should take him.

HAL The affront to my personal taste aside, I don't think it's safe or appropriate for a teenager.

ALLEN So, go with him and keep it safe, and you can figure out if it's appropriate together.

HAL Allen, when I want parenting advice, I'll look for it from people who actually have children.

ALLEN I'm fairly certain I've got a kid somewhere. *(beat)* Take your phone call, Sunshine.

ALLEN exits. HAL picks up the phone. PETER appears.

HAL Hello.

PETER Mom said you got fired.

HAL I didn't get fired.

PETER You didn't?

HAL I think you misunderstood her. Your grandpa is retiring.

PETER Yeah, but why is Allen replacing him?

HAL I don't know.

PETER You don't know?

HAL Because that's what your grandpa wants. And he's in charge.

PETER Even if he retires?

HAL Basically until he dies. More or less.

PETER Does that mean you want Grandpa dead?

HAL Only some of the time.

PETER That's fucked up.

HAL Watch your language please.

PETER You told me you wanted your dad dead and I'm supposed to watch my language?

HAL Jesus, kid, you have no sense of humor, do you? *(beat)* God, do you get that from me? *(beat)* Don't worry. I'm not going to lose my job. We're not going to be poor or anything.

PETER I don't care if we're poor.

HAL You don't?

PETER No.

HAL Well, I do. Your mother is a terrible housekeeper. *(beat)* Everything is going to be fine.

PETER You always say that.

HAL I always mean it. *(beat)* Peter?

PETER Yeah?

HAL You can go to Burning Man next year, OK?

> *PETER slams the phone down and vanishes. For a long moment, HAL sits in his office, feeling the silence of the late afternoon. He slowly puts his hands over his eyes.*

Three years, six months, nine days, one hour and eleven seconds.

Scene Five: Dusk

> *An elegant table set for two. HAL sits at it, hands still over his eyes. SERENA enters and sits opposite him. She reaches over and takes his hands in hers, lowering them.*

SERENA Someone's had a rough one, haven't they?

HAL Don't let me spoil your birthday.

SERENA Dearest, such a thing is simply impossible. You only make my life more rich.

HAL Even when I'm sad?

SERENA Sad is a color we can both wear well when we need to. And sometimes we need to. *(beat)* Why are you sad?

HAL Don't worry about it.

SERENA Don't be a bore. Tell me what's going on.

HAL Well, you've heard about Dad, right?

SERENA Mom mentioned something on the phone earlier. She didn't go into length.

HAL There isn't much length to go into. He's stepping down. He's appointing Allen as his replacement. The end.

SERENA I'm afraid I can't pretend that I'm deeply surprised he's snubbed you.

HAL I wouldn't have appointed me either, but it's the fact that he chose Allen—

SERENA Allen seems like a very natural choice, considering.

HAL Agreed, but I should think you don't need me to tell you why he's also about the last person I want to see succeed.

SERENA That's rather vindictive of you, isn't it?

HAL Well, how about succeed over me?

SERENA He hasn't succeeded over you. You yourself admit you would not have picked you as Father's replacement. And I agree. It would be a waste of your time and ability.

HAL As opposed to what?

SERENA What would you rather be doing?

HAL Endless list, really, but I doubt I'll get to any of it.

SERENA Perhaps this is a reminder to start.

HAL Yeah, well, Dad wants me to stay and assist Allen.

SERENA You don't always have to do what Dad tells you to.

HAL I don't.

SERENA What was your degree in again?

HAL You know it was in Classics.

SERENA And how does that lead to a career in finance?

HAL Serena.

SERENA Oh, that's right. It doesn't. You just went where Dad told you to.

HAL I went where I could make some money. So did you.

SERENA Yes, but I like my job.

HAL Yeah, well, I would hope so.

SERENA I wish I could say the same for you. And I'm not being a bitch there.

HAL I know you're not being a bitch. *(beat)* Dad sends his best wishes, by the way.

SERENA Tell him thank you, and that I hope he's well.

HAL It would be easier if you just spoke to him yourself.

SERENA Yes, but that's not something I want to do just yet.

HAL Serena, it's been ten years. To the day.

SERENA Not for another fifteen minutes. As you know.

HAL You can't keep blaming him for Adam.

SERENA We've been over this before.

HAL Well, it's my duty to bring it up again and again until you relent.

SERENA Is this more Daddy duty, or did you assign yourself the job?

HAL He's very sorry.

SERENA I know he's sorry. I've known he's sorry from the beginning. I suspect he was sorry the moment after he said what he said, perhaps even before the words were done leaving his mouth. That's never been the issue, though, how sorry he is or isn't. And my willingness to forgive is not the same as my willingness to engage. And though I have completely forgiven him I am still not yet willing to engage.

HAL He's already cut you out of the company. He'll cut you out of the will.

SERENA I rather hope he does. It's not like I need the money. And when at last I do engage with him I'd rather he knew it was because of everything but the prospect of either losing or gaining the money. I think it would be good for our father to know that not everybody in the world wants a piece of him. Some of us just want to be respected and loved for who we actually are and not who he wants us to be.

HAL The way you want him to be someone he's not?

SERENA Ah, see, that's the difference: you talk to Father, you work down the hall from him—

HAL Three floors below, actually, but what's your point?

SERENA I do not talk or interact with him but I still think, fundamentally, that he is a good man, capable of great benevolence. And I don't think you do.

HAL Are you saying I don't love Dad?

SERENA I'm not saying that at all.

HAL Because I do love Dad.

SERENA I never said you didn't.

HAL You said I didn't think he was a good person.

SERENA You can love someone who isn't a good person. People do it all the time.

HAL But don't you think we should love good people?

SERENA Yes. Absolutely. We should also love bad people too.

HAL Of course. I mean, once you get old enough… who else is there? *(beat)* Pan says hi, by the way.

SERENA Using my discomfort to mask your own?

HAL No, just changing the subject. I don't want to dwell on my unhappiness.

SERENA I don't want to dwell on mine.

A pause.

HAL Well then what are we going to talk about?

Scene Six: Night

A divey bar where you can still smoke. HAL is having a beer. CHLOE, enters, dressed for the evening. She sees him, walks over, and sits down.

HAL This is my eighth drink since five o'clock today. I actually did a shot, at work, with our mail clerk. Then three glasses of wine over dinner with my sister. Then two beers and a shot at the bar I went to before this. That's the kind of day I've had. And now I'm drunk in a bar on a weeknight. I've become *that* guy. *(beat)* Hello.

CHLOE Hello. Mind if I join you?

HAL I'm not going to be any fun. You're going to have to listen to me talk about how I hate my life.

CHLOE Could be worse.

HAL Could it?

CHLOE Always. But don't speculate in the negative. Just makes you more depressed.

HAL You're right. I wish I could learn how to learn how to be that way.

CHLOE So can I ask you something?

HAL Sure.

CHLOE Why do you still wear your wedding ring?

HAL I don't.

CHLOE Yes you do.

HAL Do I? I do, don't I?

CHLOE That's why I'm asking.

HAL It doesn't mean anything. I'm divorced, you know.

CHLOE I know. Everybody knows.

HAL I've been divorced for two years, four months, twenty-one days, five hours, nineteen minutes and forty seconds—and the ring stopped being significant a year before that.

CHLOE So why do you still wear the ring, if it don't mean a thing?

HAL Well, it means *something*—

CHLOE Nothing good apparently—

HAL Look, I barely ever remember I even have it on, so it's just as if I didn't wear it.

CHLOE I don't see the logic in that but… it's your hand.

HAL Yes it is. Thank you for conceding that my hand belongs to me, if nothing else.

CHLOE Nothing else?

HAL I am overdramatic sometimes. If you're going to sit here you need to be OK with that.

> *HAL's cell phone rings. He shuts the ringer off without checking it and puts the phone back in his pocket.*

Can I buy you anything?

CHLOE You think that's wise?

HAL About as wise as you sitting here in the first place.

CHLOE I'll take a whiskey sour.

HAL That's like a college girl drink.

CHLOE Well, I went to college.

HAL I know you went to college. I remember your resume.

CHLOE Oh? Did it say that I have a degree in whiskey sours?

HAL I pegged you as more of a Pinot Grigio girl to be honest.

CHLOE Is that a compliment?

HAL If you want it to be.

CHLOE Are you actually flirting with me? Like flirting back?

HAL I'm just being friendly. And drunk. *(beat)* I'm your co-worker. I'm your boss. It's a bad move.

CHLOE Bad moves can be fun.

HAL When you're young.

CHLOE You are not old.

HAL Well, in that case, I think you're beautiful. Or is this a bad time to admit that?

CHLOE There is rarely a bad time to admit that. And we're clearly pushing boundaries here.

HAL Are we?

CHLOE Don't play dumb.

HAL You don't find that cute?

CHLOE Not particularly.

HAL I could play vulgar and tell you that I'm sporting a massive erection right now.

CHLOE Wow. From zero to sixty, huh?

HAL Believe me, I'm just as surprised I said it as you are. I'm not normally like this. Not since the time of the ring.

CHLOE I like that. It reminds me of *The Lord of the Rings*.

HAL You like *The Lord of the Rings*?

CHLOE I like a lot of things. But yeah, I like *The Lord of the Rings*.

HAL Does that mean you're into hobbits?

CHLOE I'd say I'm more into elves.

HAL Why?

CHLOE I don't know. They speak in poetry. They love each other forever. They glow in the dark.

HAL I can do all those things.

CHLOE Really?

HAL My mistress' eyes are nothing like the sun;
Coral is far more red than her lips' red;
If snow be white, why then her breasts are dun;
If hairs be wires, black wires grow on her head.
I have seen roses damasked, red and white,
But no such roses see I in her cheeks;
And in some perfumes is there more delight
Than in the breath that from my mistress reeks.
I love to hear her speak, yet well I know
That music hath a far more pleasing sound;
I grant I never saw a goddess go;
My mistress, when she walks, treads on the ground.
And yet, by heaven, I think my love as rare
As any she belied with false compare.

A long moment. She smiles at him.

CHLOE Your day is getting better, isn't it?

HAL Yes, actually. How about you?

She smiles. HAL waits.

Scene Seven: The Witching Hour

HYPERION's office. Late in the evening. HYPERION sits at his desk, writing out his will. ALLEN enters.

ALLEN You're here late.

HYPERION And you're in my office. Planning to come try out my chair?

ALLEN Maybe.

HYPERION Give it a few weeks, boy. Let me clean out my desk first, at least.

ALLEN You're very funny.

HYPERION I'm not joking. Neither were you.

ALLEN Oh come on, Uncle.

HYPERION Allen, we both know you have better places to be on a Thursday night. I do.

ALLEN So why are you here?

HYPERION Just finishing up some paperwork.

ALLEN Anything I should know about?

HYPERION Yes.

ALLEN Interesting.

HYPERION Frustrating, I'd imagine.

ALLEN What is?

HYPERION The part where you'll have to wait to find out. You've already been appointed my successor, Allen. You were the third person I told after my wife and my son. That will be the last favor you receive from me any time soon.

ALLEN Oh calm down. I know my place, Uncle.

HYPERION If that were true I'd never have hired you in the first place.

ALLEN Not even for the mailroom?

HYPERION I don't hire for the mailroom, Allen. And I don't tell the people who run the mailroom who to hire. Frankly, I don't know what it takes to be a good mailroom clerk but I'm guessing you don't have the skills.

ALLEN Not regretting your choice, are you?

HYPERION I don't regret anything. Ever.

ALLEN Well, what's the point?

HYPERION Exactly.

ALLEN But then, what's the problem?

HYPERION There isn't a problem. Except the one where you're in my office talking to me, and I have work I want to finish. Why don't you go find my son's wife and fuck her? Or do whatever else it is you do when the grown-ups aren't watching.

ALLEN Ouch. You are regretting your decision, aren't you? What happened? Did Hal cry?

HYPERION Hal reacted exactly the way I expected him to.

ALLEN None of us ever surprise you, do we?

HYPERION Rarely.

ALLEN You really have mastered the friendly kick to the groin, haven't you?

HYPERION Worried you won't be able to live up to my standard?

ALLEN Just showing my teacher some respect. While I still have to. *(beat)* I'm taking tomorrow off. I'll catch you next week, Your Highness. Assuming you're in on Monday.

HYPERION I'm always in on Monday. You'll have to be too, once you take over.

ALLEN I don't know. I plan to take more advantage of our liberal vacation policy than you do.

HYPERION We'll see about that. *(beat)* Have a good evening, Allen. Tell your mother that I said hello when you let her know the good news.

ALLEN I already called.

HYPERION Oh? And what did she say?

ALLEN That you're still an asshole.

HYPERION Well then she must be real proud of you.

ALLEN All the best people are.

HYPERION Trouble is, boy, nobody can ever quite agree who the best people are.

Scene Eight: Pre-Dawn

> *HAL's apartment. A cool, simply decorated bedroom. HAL stands at a window, smoking a cigarette, mostly naked, glancing at his cell phone. The light broadens to reveal CHLOE sitting on the bed, watching him.*

CHLOE Is it strange that I find smokers sexy? I mean, still? Knowing everything that we know about smoking?

HAL Perhaps you're in love with danger.

CHLOE Maybe.

HAL I try not to smoke very often. But it's hard because I really love it.

CHLOE Bad habits are usually habits because we enjoy them.

HAL What are yours?

CHLOE I'm a slut. Clearly.

HAL Well... that's not so bad. Or at least... I don't mind.

CHLOE That's a pretty unprofessional thing to say.

HAL It's been a pretty unprofessional evening.

HAL tosses his cell phone aside. A long moment.

As long as it's not because you felt sorry for me I'm fine with it.

CHLOE Why would I feel sorry for you?

HAL I don't know. I just assume everybody does.

CHLOE Well, I believe in honesty and I didn't feel sorry for you. But I did guess you needed a friend. Someone a little less sisterly and maybe a bit more…

HAL Slutty?

CHLOE Sure. Anyway, I'll admit it was a bit calculated.

HAL Well, your guess was good.

CHLOE Considering I'm your statistics analyst I should hope my guess was good.

HAL I thought you were my assistant.

CHLOE No, I just hang around your office making myself indispensible because I like you. *(beat)* The rules are different at night. Why shouldn't people be?

HAL What?

CHLOE Something my stepmother says.

HAL Your parents aren't together?

CHLOE To put it lightly. *(beat)* You miss your wife, don't you?

HAL Sure. When we're not at each other's throats.

CHLOE She's always seemed nice.

HAL She's a lovely woman. Very different from… well, my life. She thinks I'm an enormous spoiled brat and she's right, but the real divide between us, if you will, is that I divorced her, and then she basically replaced me—and I'd like to think I'm irreplaceable.

CHLOE People will do what they have to do to fill a hole—in themselves, or in their lives.

HAL Yeah, but what if the same person in your life seemed to always be the person people chose to fill their holes? What if, actually, you felt like you were perpetually in competition with that person? Someone who was younger and better-looking and faster—

CHLOE And named Allen?

HAL Exactly. *(beat)* Prior to working for me, did you know who I was?

CHLOE Of course. I work in finance and you're a billionaire's son.

HAL Yes, but did you know what I look like? Did you know it was me when we first talked?

CHLOE I would have talked to you regardless.

HAL That's not what I asked you.

CHLOE No, I didn't know it was you.

HAL But if I was Allen, would you have recognized me?

CHLOE Well, yeah, of course—

HAL Why?

CHLOE Well, he's... very prominent.

HAL He is, isn't he?

CHLOE He's done a lot for someone his age.

HAL That statement is like nails on a chalkboard to me.

CHLOE He used to front a band I was into.

HAL Before he became the youngest district supervisor in San Francisco history?

CHLOE Well, he wasn't like... amazing at it.

HAL Doesn't matter. He still got a clinic named after him.

CHLOE He raised a lot of money for that clinic.

HAL Half that money came from my ex-wife. Which means it came from me.

CHLOE If you wanted a clinic named after you, you should have opened one.

HAL I opened a fucking hospital. The Adam Ward at Davies Campus is named for my sister's dead boyfriend. But if you access the financial records you'll note there is only one principal benefactor. My sister is a doctor and her boyfriend, who my father kicked out of her birthday party, died in a coma after he wrecked his car trying to drive home drunk. So I built her a trauma ward and we named it after him.

CHLOE That's incredibly generous of you.

HAL Please, it couldn't be more selfish. I love Serena and I did it for her because it's what she wanted because she is a good person, but if drinking the blood of babies would have made her happy, believe you me I would have been on the phone with a Romanian orphanage in a heartbeat.

CHLOE I don't think acting selfishly and acting for the greater good are mutually exclusive.

HAL That's because you are young and beautiful and you have not yet passed the point where you realize you are never going to leave your mark on this world.

CHLOE And you have?

A moment. He takes a breath.

HAL We were in Libya because I was on a vacation with my family—my ex-wife, my son, and Allen. We were touring the countries of the Mediterranean in an attempt to bond as a unit and my wife—my ex-wife—in her great wisdom and because she thought he was going to propose—booked a desert camel ride for myself and Allen, hoping we could use the time to bury the hatchet or… something. So here we are, Allen, myself, the guide, an Australian couple whose names I can't remember and, surprise of surprises, Hercules Olympus, world famous

Olympus Airlines heir and big-game hunter, never leaves home without a gun but usually neglects to pack his brain. Here we are, on camels, in the fucking Libyan desert and dear God is it hot and Hercules keeps looking at me funny from the outset because he knows he's seen me somewhere before and he knows he's supposed to know who I am but he can't place how or why. And we stop for lunch in the ruins of a Roman temple that's ostensibly for Sol, the Sun, but it's Roman and why the fuck do you need to worship the sun in the desert so it's essentially just about being Roman, and Allen chooses this moment to take me aside and try to bond by asking me, "So, I think your ex is hoping that I'm going to propose to her, and the truth is, dude, I don't think I'm ready for marriage—how do I let her know that without killing a good thing, you know?" And I swallow my first-ever urge to punch another man and say, "Boy. You know… I'm gonna have a smoke. Excuse me." And I go over to the far side of the temple, away from everyone else—or so I think—and there is our guide, also grabbing a minute alone and we light up together and chat a bit in Greek—

CHLOE You speak Greek?

HAL I do. And I ask the guide, "Why do you think someone would build a temple to the sun in the desert?" And he says to me, "Sol was not just the god of the sun. He was the god of truth, and the protector of oaths. From his place in the sky he could see all things—and his light dispelled fear and sorrow. So the other gods made him the watchman of honor, someone of great value if you're hoping to survive in a desert." That's when the bullet goes whizzing past my head and into the guide's shoulder because Hercules had just decided he recognized me from a file of known airline terrorists and, because he's a total dumbass, thinks the Greek we're speaking is actually Arabic. The worst part? Before he can get a second shot off, Allen of all fucking people tackles him. So, on top of everything else, I probably owe that golden turd my life.

CHLOE Oh wow.

HAL Yeah, so, there you go. But to me, the most humiliating part is that here's a guy who is a peer of mine, my own generation, my extremely narrow and exclusive echelon of society, whose parents are friends with mine, who owns twelve percent of our stock, who calls my office all the time and who has met me at numerous conventions and summits. No, we aren't friends or even business associates, but still, I knew who the fuck he was despite his ridiculous hat-and-sunglasses routine and bullshit alias he was traveling under and so he sure as shit should have known who I was since I introduced myself as Hal Hyperion.

CHLOE Did he recognize Allen?

HAL Allen had a beard at the time and was going by the name of Samuel Clemens.

CHLOE And that worked for him?

HAL Again, Hercules is not exactly bright, and we were in Libya.

CHLOE Well, look at it this way: do you remember the Australian couple's names?

HAL That's different. They were just travelers. They weren't important people.

CHLOE I bet they don't think they're unimportant—

HAL You know what I mean. They're not important the way—

CHLOE You are?

HAL The way I'm supposed to be.

CHLOE According to who?

> *HAL's cell phone goes off.*

HAL Shit, I thought I'd turned that off. *(retrieves the phone)* Oh fuck. *(answering the phone)* Clara, hi.

> *CLARA appears in her own space.*

CLARA Why have you not been answering your phone?

HAL I've been—it's none of your business.

CLARA I have called you five times. How did it not occur to you that perhaps this was an emergency?

HAL I haven't exactly been staring at my phone all night.

CLARA Are you home?

HAL Yes.

CLARA Allen is on his way over to get you. Peter is missing.

HAL What?

CLARA Your son is gone and you are coming to find him. Get dressed.

HAL Wait, Clara—

CLARA He's taken your company car.

HAL What?

CLARA Pan is with him.

HAL Oh shit.

CLARA They're going to Burning Man and yes it is your fault this has happened and so you can come help fix it. Allen will be there soon.

> *CLARA hangs up the phone and vanishes. Almost immediately his phone rings again. He answers without looking at it.*

HAL I'm getting ready, OK?

> *SERENA appears.*

SERENA Hal. It's Serena.

HAL I'm sorry, I thought you were—

SERENA Dad's in the hospital.

HAL What?

SERENA He's here at the ward. He had a heart attack.

HAL Is he... is he OK?

SERENA I don't know. He's family and so I can't treat him. He's not conscious. Can you come?

HAL I... of course, but... there's... something else going on.

SERENA What?

HAL Peter has gone missing.

SERENA What?

HAL It's a long story. Look, I need to deal with that first but I will get there as soon—

SERENA I'll call Erin. And Mom. Just get here as soon as you can, OK?

HAL I promise I will do my best. Are you going to be there?

> *SERENA hangs up the phone without answering and vanishes. ALLEN walks in.*

ALLEN Hey Bright Eyes, hope you're awake. I borrowed Clara's emergency key 'cause we have an emergency on our hands. *(sees CHLOE)* Well hello, Nurse. *(to HAL)* No wonder Clara couldn't reach you! *(to CHLOE)* Dandelion, does this means we can finally tell Hal about our little affair? *(to HAL)* Surprise!

> *HAL walks over to ALLEN and punches him in the face.*

Interlude: Yesterday

> *PETER stands in a spotlight, strumming a guitar. The more worked up he gets, the more he strums.*

PETER "Who is my father?" This was an essay question we were given in the eighth grade—which was like over a year ago for me. It was part of a contest that we all had to participate in because my school believes in, amongst other things, fostering a "healthy sense of competition" which basically translates to everyone always trying to show everyone else how fucking smart they are, like anyone gives a shit. My father says that I'll be grateful for the experience when I'm older, which is the quote I use to start my essay so joke's on you, Dad. The rest of the essay is sort of depressing, I guess. I mean, I started it out trying to be all like, "So my dad is an asshole," but it just kind of devolves into how pathetic he is. Like how he's still hung up on my mom even though he was never fucking around and like, come on, I'm gonna be fifteen in a few months and even I know you're not supposed to moon over people who aren't into you. Like I asked this girl to winter formal last year and she said yes and we made out a bit there and then we sort of went on dates and held hands for a while and I liked her and then right after spring break she tells me she kissed some guy she met on her trip to Nantucket and now they write e-mails to each other every day and she wants to lose her virginity to him, not to me, and fine whatever I went and played guitar in my room all that weekend and I'm fucking over it. And my dad says it's not the same when you're older, people don't feel so disposable, and I was like, "Well, if that's the case, Dad, why the fuck weren't you around more until Mom replaced you with Allen?" And he didn't answer me. He just looked at me for a long time and then he apologized—which is what he's always doing. My dad is perpetually sorry. I put that in my fucking essay too. I wrote, "My father is always sorry for something, and everything I do makes him sad and everything he does makes me sick and I pray every night to a god I don't believe in that I will not end up like him." I spent two paragraphs on how he's such a weakling and one paragraph on how he never knows the right thing to say to me. A full fifteen hundred and thirty-six words went into how all any son wants is a titan and instead what I got was just some guy who, OK, fine, he's trying, but mostly he's just fucking it all up and it's like he has no idea what he's doing but I'm sure I'll really fucking be grateful for it when I'm older. And the worst part is that I won that contest. I won that fucking contest and I had to read the essay aloud in front of my whole goddamn school and my dad was there and afterwards he congratulated me. I mean, seriously? Seriously? Don't you care that I think you're totally… fucking… lame? "I thought you made me look human, son," he said to me. Right. Like that's a fucking good thing? I swear to Christ I am never having kids—never.

He begins to play in earnest. Blackout.

End of Act One.

Act Two: Lunar Eclipse

Entr'acte: After

SERENA stands in her own spotlight, drinking a cup of coffee.

SERENA "Who is my brother?" Erin said to me as we waited in the airport terminal in Fort-de-France for Hal to arrive. She was joking, of course, alluding to the fact that she hadn't seen either of us for five years, but within the joke was the unspoken fear that she wouldn't recognize him. She hadn't recognized me. But then, I'd definitely changed. Sad things had happened, and too many nights working late. Erin was the same, rosy and unflappably cheerful, and Hal was too—she recognized him right away when he arrived—still golden, still good. It was a nice reunion. There were happy tears. Erin had allowed herself the luxury of a destination wedding and since Father wouldn't approve of her marrying a foreign man of small financial means and twice her age, he wasn't in attendance—though he paid for everything. Thus we were allowed the luxury of a week together without our parents. It is still one of the best experiences of my adult life. Peter was nine then and all he wanted to do was swim. I remember Clara, radiant in a sarong, telling me he'd never been to a warm sea before, and the two of us watching Hal carrying him above the turquoise waves, sometimes in his arms, sometimes on his shoulders. There was a lot of laughter. The nights were warm and dark, moonless it seemed, and we would dance as a family, drink too much, and have conversations that meandered and echoed. On the last night I lost myself so completely I went to bed with the son of a family friend—barely out of his teens then. The next morning, quietly packing, watching the sun creep across him where he still slept, I thought about Adam for the first time since I'd landed on the island. When the boy on my bed opened his eyes they smiled even though he didn't. "Where are you going?" he asked me. My bag over my shoulder, I responded, "Home." And then I slunk out the door like I was retreating. Hal drove me to the airport. He and the others were staying on a few days longer. We didn't speak the whole way, but he could tell something was wrong. He held my hand in his right one while he drove with the left, and I could feel the hug he gave me at the terminal linger in the muscles of my arms all the way back to San Francisco.

Scene One: Dawn

> *The car has stalled on the side of the highway. PAN and PETER are sitting in it trying to figure out what to do.*

PAN Shit. Your dad is never gonna trust me again.

PETER It's not your fault we got lost.

PAN Actually... yes it is. I should have told you I've never driven there before.

PETER What?

PAN I mean, usually, other people have driven. And by usually I mean every single time.

PETER Yeah, but don't you pay attention?

PAN I've…never… actually… been sober.

PETER Oh. Well, it's not your fault the car died.

PAN Actually it… kind of is.

PETER How?

PAN Well… OK. Don't get angry at me, but… we're out of gas.

PETER What?

PAN I know.

PETER When we passed that last gas station I asked you—

PAN I realize now I was looking at the wrong dial on the dashboard. Your dad's car is really complicated. I have no idea what half of these buttons do. Goddamn it, why do you have to be so fucking rich?

PETER What?

PAN Sorry. I'm sorry. That's not your fault, I know. I'm just freaking out.

PETER I can't believe this is happening.

PAN Yeah, I know, it's totally lame, but, whatever, we can just suck it up and call your dad—

PETER We can't call him.

PAN Why?

PETER Because he's like… I mean… you know.

PAN Oh shit.

PETER Don't be angry with me!

PAN You didn't get his fucking permission, did you?

PETER Hey, I didn't get angry at you—

PAN Did you get his permission?

PETER Not… exactly.

PAN Oh, fucking A, Peter…

PETER Look, what's worse? That I lied to you or that you didn't even bother to check if I was telling the truth.

PAN I didn't bother because I trusted you.

PETER Pan, please, I'm fourteen. That was clearly a mistake on your part. And hello, we had to go "borrow" his car in the middle of the night? How does that make any sense?

PAN Dude, I am very trusting and I am not like an analytical person—

PETER You play the guitar!

PAN There's a reason I don't play the fucking piano! Your parents could have me arrested for kidnapping you.

PETER Oh please. I'll just tell them—

PAN It doesn't matter what you tell them. I took you across state lines without their knowing. Do you have any idea what that looks like to other people?

PETER My parents aren't going to press charges, even if you do get arrested.

PAN That makes me feel so much better. *(beat)* I need to take a walk.

PETER We're in the middle of nowhere.

PAN I know. But I have a ton of drugs in my bag and I need to dump them somewhere before a highway patrolman notices us.

PETER Will they?

PAN Probably. I don't know. We haven't been on an actual highway for a long time. Oh God, this is all way too *The Hills Have Eyes* for me to deal with.

PETER We can use my cell phone to call Triple A or something.

PAN What are we going to tell them? We don't know where we are.

PETER I saw a sign for an Indian reservation a few miles back.

A light bulb goes off in PAN's head.

PAN How many miles?

PETER I don't know. Ten?

PAN That's walkable. Especially now, before it gets too hot.

PETER Well, and once we told Triple A where we were in proximity to the sign—

PAN Oh, fuck that. We'll find help much faster at the reservation. I have a brick of weed in my bag.

PETER Isn't that drug trafficking?

PAN In America.

PETER We're in America.

PAN No, we're on an Indian reservation. Grab your hat and some sunblock, kiddo. We're gonna find us a casino.

Scene Two: AM

ALLEN's car. CLARA is driving. ALLEN sits next to her, holding an ice pack to his face. HAL sits in the back, holding an ice pack on his right hand.

ALLEN Well… you sure are silent this morning, aren't you, Glitter Boots?

HAL I'm hung over.

ALLEN Clearly.

HAL I have been up for twenty-seven hours and thirty-two minutes so back the fuck off. *(beat)* I wish you had let me shower before we left.

ALLEN Me too, but we were in a hurry, and what with getting your friend on her way and your vicious attack on me—oh, did I mention I've fucked her?

HAL Yes. Three times now.

ALLEN Well, I'm having a hard time getting over it.

HAL Funny. I'm not.

ALLEN Yes, well, you're used to me sleeping with everyone you know. Whereas I am finding being on the reverse side of the situation a unique new experience. *(beat)* Does she still bite her inner arms when she comes?

HAL What?

ALLEN She used to do this thing when she came, if she was on her back, where she would bite her inner arms. It was kind of hot. Though it also sort of made her look like a junkie.

HAL Well, she doesn't do that any more.

ALLEN Maybe she didn't come with you.

HAL I'm pretty certain she did.

ALLEN How do you know? I mean, if she didn't do her arm-biting thing?

HAL How do you know that really means she came? How do you know that's not just an act?

ALLEN Because I asked her.

HAL And women never lie?

ALLEN I can tell when women are lying to me. Plus there was no need. I mean, why lie about if you've had an orgasm?

HAL Because you want to make someone feel like a good lover.

ALLEN Well, and again, with me, there's no need.

HAL I don't think anybody is surprised by your incredible overconfidence, Allen.

ALLEN It's not overconfidence, Hal. It's just being polite. I know I'm a good lover because I'm an attentive lover.

HAL I'm not inattentive myself.

ALLEN You're certainly not the most attentive parent, are you?

HAL Do you want to clarify the connection between these two completely—

ALLEN We're in the car chasing down your kid. I don't think we need any other clarification.

HAL You know what, bucko? He vanished on your watch—

ALLEN Well hold on Bright Eyes, who is the one who never takes his turn being the good parent? Oh, and who hooked him up with that dumbass gutter-rat musician in the first place?

HAL You know why I hired Pan to be Peter's music teacher?

ALLEN Because he's your friend's son and you're a douche that way?

HAL No. Because I know you think he's a bad musician.

ALLEN I wouldn't say he's bad, I'd just say he's rustic and mediocre.

HAL Either way, he's not you.

ALLEN And believe me, it's reflected in the playing—

HAL Just because you don't think he's a good musician doesn't mean he isn't—

ALLEN No, but that's what you're banking on as the way to ruffle my feathers, isn't it? The fact that I look down on him.

HAL Is there anybody you don't look down on?

ALLEN I have a high standard and I expect people to live up to that—

HAL Oh please, you are just another fucking snob—

ALLEN And you think you're not?

HAL I know I'm a snob! I embrace that. Which at least makes me consistent. Whereas you, you sycophantic sniveling fountain of bullshit, you change your tune to whoever you can brown-nose the hardest into getting you wherever you're going next—

ALLEN Because I play a good game of cards doesn't make me—

HAL You have as much sincerity as a Facebook status update and what's more, you are not just an opportunistic brown-noser you are a condescending opportunistic brown-noser. You treat people like shit and you are so completely oblivious to everyone else—

ALLEN Right and you're this really nice guy who the whole world craps on—

HAL Well at least, as the principal anus, it's nice to hear you admit it—

CLARA WHO ARE YOU? WHO THE FUCK ARE YOU? BOTH OF YOU SHUT THE FUCK UP OR I WILL FUCKING KILL YOU WITH MY FUCKING BARE HANDS AND BURY YOUR FUCKING BODIES ON THE SIDE OF THE FUCKING ROAD!!! Jesus Christ do either of you know what it's like to sit in the same room with one of you? It's like having dentistry done on my skull only I would rather listen to my impacted wisdom teeth be broken in my mouth over and over again than sit through another minute of listening to the two of you piss in each other's faces! I get that you don't like each other. I get that you think you are in competition with one another. But the fact of the fucking situation is this, you phenomenal pair of assholes: I do not rely on either of you to be a role model for Peter because I am still praying that he will grow up to be the kind of guy who knows better than to sit in a car and talk about some woman they have both fucked, in front of another woman they have both fucked, who by the way has faked orgasms with both of them and for the exact same reason—namely to get them to shut the fuck up—something I wish they would fucking do right now BECAUSE I AM JUST ABOUT HITTING THE LIMIT OF BEING ABLE TO STAND THE SOUND OF THEM BREATHING LET ALONE TALKING. SO JUST SHUT UP! SHUT UP! SHUT THE FUCK UP! SHUT UP! PLEASE SHUT UP!!!!

A long pause.

I mean, does it even occur to you two that there are people out there who don't have money to eat? They don't have money to eat, they can't afford to send their kids to college, they will never be able to retire, they might not have health care and the biggest problem the two of you have is whose dick makes a better sundial.

Another long pause.

ALLEN You don't fake all of your orgasms, do you?

CLARA No, of course I don't.

HAL Oh my God, I can't believe you just asked that.

ALLEN What about with him?

HAL You fucking turd!

ALLEN Don't you want to know?

HAL Not because you fucking asked, you douchebag! Why do you insist on being like this?

CLARA Because he's intimidated by you, Hal, obviously.

HAL What?

ALLEN What?

CLARA Look, no matter where we are now Allen knows I loved you first and that's always going to be the case, just like he knows you're really Peter's father and you'll be the next owner of Sun Enterprises—

HAL Yeah, and it's so great always being the guy behind the scenes—

CLARA What is this? The seventh grade? Why do you care so much about a popularity contest?

HAL Because that's all there is. That's all modern life is and anyone who says anything different is lying because they either can't win it or they don't want to feel bad about winning it. And if you think I'm being overdramatic here ask your fucking boyfriend if I'm right because he's a textbook example of someone who is winning it and doesn't give a fuck about how he's getting the votes.

ALLEN Well, Lite-Brite, like I said: I play to win. I don't think you can blame me for that. Or maybe you can, but maybe you should put that energy into winning yourself.

CLARA And what do you win, Allen? Me?

ALLEN Honey… no. Let's not… I mean, come on, it's not like that, there's no prize—

HAL There isn't?

ALLEN It's a way of looking at your life.

HAL And how your life is looked at.

ALLEN If you think of yourself as being a loser you will be looked at as a loser.

HAL I don't think of myself as a loser.

ALLEN Don't you?

HAL No. But I can tell you think I am one.

ALLEN I actually do, or you just need me to?

HAL You aren't exactly hard to read.

ALLEN I am also not as simple as you think.

HAL Neither am I.

CLARA Good. Let's call it a draw. Please.

> *Another long moment.*

ALLEN But my dick is bigger.

CLARA YOU ARE BOTH SIX AND A HALF INCHES NOW SHUT THE FUCK UP!!!

Scene Three: Noon

A hospital. HYPERION lies unconscious in a hospital bed. SERENA sits in a chair, watching him. CHLOE enters, knocking on the door. She brings flowers.

CHLOE Is it OK if I come in?

SERENA Hello?

CHLOE You must be the sister. Dr. Hyperion, yes?

SERENA Yes. Can I help you?

CHLOE Chloe Orchamus. I work for your father.

SERENA Oh, you're my brother's assistant, aren't you?

CHLOE No, but… I know why you would think that.

SERENA You've bought my birthday gift for the last three years.

CHLOE That's me. *(beat)* I heard the… terrible news. Please accept my gift for your father and my hopes for a speedy recovery.

SERENA *(takes the flowers)* Thank you.

CHLOE Has he come out of the, um…

SERENA Coma. It's officially a coma at this point. And no.

CHLOE Ah. And do they expect him to? I'm sorry, that must seem terribly rude—

SERENA It's a perfectly natural question. It could go either way.

CHLOE Such a shame. Such a brilliant man, such a brilliant life. Not much older than my dad. Not that this is about me, of course.

SERENA I have observed that it is a fairly normal reaction to think of oneself when confronted with someone who is dying.

CHLOE So you think he's dying?

SERENA I think his chances of a full recovery are quite slim.

CHLOE And that's your professional opinion?

SERENA Yes. Technically, I'm not supposed to have one, being his family.

CHLOE Oh right. Of course. I'm sorry. Again.

SERENA Don't be. I'm no more prepared to deal with this than you are.

CHLOE Who is? I mean, your father had a heart attack and that's always very sudden but even when someone does die slowly, you think it's not a surprise? Even when someone is old or lives an unhealthy lifestyle, no one ever really sees it coming. Especially not them. You think we're not prepared? I can only imagine how shocked your father would be to know this was happening to him. If you're prepared to die I kind of question if you're actually living your life. Personally, I think we fill our days because when they feel full we forget the end is always sneaking up on you, slipping in from behind to catch you unawares… which is scary, but it beats Death staring you in the face, counting down the minutes until… you know. Time's up. I remember your father once told me, "The trick to life isn't so much taking time to stop and smell the roses—roses are covered in thorns and bees and who knows what else, just waiting to get you—no, the trick to life is being grateful that the roses are pretty and more or less hide all that shit. So smell the roses, pussycat, but don't get too close." That's probably the best advice I've ever gotten.

A pause.

SERENA What… exactly… do you do for my father?

CHLOE I'm a statistical analyst. It's more philosophical than you'd think. Anyway, I won't take up any more of your time to be with him again. It was nice to finally meet you. Sorry it wasn't under better circumstances.

SERENA Thank you for the flowers. If he wakes up I'll let him know who they came from.

CHLOE Thank you. Get some rest yourself.

SERENA I will. Goodbye.

CHLOE Goodbye.

CHLOE leaves.

HYPERION Serena?

SERENA You're awake.

HYPERION Would you prefer I wasn't?

SERENA That is a cruel thing to say and you know it.

HYPERION I was just asking. There were no cruel intentions. Where is your mother?

SERENA She's gone to pick up Erin from the airport.

HYPERION Erin's coming? And you're talking to me. I *must* be dying. *(beat)* Well. Could be worse. Could be raining.

SERENA You're in the Adam Ward.

HYPERION Am I? It's nice. Are you my doctor?

SERENA No. Would you like me to get him?

HYPERION No. *(beat)* It's nice to hear your voice again.

SERENA Is it?

HYPERION Yes. Can I say that?

SERENA You can say whatever you want.

HYPERION I always say whatever I want. *(beat)* Throw those flowers away.

SERENA They're pretty.

HYPERION I detest cut flowers. They look like they belong on a grave.

SERENA Maybe we'll put them on yours.

HYPERION We can afford fresh ones when the time comes, thank you very much. *(beat)* So how have you been, Little Girl?

SERENA I'm fine. I'm sure you've heard plenty from the others.

HYPERION Yes. But I want to hear it from you.

SERENA I'm fine.

HYPERION Glad to hear it. Up until yesterday, I was fine as well. Better than fine. But then I did the thing I wasn't supposed to do, and it got me.

SERENA What got you?

HYPERION The world got me. I was never supposed to give up my empire.

SERENA You mean announce your retirement?

HYPERION Yes. I always knew the moment I did, I would lose everything.

SERENA That's ridiculous. You didn't have a heart attack because you decided to retire.

HYPERION I didn't?

SERENA No.

HYPERION How do you know?

SERENA There's just no evidence that's how it works.

HYPERION It seems to me there's plenty of evidence. But you're the doctor.

SERENA Well, I'm not a cardiologist.

HYPERION That's fine, Little Girl. Anything you say. Where is your brother?

SERENA He and Clara and Allen are heading to Nevada. They left very early this morning.

HYPERION Nevada?

SERENA Peter has gone missing. They have a fairly good hunch he's on his way there so…

HYPERION Is he going to Las Vegas?

SERENA He's going to Burning Man.

HYPERION When I was young, and we wanted to get into trouble, we would go to Las Vegas. What is Burning Man?

SERENA Um… I don't know, it's… this sort of art festival, I suppose. Like an art festival crossed with a party in the desert.

HYPERION It sounds awful.

SERENA Yeah, I don't think you'd like it, but Peter wanted to go and, so, I guess he stole Hal's company car.

HYPERION That's hysterical. I like Peter.

SERENA Yeah, he's a good kid.

HYPERION He reminds me of…

Beat. He doesn't finish the thought.

SERENA You know, Adam went to Burning Man once. When he was twenty-one. He liked it. He said he learned a lot. About how the world was bigger than him. I guess that's why I've never felt a need to go. I've always felt like I wouldn't get very much out of it all. I already know the world is so much bigger than me.

HYPERION Well, you've always been a little on the outside of it.

SERENA Yes, I suppose that's true.

HYPERION You miss Adam a lot, don't you?

SERENA Oh, I'd prefer not to talk about him, thank you.

HYPERION I don't believe you.

SERENA I don't care. *(beat)* I'm not ready.

HYPERION There isn't much time left to be ready… is there?

They sit for a long moment, looking at one another.

SERENA Perhaps you should have thought of that before now.

Scene Four: Afternoon

A gas station. CLARA is sitting on the curb. HAL enters and hands her some coffee.

HAL I got you some coffee. Allen is inside trying to find out if anyone's seen the kids.

CLARA According to the surveillance cameras, they left just after midnight. It doesn't take that long to drive to Burning Man. They're probably already there.

HAL If they were I think we would have heard by now.

CLARA How? I read on the website that cell phones don't work out there.

HAL There's a satellite phone in the car. Peter wouldn't want us to worry. Especially if he thought he was already safely out of reach.

CLARA Oh, he knows we'll come after him. He's not stupid. That's why he did this.

HAL Well, then, maybe you're right and they are already there.

CLARA I prefer that to the alternative.

HAL Which is?

CLARA That they're dead in a car wreck somewhere. That they've been arrested. That they've been kidnapped by hitch-hiking felons. Take your pick. Come up with something fun and terrifying of your own invention.

HAL Don't speculate in the negative. Think about something else.

CLARA Like what?

HAL Like what we're going to do when we find them. Because we will find them. And then we'll punish them.

CLARA Pan's not our kid to punish.

HAL Well, we employ him.

CLARA *You* employ him. You ready to fire him?

HAL Don't you think I should?

CLARA I think it's a fantastic way to catapult Peter into full-scale rebellion.

HAL And we're not already there?

CLARA You don't teach a kid to be responsible by denying him artistic expression.

HAL Not according to my dad.

CLARA Yes, and look how happy *you* are, Hal.

HAL I'm happy enough.

CLARA If you say so.

HAL Oh fuck you, Clara. *(beat)* We could have raised him on a classics professor's salary.

CLARA If you could have found a job.

HAL Yeah, OK, fine, that was harder than I thought it was going to be. I'm sorry that my lack of distinctive brilliance in the field of my choice forced me to end up working for my parents so I could support you and our son.

CLARA You weren't undistinguished in anything but ambition, Hal. You could have looked harder than you did. You could have taken something else. You didn't have to say yes when your father called.

HAL I was afraid to say no.

CLARA Things weren't that desperate.

HAL *I* was that desperate. I thought I was fucking up my life and your life and Peter's life and it was a good solution at the time and before you get on your high horse about it I want you to remember that the first time I wanted to quit Sun Enterprises, *you* said, "Most men would kill for your job."

CLARA Most men would.

HAL Including your boyfriend.

CLARA He doesn't have to kill for it, Hal, and you know that.

HAL Well I'm sorry that I am not as good at life as Allen is.

CLARA When did I say that? And why does it always come down to him? Why are you so angry at *him*? There is plenty of room for both of you in the world!

HAL You know, I don't need room in the world, Clara, just in my own family!

CLARA Wonderful! We'd love to have you back! That space is already there, waiting!

HAL FUCK YOU! YOU KICKED ME OUT OF THAT SPACE! YOU!

CLARA I KNOW! I KNOW! I FUCKED UP AND I'M SORRY AND I CAN'T TAKE IT BACK AND YOU NEED TO FORGIVE ME!

A long moment.

You need to forgive me.

HAL It's hard. We made a promise. One I took very seriously.

CLARA So did I.

HAL You still broke it. *(looks at his watch)* Three years, six months, ten days, three hours, fourteen minutes, fifty-two seconds. I can time my life from the day I found out.

CLARA Why are you still holding onto that?

HAL Because I own it. Because it's the last part of us that belongs to me.

CLARA But it's not a good part, Hal. And I can't imagine it's easy to hold. Where do you get the strength?

HAL It's all the energy I would have put into loving you.

He turns away from her. A moment.

CLARA I imagine… that you must be… so tired.

HAL You have… no idea.

CLARA Yes, Hal. Yes I do.

ALLEN enters.

ALLEN I found them.

CLARA Where?

HAL How?

ALLEN Peter called. They're in a casino on an Indian reservation. They got lost. The car ran out of gas.

CLARA Oh God…

ALLEN It gets better. Pan got busted for marijuana possession.

HAL Are you fucking kidding me?

ALLEN Nope, Sunshine. Good hire there, by the way.

HAL You really want to start that up again, buddy?

CLARA No, he doesn't and neither do you. Do we know where this casino is?

ALLEN Yes. The guy at the counter helped me find it on the map. We can be there in an hour.

CLARA Let Hal drive.

ALLEN What?

CLARA You heard me, Allen, let Hal drive. You can sit in back.

ALLEN It's my car.

CLARA It's our kid, Allen. We need to lead the parade, OK?

HAL Clara, I appreciate it, but this isn't necessary—

CLARA When I want your opinion, Hal, I will ask it. Allen, give him the keys.

ALLEN *(fishing the keys out of his pocket)* Oh for fuck's sake.

CLARA *(as ALLEN hands over the keys)* Thank you. *(to HAL)* Go get in the car.

HAL Yes ma'am.

> *He exits. She turns to ALLEN.*

CLARA I'm only going to say this once: stop picking on him.

ALLEN Stop picking on him? He's the one who hit me! I'm not picking on him!

CLARA Yes, you are. Stop. The man is thirty-nine years old—

ALLEN So he should be able to stick up for himself.

CLARA He also shouldn't have to stoop to your level—which is the only reason why he doesn't defend himself. Because unlike you he can keep himself in check.

ALLEN Oh yeah, he really kept himself in check this morning.

CLARA You have no idea how many years you've had that coming, do you? Now be a grown-up because I am not interested in a man with a mommy complex.

ALLEN Now you tell me.

CLARA Very funny. Get in the fucking car.

ALLEN I love it when you talk to me that way.

CLARA Allen!

ALLEN I'm going, I'm going.

> *He exits. A moment. CLARA closes her eyes, takes a deep breath, and follows him.*

Scene Five: Evening

> *A holding cell. PAN and PETER sit on a bench in a blank room. PAN is handcuffed.*

PAN I don't want to say that this is the shittiest trip I've ever taken because I recognize that you're young and stuff and I don't want to like… stunt your emotional growth or anything… but this is the shittiest trip I've ever taken.

PETER I'm sorry.

PAN It's not your fault.

PETER Well, it kind of is.

PAN No, it totally is. I was just being nice.

PETER Oh. Sorry.

PAN It's OK. *(beat)* You know your dad and my dad spent the night in jail once?

PETER Really?

PAN Yeah. My dad tells the story all the time.

PETER That doesn't sound like my dad at all. I mean he never does anything wrong. I mean, like, in a breaking-the-law sort of way.

PAN Yeah, well, I think my dad was the primary idiot that time around. I guess they stole a cow or something. It was out in Mendocino.

PETER What the hell did they want with a cow?

PAN They were just goofing off. They were probably stoned or something.

PETER My dad has never been stoned in his life.

PAN Please. My dad has a picture of the two of them holding a bong longer than my arm.

PETER That's ridiculous.

PAN No, what they're wearing is ridiculous. Two guys in their twenties getting stoned in Mendocino is just like… Tuesday.

PETER I still don't believe it.

PAN Dude, your dad smoked me out for the first time when I was seventeen.

PETER Really?

PAN Yeah, he bought me my first beer too. But don't tell him I told you. In fact, forget everything I've said. Drugs are bad. Clearly.

PETER How come my dad never wants to corrupt me?

PAN 'Cause you're his son and it's different. Plus you're still a little kid.

PETER I'm not a little kid!

PAN Enjoy it while you can, little dude. Enjoy it before all you get is like one week a year to have fun and you can't relax without two cocktails or an assload of Valium or whatever. *(beat)* If I can get through this without jail time, I'm totally going back to school.

PETER School is lame.

PAN I'm talking about college, not high school.

PETER It's still lame.

PAN Please. You're gonna love college. You'll be the biggest nerd too. Just like your dad was.

PETER I'm not gonna be like my dad.

PAN We all end up like our dads sooner or later. At least yours is a nice guy.

PETER I don't want to be a nice guy.

PAN On a day full of stupid shit—that has to be the stupidest shit I've heard all day. *(pause)* I'm in love with your aunt.

PETER Oh my God, why do you keep talking?

PAN She's like… perfect. And totally unattainable. Which is my type. Actually, that's everybody's type. People who say that they're not into that are lying. You will grow up to discover this is true.

PETER I don't believe in love.

PAN You are fourteen. Shut the fuck up.

PETER You shut the fuck up.

PAN Who is anybody? That's the point. Who are you? Who am I? Who was she? Who's, like… that guy down the street or like those people over there? Where is this place and how did we get here? Why this moment in time? Why now, why then, why tomorrow? What is that big glowing thing in the sky and what put it there and what does it want from us? I don't know. Do you? Do you actually or do you just think you do? Because I suspect, more and more, that all the people who know shit out there are either deluded or lying. And I think that's how it works. Because we don't really know anything. I mean, I don't know anything. I just know what I like. And sometimes, I'm not even sure I know that. All I know is that I need to like more than one thing or I'm just gonna have a miserable fucking time. And that is so not an option.

PETER Wow.

PAN No shit huh?

PETER You just had a total meltdown, didn't you?

PAN Yup. Welcome to being a grown-up.

Scene Six: Darkness

Outside. The sun has just set and illuminates the desert. HAL is standing by himself, smoking a cigarette. PAN enters.

PAN How... mad... are you?

HAL Haven't you noticed? Getting mad really isn't my thing. I'm much more the "sit and quietly stew about something till it eats me alive" type.

PAN That's really unhealthy.

HAL I'm not really a healthy person. *(beat)* You still have a job, in case you're wondering.

PAN I was... sort of wondering.

HAL I doubt Clara and Allen will let you come to their place though, at least for a while, so, you can meet up with Peter at mine on Saturdays. Does that sound good?

PAN That sounds great. That sounds... amazing. Thank you, man. For everything.

HAL It's music lessons.

PAN Well, and bail.

HAL Yeah, about that: let's never be in this position again, OK?

PAN Not a problem, man, I swear.

HAL Because I like you, Pan, I really do, and I like your father, you've both always been here for my family but if I have to grow up at some point then you do too, you understand?

PAN Completely. I really am sorry.

HAL I know you are. But we're good. Just don't fuck up again.

CLARA, PETER and ALLEN come in.

PETER I said I'm sorry.

CLARA Sorry really isn't going to cut it, young man.

PETER I don't see why it's such a big deal. I mean it's not like anybody fucking died—

CLARA Oh well thank God for small miracles. You stole a car, Peter.

PETER We didn't steal it, Pan borrowed it.

PAN Hey, dude, I just got out of the doghouse, so, um… shut up.

CLARA Needless to say, you are grounded.

PETER Oh come on, what am I? Ten?

ALLEN Not eighteen, Peter, which is about all that matters.

PETER Stay out of it, you're not my dad, Allen!

CLARA Don't talk to Allen like that.

PETER Dad—!

HAL Your mother's right, Peter. Apologize to your… mother's boyfriend.

CLARA See, this is why we need to get married. Doesn't that just sound awkward?

ALLEN Right. *That* is why we need to get married.

PETER Please, Mom, Allen is never gonna marry you. Even I can see that.

HAL Peter.

>   *Beat. Everyone looks at HAL.*

Apologize to your mother. And apologize to Allen.

PETER It's nothing you haven't said.

HAL It's nothing I haven't apologized for either. *(to CLARA)* I've apologized, right?

CLARA More or less.

ALLEN Not to me.

CLARA Shut up, Allen.

HAL Peter?

PETER All right, all right. I'm sorry, Mom. I'm sorry, Allen. How long am I fucking grounded?

CLARA Till Halloween.

PETER What?

ALLEN Oh that is way lenient. Christmas at least.

CLARA Get in the car.

ALLEN Again? I'm not your kid.

CLARA I wish I agreed. Get in the car.

ALLEN Oh for fuck's sake.

ALLEN exits.

HAL You too, Peter.

PETER I need to get my stuff out of yours first.

HAL No, you can leave it. You're coming with me. I got actual directions to this… Detroit Rock City or whatever it is the little heathens are calling it. It shouldn't take us more than an hour to get there. You two were heading in the right direction, you just… I mean it's kind of astounding how you were going in circles when it's pretty much a straight line—

PETER You're letting me go to Burning Man?

HAL No, I'm taking you. So you can pretty much forget about having fun.

PETER Aren't I grounded?

CLARA The minute you get back home.

PETER Is Pan coming too?

HAL If he wants to. He's welcome to drive back to San Francisco with Allen and your mother.

PAN No offense, Mrs. Hyperion, but even if we weren't going to Burning Man, I wouldn't want to do that.

CLARA That's probably wise, Pan.

PAN *(to HAL and PETER)* I will see you both in the car.

PAN exits.

CLARA Remind me why you're letting him off so easy?

HAL Pan didn't convince him to take the car, it was the other way around. You know that.

CLARA Please. He's an adult. He should have known better.

HAL He's not an adult. He's twenty-five. Think of all the stupid shit we did at twenty-five.

CLARA You mean like get married and get pregnant?

HAL Right. But not in that order.

PETER Wait a minute. Aren't you both thirty-nine?

HAL Peter, get in the car before I change my mind.

PETER Yes sir.

PETER exits. HAL turns to CLARA.

CLARA Do not let him out of your sight.

HAL I won't.

CLARA And be nice to him. Let him have some fun before I lock him up and throw away the key.

HAL I will.

CLARA See you when you get back.

> *She starts to go.*

HAL Clara?

> *She turns back.*

Do you think we're ever going to be friends?

CLARA You and me, Hal?

> *He nods.*

We're already friends.

> *She exits. A moment. HAL takes off his wedding ring and chucks the ring into the desert, as far as he can throw it. His cell phone rings. He answers it. CHLOE appears.*

HAL Hey Chloe. We found him.

CHLOE Oh? Oh good! I'm so glad.

HAL Me too. Thanks for checking in. Oh, I'm not going to be coming into the office for the next week. So, please do what you can to hold down the fort. I have a satellite phone in the car if you need to reach me.

CHLOE Where are you going?

HAL I don't want to get into it.

CHLOE Well, all right, but… Listen, Hal, it's about your father—

HAL Oh my God. I completely fucking forgot. How is he?

CHLOE I don't know. But I went to the hospital and it did not look good.

HAL Look, I know you're gonna think I'm a bad son but I… I really need to do this thing with my kid. Maybe we won't take a whole week, maybe we'll be back in a few days, but I just… I need to do this. I think my father would understand. *(beat)* And if he doesn't, fuck him. I gave that bastard my whole life and he still didn't give a shit.

CHLOE Well, and… OK, first of all, I don't think you're a bad son, and secondly, we do need to talk about the company and Allen's appointment.

HAL Whatever. I'm quitting the moment I get back. I want to look for a teaching position—

CHLOE Hal, you can't—

HAL Look, owning this company is about the last thing I want to do, especially after all this—

CHLOE I understand, but listen, there's something you should know first.

HAL Please don't say you're quitting.

CHLOE I'm not.

HAL Oh thank God. Somebody is going to need to take care of the—

CHLOE You're not inheriting the company, Hal.

HAL What?

CHLOE I've read your father's will. Your father's actual will. It's handwritten but it's signed and dated and it's official.

HAL How did you—?

CHLOE I went snooping.

HAL Why?

CHLOE You, your father and Allen are all gone. Why wouldn't I?

HAL I really have no head for business politics at all, do I?

CHLOE Shut up. I was snooping on your behalf, OK? I was trying to find something that would stop your father from being able to appoint Allen his successor—

HAL Please, Chloe, let him have it. I know you don't like him, but—

CHLOE You don't understand. He doesn't leave it to Allen either. He appointed Allen as his replacement but not in writing, only verbally, and besides, as the sole owner of the company your sister can choose whoever she wants as the Executive Director—

HAL He left it all to Erin? She lives in South America, she could care less about—

CHLOE He left everything to Serena.

HAL Serena?

CHLOE I mean, there are financial provisions for Peter and your mother, Erin, some other people… but Serena gets the sole ownership of Sun Enterprises. And there's nothing in the will about Allen. Or you.

HAL But Dad and Serena haven't spoken in years. He told me he took her out of the will.

CHLOE Maybe, but at some point—last night, actually—he changed his mind and he took *you* out.

HAL But Serena won't want it. None of us want it. None of us want Sun Enterprises but Allen.

CHLOE Are you sure you don't want it?

HAL I just said—

CHLOE I know what you said. But we're talking about your father's company here, Hal. We're talking about a lot of money and a lot of power and lot of… a lot.

HAL Chloe, how much do you like me?

CHLOE What?

HAL How much do you like me?

CHLOE A lot. A lot and for a very long time.

HAL Is it because I'm a billionaire's son?

CHLOE Of course not.

HAL If it was a choice between me and Allen… which would you pick?

CHLOE You. If you want me to tear this thing up—I will. I will and I will take the blame—

HAL I'd much rather you hand-deliver it to my father's lawyer. As soon as possible.

CHLOE Are you serious?

HAL Only if you are.

> *Pause.*

CHLOE Will you still date me when I'm making more money than you?

Scene Seven: Midnight (Hospital)

> *SERENA sits talking to HYPERION, who lies in bed.*

SERENA How do you feel?

HYPERION Good… actually. Excited. Relieved.

SERENA Relieved.

HYPERION Yes. I would have assumed I'd feel frightened but then… have I ever been frightened of anything?

SERENA Failure.

HYPERION You can't fail at dying, Little Girl. It's the one game we're all promised to win. *(beat)* Where is your brother?

SERENA Still in Nevada.

HYPERION Did they find the boy?

SERENA They did. Everything is OK.

HYPERION Why hasn't he come back?

SERENA I'm not sure.

HYPERION Well. I suppose I had this coming, too.

SERENA What?

HYPERION Dying alone, abandoned by my children.

SERENA Erin took Mom to eat something. And I'm here.

HYPERION Yes you are. *(beat)* I want you to know that I liked Adam.

SERENA Did you?

HYPERION Yes. I lost my temper that night. He said some stupid things to me.

SERENA Who knew you were such an easily offended man.

HYPERION By sloppy drunks and bad public behavior? Certainly. How our family is perceived is important. I put a lot of work into making us feared, respected and envied, but it's a fine line that separates us from a humble beginning and when someone reminds me of that I see red. It's why I have always kept your brother on such a short leash. He has a tendency towards clumsiness and overkill. And your sister is a very nice girl but she's careless and whimsical. Not like you. You are always serious and elegant, Little Girl. My favorite combination in a woman. Floating. Distant. Entrancing. *(beat)* You are my favorite, you know?

SERENA I do.

HYPERION And you didn't talk to me. For years.

SERENA I play to win. Just like you. Dad.

HYPERION If you can call it winning. *(beat)* Your sister is happy, isn't she?

SERENA She is.

HYPERION She'll take care of your mother when I'm gone. That's comforting to know.

SERENA *(rising)* I should probably call them. Excuse me—

HYPERION Please stay.

SERENA *(stopping)* OK.

HYPERION And come closer. I want to hold your hand.

She moves to sit close, and he takes her hand in his.

Your hands are colder than mine.

SERENA My hands are always cold. I wear gloves nine months out of the year.

HYPERION I remember. We always knew what to buy you for Christmas. And Easter. And your birthday.

SERENA Three sets of gloves a year.

HYPERION Nine months without touching the world.

A long moment. They look at one another. SERENA looks away.

SERENA I miss him so much. Adam. There really aren't words for it. I mean, I know that's a cliché to say but… what else do you say? I miss him. I miss him and that doesn't begin to describe it and because I don't know how to describe it or where to begin, I… I can't. I keep circling. I keep going around and around the same three words. I miss him. It's like "I love you" but… awful. I don't blame you anymore. Really. I understand how life works, I understand the world is a place where bad things seem to happen for connected reasons but in reality there are very few actual examples of cause and effect. I know this, I'm a doctor and I deal with it all the time, with patients who are dealing with their own problems and… families and… you blame someone. You do. You have to. It's part of the process. You're easier to blame than myself. I don't think I did anything wrong. I think you did. But obviously, no, you didn't. Nobody makes the world happen. No one person can be responsible for everything. Just like no one person can protect you from it.

HYPERION But that's what I was supposed to do, wasn't I? *(beat)* Smile.

SERENA I can't.

HYPERION Try.

> *A moment. She does.*

See.

Scene Eight: Twilight

> *The playa. A desert landscape in twilight. PETER and HAL sit looking out together.*

PETER You know why I wanted to come here? Because of Rhodes.

HAL Rhodes, Greece?

PETER Yeah, that little island we went to, remember? All the little white houses. That port where the big statue was.

HAL Big statue?

PETER Well, I mean, it wasn't there anymore. It's gone now. But you know, like, in ancient times or whatever, there was supposed to be this big-ass statue of the god of the sun. For fuck's sake, Dad, you're the one who told me about it—

HAL The Colossus. It was called the Colossus. I know what you're talking about.

PETER Right, but you apparently don't remember the conversation we had—

HAL We were sitting at a café in the harbor. You were having gelato. I was smoking because your mother wasn't around. She was shopping with Allen. You were wearing a red shirt and sunglasses even though it was night. It was really hot.

PETER You pointed out into the dark with your cigarette and you said, "Do you see that empty black space right there? Once upon a time, there was a giant statue of Helios, the god of the sun. And he was so big you could sail a ship between his legs, and he stood over the entrance to the harbor and he protected it. He kept the whole island safe. And he was covered in bronze, so when the sun hit him he looked like a great big tower of fire."

HAL And you said, "Cool."

PETER And you said, "I really wish I could have seen that." And you looked like… I don't know. All happy. Like happier than I'd seen you since…

HAL Four years, four months, six days and… who knows? *(beat)* It's funny, but I never remember that part of that trip.

PETER That's the part I remember the most. Anyway—check it out. There's a big statue of a guy and it's… you know. On fire.

HAL Huh. You're right.

Epilogue: Tomorrow

> *A spotlight rises center stage. HAL steps into it.*

HAL Who am I? Can I tell you who I'm not? That always seems easier to me. Or better yet, can I tell you who I don't want to be? Because that I know, that I've always known, and while it has messed up a great deal of my life it's also been the one thing I could cling to, even as I watch myself become the person I never wanted to be. But that happens to all of us, right? Or am I just comforting myself there? I don't want to be someone who lives for comfort and normally I'm not but I also don't want to be someone who lives for pain either: I don't know that I agree with the idea that what doesn't kill us makes us stronger. I think it just doesn't kill us. We tell ourselves it makes us stronger because we have to talk ourselves into engaging with the world, knowing the odds of being cauterized one way or another are very high but also because nobody wants to be someone who lives to regret. But do you really regret the things you didn't do more than the things you did? I don't know. I've done some things I definitely regret, and when I feel tired now it's not acute. It's cumulative. I want to be someone who can laugh at the world. I want to be someone who can laugh at the world and inspire laughter in others, or some kind of joy. I want to feel good about receiving and I want to feel like I have something to give. But it takes a lot of energy, to really do something. About the most I can manage these days is a sort of benevolent vigil, but that seems so useless and I don't want to be someone who gives up. I'd like to think I'm still too young for that.

Sometimes I look back—though a man never should—and I see more clearly, as we all do, the things I should have done different. But I don't want to be a man who regrets. A man who regrets doesn't understand how life works. He's betrayed his roots and missed the point of time. He believes that we can only be victims or we can only be witnesses. Why become that man? Why become that man when there are so many more things we can be?

> *A moment. The light sits on him. He looks up into it and smiles. Blackout.*
>
> *End of play.*

WRITERS AND ARTISTS

Molly Benson (artist, *Cassiopeia*) is a native of Sacramento, CA, a graduate of Oberlin College with a B.A. in Theatre, and a San Francisco-based artist, actress and voiceover artist. A mostly self-taught artist, she has been exploring art most of her life in various media including painting with acrylics, collage, clay sculpture, drawing and, of course, mosaics. The Olympians Festival was her first attempt at working with mosaics using a theme, and as she has loved Greek mythology since childhood, it was an ideal collaboration. The design of this particular piece, "Cassiopeia," was inspired by the Picasso exhibit that toured at the de Young Museum in summer 2011, as well as by the description of the play given by the playwright. Molly wanted the eyes of Cassiopeia to be abnormally large, taking in and reflecting the image of her naked daughter, Andromeda, bound to the cliff. She hoped to convey the queen's sense of resolve in her decision, yet also a connection to the actions she was taking against her own flesh and blood. As an actress, Molly has performed on stage and in readings all over the Bay Area and Los Angeles with companies including Word for Word, Theatreworks, Killing My Lobster, Atmostheatre, Dark Porch Theatre, Town Hall Theatre, Theater Pub, Stagebridge, Cutting Ball, Grove Theatre Center, Old Man Buckle, Chautauqua Theatre Company, at the El Portal and Complex Theatres, and, of course, No Nude Men, producer of the Olympians Festival. To learn more about Molly's voiceovers, acting and art, or to contact her, please go to www.mollyrbenson.com.

Stuart Eugene Bousel (playwright, *Hyperion to a Satyr*) graduated from Reed College in 2000 with a degree in English and Creative Writing. He has served as the artistic director of three theater companies: Quicksilver Productions, Inc. (1997-2000) and Horror Unspeakable Productions (2000-2002) in Tucson, and No Nude Men Productions (2003-present) in San Francisco. For all three companies he has directed a number of classic plays, including *Lysistrata*, *The Oresteia*, *Faust Part One*, *Salome*, *Edward II*, *Le Cid*, *Love's Labors Lost*, *Hamlet*, *Phaedra*, and Derek Walcott's *Odyssey*, as well as the world premieres of David Duman's *Fishing*, Alison Luterman's *Oasis*, Nirmala Nataraj's *The Monk* and *The Book of Genesis: Remixed and Remastered*, Claire Rice's *Woman Come Down*, and Susan Sobeloff's *Merchants*. He has frequently directed for Atmostheatre/Theatre In the Woods (*A Midsummer Night's Dream*, *Twelfth Night*, *The Frogs*), Wily West Productions (*Ruth and the Sea*, *Universe Rex*), and Custom Made Theatre (*M. Butterfly*, *The Merchant of Venice*), and is a Founding Artistic Director of the San Francisco Theater Pub, for which he has directed numerous readings and a full production of *Measure For Measure*. A writer first and foremost, his produced work includes the plays *The Exiled, The Edenites, Speak To Me, Love Egos Alternative Rock, Troijka, Housebroken, Speak Roughly, Brainkill, A Late Lunch, Juno En Victoria, Polyxena In Orbit, The Boar's Head, Vincent of Gilgamesh, Wild Blue Peaks, Mathew 33:6, The Attack Of The Killer Space Zombies, Men and Women, Joe And Cleo: A Romance, Three Liars, Queen Mab In Drag* and *The Vampire Sorority Babes vs. The Inter-Galactic Frat Zombies: A Ballet*. Two of his screenplays have been produced as the short films *Insomnia* (with Chris McCaleb and Amanda Karam, winner of the John C. Cosgrove Award) and *Wish U Were Here*, and he has published one novel, *Dry Country*. He has been nominated for the MAC Award and the Heideman Award, and was a finalist for the Sky Cooper Award. Places his work has been performed include New York City, San Francisco, Chicago, Melbourne, Dublin, Tucson and Portland. He occasionally acts as well, has sung opera with the Arizona Opera Company, and has voiced a number of television and radio commercials. He is the creator and the Executive Director of the San Francisco Olympians Festival, and his partner is artist Cody Rishell. His website is www.horrorunspeakable.com.

Megan Cohen (playwright, *Joe Ryan*) is the most frequently produced female playwright in the San Francisco Bay Area, with over 20 shows and readings in 24 months for companies including Playwrights Foundation, SF Theater Pub, and PianoFight. She's also had scripts performed Off-Broadway, Off-Off-Broadway, and even in Seattle. In 2011, *The San Francisco Chronicle* called her "a local luminary" and the *San Francisco Bay Guardian*'s "Year in Theater" awarded one of her shows "Most Memorable Food Fight." She studied drama at Stanford University (B.A. with Honors '05), and is a former staff member at American Conservatory Theater (Dramaturgy Fellow) and Cutting Ball Theater (Literary Manager). She currently writes interactive game stories for mobile and social platforms. She would love to hear from you on Twitter (@WayBetterThanTV) and warmly invites you to visit her website, www.megancohen.com.

Jeremy Cole (playwright, *Too Near the Sun*) has dabbled in all areas of theatre, receiving awards and nominations for his directing (*The Kentucky Cycle, Metamorphoses, for colored girls…*), designing (*The Illusion, Bent, Tales of the Lost Formicans, The Mineola Twins*), acting (*Burn This*) and playwriting (James Joyce's *The Dead*). He has served as the Artistic Director of Backstage Theatre in Breckenridge, Colorado; as the president of Colorado Dramatists; and on the boards of several theater groups, including The Theatre on Broadway, Hunger Artists Ensemble Theater and Actors Ensemble of Berkeley. His produced plays include *James Terry, Dreams That Money Can Buy, The Women's Ward,*

Traces of the Western Slopes, Hot? Or Not…, English for the Romantically Challenged, Might Makes Right and *A Cry in Ramah*. His adaptation of James Joyce's *The Dead* ran for six seasons, picking up two "Best of Denver" citations from *Westword* magazine. *Too Near the Sun* was his first play for the San Francisco Olympians Festival, and as this goes to press, he is madly typing away at his second: *Playing with Fire*, based on the Prometheus myth. For his writer pals Tamara Chapman and Lee Patton, who always have to suffer through his first drafts, he "can no other answer make than thanks, and thanks, and ever thanks."

Liz Conley (artist, *Europa* and *Leda*) is a book artist and printmaker living in San Francisco. Working primarily in intaglio, she also uses silkscreen, letterpress, and even digital methods for creating her art. Her work can currently be purchased at 23 Sandy Gallery in Portland, Oregon. You can contact her at liz@lizconley.com.

David J. Duman (playwright, *Nyx*) David J. Duman's playwriting credits include *Fishing*, produced in 2012 by Playwrights6 and D3M in Los Angeles; in 2011 by Open Tab Productions in San Francisco and in 2008 by No Nude Men Productions in Emeryville, California; *Goliath*, workshop and reading by Playwrights6 in Los Angeles; *Five Short Episodes in the Life of Sacagawea*, produced by No Nude Men Productions at the San Francisco Theatre Festival; and *Lobsters in a Pot* (co-written, directed, and performed with Meghan Kane) which won the Audience Choice award at the 826 Valencia 10-Minute Play Festival. Additional credits include the short plays *Nyx* at EXIT Theatre and *A Second Life* at the Jon Sims Center, and a new adaptation of *Othello* (co-written with Claire Rice), performed at the Studio Theatre at San Francisco State University. His web series Vlog Star (www.vlogstarshow.com) was a three-time selection of the Los Angeles Web Series Festival, where it received awards for Outstanding Comedy Series and Outstanding Writing in a Comedy Series. David is also a regular contributor to The Satellite Show pop culture blog (www.thesatelliteshow.com), where he writes about food and wine, and he has been a contributing wine blogger for The Huffington Post since 2011. He's a graduate of UC Berkeley and has a Creative Writing MFA from San Francisco State University. David is a member of the Dramatists Guild of America. www.davidjduman.com.

Bennett Fisher (playwright, *Chronus*) Bennett Fisher's plays, including *Hermes, Don't Be Evil, The Dark Backward, Devil of a Time, Chronus, Exchange, Query, Pure Baltic Avenue, Disinfect, No Bull, Solstice, The Bird Trap, Daedalus,* and *This Is What It Means To Get Hit By A Bus*, have been produced in the United States and internationally. As an actor, playwright, dramaturg, director, and producer, he has collaborated with the Cutting Ball Theater (where he is the literary manager), the National Theater of Northern Greece, Campo Santo and Intersection for the Arts, Threshold Theatre, AtmosTheater, California Shakespeare Theatre, Adirondack Shakespeare Company, Marin Shakespeare Company, Stanford Summer Theater, the Pear Avenue Theatre, New Conservatory Theater Center, San Francisco Theater Pub, Three Wise Monkeys, Theater Pop SF, PianoFight, Misfit Toys Rep, Bread and Water Theatre, Playwright's Foundation, No Nude Men, and others. He is an associate artist with AtmosTheatre and Threshold Theatre, and a founding artistic director of both the San Francisco Theater Pub and the Flying Island Theater Lab. He lives in San Francisco, where he teaches English literature and playwriting.

Chelsea Harper (artist, *Joe Ryan*) was born a storyteller and an artist. Dabbling in all manners of storytelling including acting, singing, drawing and writing, Chelsea has become a jack of all trades, but has since narrowed down her scope of interest to art and writing in hopes of honing those skills instead of spreading herself thin. She taught herself to draw in childhood and expanded her skills by takng classes at Santa Rosa Junior College. She has also been an avid writer since childhood and, thus, she has become an avid and dedicated participant in National Novel Writing Month and Script Frenzy, winning these challenges every year since 2006. She is working on her own novel which she hopes to publish oned day as well as her original pop-up book. Having transferred from the Santa Rosa Junior College to the Academy of Art, Chelsea is very excited to finally get a chance to stretch and expand her artistic skills in her pursuit of a BFA in Illustration. Afterwards, she hopes to make her way to Pixar, the storytelling behemoth that she's dreamed about joining since she was eleven, and make a niche for herself in the story department. For now, she's working hard on collecting scholarships and finishing her personal projects. Her portfolio is available at Etherelle.com.

Emily C. Martin (artist, *Pleiades*) is an art instructor by day, and an illustrator and comic artist by night, when she is not otherwise gaming, gallivanting or fighting crime. Her past is complex and mysterious and full of intrigue. She graduated from Sonoma State University with a BFA in Printmaking in 2006. Emily is the founder of Megamoth Studio, a collective of artists and students, where she teaches after-school classes in comics and illustration. Her current projects include "Princeless" with Action Lab comics, as well as her own webcomic, "Otherkinds." Her hobbies include gardening, Tae Kwon Do and watching other people play video games.

Lise Miller (playwright, *Boreas*) grew up in New Hampshire, the site of the fastest recorded (freezing) wind. She earned her B.A. in Creative Writing from Bennington College and has won the PEN New England North Fiction Discovery Prize.

Claire Rice (playwright, *Europa*) is a playwright, director, and producer. She has worked with Thunderbird Theatre Company, No Nude Men, Three Wise Monkeys, PianoFight, AtmosTheatre, and the San Francisco Theater Pub, and is co-founder of Ann Marie Productions. Her plays include *Once a Boy*, *The Carmine Lie*, *It Ain't Me*, *Pride and Succubus*, *Waterline*, *Demeter's Daughter*, *Woman Come Down*, *Sex in the Next Room*, and the blog play *English for Beginners*. She has directed the sketch comedy *Serve by Expiration* for Thunderbird Theatre Company, and the plays *Horrible In Between Place* for Ann Marie Productions, *How I Learned to Stop Worrying and Lost My Virginity* for the 2011 New York International Fringe Festival, and *Juno en Victoria* for Wily West Productions. She has worked as a lecturer in Theatre at San Francisco State University and as a Membership Associate at Theatre Bay Area. She lives in San Francisco with her loving husband, actor Matt Gunnison.

Cody Rishell (artist, *Helios* and *Nyx*) is a graphic illustrator who is continually inspired by the Greek gods and their stories. He attended the Academy of Art University and received a BFA in Illustration. He's worked within the Bay Area theater scene for the past five years, and his work has been on display in Italy, Turkey, and San Francisco. You can see his work at www.codyrishell.com.

Celeste Schulte (artist, *Chronus*) is originally from the Midwest, and now works as a freelance illustrator and game artist/animator in San Francisco. She loves exploring myths and fables through a variety of media, including paint, print, graphic novel, collage, animation and sculpting. Please feel free to view a portfolio of her work here: www.celesteschulte.com.

Kirk Shimano (playwright, *Leda and the Pr0n*) In addition to writing plays about Leda, Cetus and Hermes for the San Francisco Olympians Festival, Kirk Shimano has also created the official iPhone app for the festival for two years running. His first full-length play, *Love in the Time of Zombies*, was produced by San Francisco Theater Pub in October of 2012 and introduced the word "GWAAAAAH!" into the zombie vernacular. He is a member of the PlayGround Writers Pool, where his play *Miss Finknagle Succumbs to Chaos* was featured in the 16th Annual Best of PlayGround festival. He adapted the same play into a short film for the 2nd Playground Film Festival, where it received the 2013 People's Choice Award. His works have been performed by PianoFight Productions, Wily West Productions, and the Playwright's Center of San Francisco. He is also a member of the Asian American Theater Company NewWorks Incubator. By day, Kirk works in the visual effects industry as a Lighting Technical Director, where he recently helped ninjas to fight in an avalanche. For more information, please visit www.kirkshimano.com.

Christian Simonsen (playwright, *Cassiopeia*) Christian Simonsen's plays include *Cassiopeia*, *The Road Less Traveled Agency*, *Dream Date*, *Eve of the Vertebrates*, *Taxi!*, *Neanderthal Tech Support*, *Chronus*, *The Genesis Project*, and *Io: A Sequel to Prometheus Bound*. In addition to the San Francisco Olympians Festival, his work has appeared at Eat Street Players, San Francisco Theater Pub, The Darkroom, The Chameleon Theatre Circle, Please Leave the Bronx, and PianoFight Productions. He is also a founding member of the sketch comedy troupe 5by5. He lives in San Francisco.

Marissa Skudlarek (playwright, *Pleiades*) Marissa Skudlarek's extensive involvement with the Olympians Festival began when she served as its box-office manager in 2010. Subsequently, she has written the introduction to *Songs of Hestia: Five Plays from the 2010 Olympians Festival*; served as associate producer of the 2011 festival; and written two works for the Festival, *Pleiades* (2011) and *Aphrodite, or The Love Goddess* (2012). Her other full-length plays include *Deus ex Machina* (Young Playwrights Festival National Competition winner, 2006), *Marginalia*, and *The Rose of Youth* (Marilyn Swartz Seven Award and Vassar College production, 2008). Her shorter plays have been produced by San Francisco Theater Pub, Un-Scripted Theatre, and the San Francisco One-Minute Play Festival. She served as the dramaturg and copy-editor for the 2012 Bay One-Acts Festival, and has translated Jean Cocteau's *Orphée* from the French. Marissa holds a B.A. in Drama and French from Vassar College. She writes a twice-monthly column about Bay Area theater for sftheaterpub.wordpress.com and maintains a personal blog at marissabidilla.blogspot.com.

Gintah Tran (artist, *Boreas* and *Icarus*) is an illustrator living in San Francisco. He was trained in traditional illustration at the Academy of Art University and has worked in character design, comics, packaging art, restaurant design and children's illustration. He's a lover of art and storytelling, being especially enamored with the medium of comics. Currently, he is writing and illustrating his first full-length comic series. You can visit his website at www.gintah.com.

No Nude Men and the San Francisco Olympians Festival

In July of 2010, No Nude Men Productions produced the first San Francisco Olympians Festival, a new works development project that included participation by over 100 Bay Area writers, fine artists, directors and actors. The festival continues to be a yearly event (the second installment was in October of 2011, and the third in December of 2012), with new and returning writers submitting proposals for new plays, which are completed over the course of the year and then given staged readings during the twelve nights of the festival. Visual artists are commissioned to create original images inspired by each of the plays, and these images are displayed in a public gallery during the month of the festival. Since the festival began, six works have gone on to be developed for full productions, with plays first crafted for the Olympians festival showing up in theaters around the country and the world.

No Nude Men was born in March of 2003 with a production of Marlowe's *The Troublesome Reign of Edward II*, and was not intended to exist beyond its first show. Since then the group has produced a number of classics, including *Phaedra*, *Love's Labors Lost*, *No Exit* and *Hamlet*, but it primarily focuses on developing new works or producing shows by lesser-known, contemporary authors. No Nude Men's list of premieres and contemporary remounts include works by Stuart Bousel (*Speak To Me, Troijka, Love Egos Alternative Rock, The Exiled, Polyxena In Orbit, Mathew 33:6, Housebroken, Edenites*), Erin Bregman (*I.S.O. Explosive Possibility*), Ashley Cowan (*Word War*), David Duman (*Five Short Episodes In The Life Of Sacagawea, Fishing*), M. R. Fall (*Test Preparation*), Ryan Hayes (*Boys Together Clinging*), Wylie Herman (*Better Homes and Ammo*), Hilde Susan Jaegtnes (*Spook Justice, Learning From Hilde's Mistakes, Oily Replies*), Bennett Fisher (*Hermes*), Alison Luterman (*Oasis, A Night In Jail*), Nirmala Nataraj (*The Book of Genesis: Remixed and Remastered, The Monk, A Grave Situation*), Claire Rice (*Woman Come Down*) and Susan Sobeloff (*Merchants*).

The group has performed at EXIT Theatre, Build Space, Spanganga, Langton Center For The Arts, Periscope Cellars, the Xenodrome, and the Dramatists Guild of Los Angeles, and they were the resident company at the Climate Theater in 2006. They regularly participated in the San Francisco Theater Festival from 2005-2011, and have annually produced a show with the Bay One Acts Festival since 2010. Directors over the years have included Jesse Baldwin, Stuart Bousel, John Dixon, Ryan Hayes, Julia Heitner, Wylie Herman, Sara Judge, Christopher P.

Kelly, Stacy Malia, Claire Rice and Tore Ingersoll-Thorp.

In 2010 the group collaborated with Conlan Media to create *Giant Bones*, the official stage adaptation of several short stories by renowned international fantasy writer Peter S. Beagle.

In addition to its producing presence within the community, No Nude Men has raised money for the San Francisco AIDS Walk and Equality California, and has contributed food to homeless shelters and food banks around the Bay Area. They ran a traveling salon from 2009-2011, bringing actors, directors and writers together on a monthly basis to share food and discussion over a published play. An annual retreat open to the larger theater community and centered around the discussion of the Bay Area theater scene and the development of new work was part of the company's season from 2009-2011.

Independent from the beginning both financially and in spirit, No Nude Men remains outside both the corporate and non-profit sectors and is unaffiliated with any unions or artistic collectives, schools of theater or production trends, existing entirely off of ticket sales and private donations. The loose structure of the group allows it to morph and change from year to year, alternating between sporadic productions and full seasons, with various elements coming and going depending on the artistic whims and pragmatic means of those who currently inhabit the confederacy. As of June 2012, the group is on hiatus, but having gone on hiatus twice since 2003, they are expected to return at some point, in one capacity or another, in the future.

In the meantime, The San Francisco Olympians Festival, first produced by No Nude Men, continues as the most prominent legacy of a company that officially never existed.

More Plays From EXIT Press

Songs of Hestia: Five Plays From the 2010 San Francisco Olympians Festival
Playwrights Nirmala Nataraj, Bennett Fisher, Stuart Eugene Bousel, Claire Rice, and Evelyn Jean Pine adapt some of Western culture's oldest stories, illuminating our present-day concerns with imagination, creativity, curiosity and passion.

Woyzeck, Pelleas and Melisande, Ubu Roi: translated by Rob Melrose
"Rob Melrose is a kind of magician, and his theater, Cutting Ball, is one of the most exciting and integrity-filled enterprises going in the sometimes-shabby field of the American theater. These translations, lucid and sharp, are a beautiful testimony to the value of Rob's achievement." — Oskar Eustis

Three Plays by Mark Jackson
"Playwright/director Mark Jackson has made his name as a first-class theatrical provocateur. Gutsy showmanship, brainy literary instincts and laser-sharp satire mark his canon." — *San Jose Mercury News*
The second collection of plays by Mark Jackson includes three plays based on incredible historic events: *God's Plot*, *Mary Stuart*, and *Salomania*.

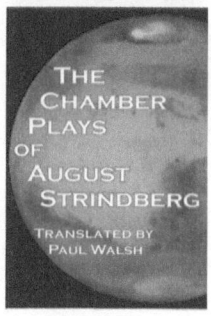

The Chamber Plays of August Strindberg translated by Paul Walsh
The Ghost Sonata, *The Pelican*, *The Black Glove*, *Storm*, and *Burned House*. Yale professor Paul Walsh provides modern translations while keeping Strindberg's "curiosity and his strangeness as specific and opaque as they are in the Swedish."

EXIT Press, the publishing division of EXIT Theatre, a San Francisco theater company founded in 1983, is distributed by Small Press Distribution.   www.exitpress.org   www.spdbooks.org

www.ingramcontent.com/pod-product-compliance
Lightning Source LLC
Chambersburg PA
CBHW021829220426
43663CB00005B/184